BIMSTEC MASTER PLAN FOR TRANSPORT CONNECTIVITY

APRIL 2022

 Creative Commons Attribution 3.0 IGO license (CC BY 3.0 IGO)

© 2022 Asian Development Bank
6 ADB Avenue, Mandaluyong City, 1550 Metro Manila, Philippines
Tel +63 2 8632 4444; Fax +63 2 8636 2444
www.adb.org

Some rights reserved. Published in 2022.

ISBN 978-92-9269-069-4 (print); 978-92-9269-070-0 (electronic); 978-92-9269-071-7 (ebook)
Publication Stock No. TCS210388-2
DOI: http://dx.doi.org/10.22617/TCS210388-2

The views expressed in this publication are those of the authors and do not necessarily reflect the views and policies of the Asian Development Bank (ADB) or its Board of Governors or the governments they represent.

ADB does not guarantee the accuracy of the data included in this publication and accepts no responsibility for any consequence of their use. The mention of specific companies or products of manufacturers does not imply that they are endorsed or recommended by ADB in preference to others of a similar nature that are not mentioned.

By making any designation of or reference to a particular territory or geographic area, or by using the term "country" in this document, ADB does not intend to make any judgments as to the legal or other status of any territory or area.

This work is available under the Creative Commons Attribution 3.0 IGO license (CC BY 3.0 IGO) https://creativecommons.org/licenses/by/3.0/igo/. By using the content of this publication, you agree to be bound by the terms of this license. For attribution, translations, adaptations, and permissions, please read the provisions and terms of use at https://www.adb.org/terms-use#openaccess.

This CC license does not apply to non-ADB copyright materials in this publication. If the material is attributed to another source, please contact the copyright owner or publisher of that source for permission to reproduce it. ADB cannot be held liable for any claims that arise as a result of your use of the material.

Please contact pubsmarketing@adb.org if you have questions or comments with respect to content, or if you wish to obtain copyright permission for your intended use that does not fall within these terms, or for permission to use the ADB logo.

Corrigenda to ADB publications may be found at http://www.adb.org/publications/corrigenda.

Notes:
In this publication, "$" refers to United States dollars, unless otherwise stated.
ADB recognizes "China" as the People's Republic of China.

The main work for the preparation of the Master Plan was undertaken in 2018, and accordingly 2018 was the base year used. Periodic updates were made between September 2018 and the fourth quarter of 2020 based on inputs from the BIMSTEC member states. However, since not all projects were updated, some data may not reflect the current status of project development and implementation.

Cover design by Josef Ilumin.

 Printed on recycled paper

Contents

Tables, Figures, and Boxes	vi
Foreword	viii
Preface	x
Abbreviations	xi
Executive Summary	xiii

I.	**Introduction and Background**	1
	Background	1
	Objective	2
	Vision and Mission	3
	Scope	3
	Key Principles of the Master Plan	4
	Structure of the Master Plan	7
II.	**Overall Master Plan Framework**	8
	Overview of the Bay of Bengal Initiative for Multi-Sectoral Technical and Economic Cooperation Region	8
	The Transport and Trade Environment of the Bay of Bengal Initiative for Multi-Sectoral Technical and Economic Cooperation Region	9
	Key Regional Transport Issues	11
	Key Strategies	13
	Cross-Cutting Issues	15
III.	**Roads and Road Transport**	16
	Sector Overview	16
	Enhancement of Arterial Links to Borders and Ports	17
	Upgrading of Border Roads	23
	Upgrading of Port Access Roads	27
	Road-Based Buddhist and Temple Tourism Circuits	29
	Coordination of Road Programs	30
	Through-Transport Agreements	33

IV.	**Railways and Rail Transport**	**37**
	Sector Overview	37
	Enhanced Rail Connectivity between Ports, Dry Ports, and Borders, and Their Hinterlands	38
	Rail Connectivity for Landlocked Member States	40
	Rail-Based Buddhist and Temple Tourism Circuits	42
	Coordination of Railway Programs	42
V.	**Ports and Maritime Transport**	**44**
	Sector Overview	44
	Development of Deeper Water Ports	45
	Improvement of Container Handling Performance at Bay of Bengal and Andaman Sea Ports	48
	Development of Coastal/Short-Sea Shipping	49
VI.	**Inland Water Transport**	**52**
	Sector Overview	52
	Issues	53
	Policy	54
	Strategy	54
	Projects	55
VII.	**Civil Aviation and Airport Development**	**56**
	Sector Overview	56
	Expansion of Airport Capacity	57
	Development of Airfreight Facilities and Services	61
	Development of Support Facilities for Low-Cost Carrier Operations	63
VIII.	**Multimodal and Intermodal Transport**	**64**
	Sector Overview	64
	Issues	64
	Policy	64
	Strategy	64
	Projects	64
IX.	**Trade Facilitation**	**68**
	Sector Overview	68
	Development of Border Infrastructure and Facilities	68
	Development of Inland Clearance or Inland Container Depots	72
	Simplification and Harmonization of Import–Export and Transit Documentation	73
	Further Development of Automated Clearance Systems	76
	Advanced Logistics	79
X.	**Human Resource Development**	**81**
	Sector Overview	81
	Capacity Building in the Transport and Related Sectors	81
	Capacity Building in Trade Facilitation	83
	Training in Border Management	84

XI.	**Implementation**	**86**
	Critical Success Factors	86
	Project Financing	86
	Monitoring	87

References   **90**

Appendixes

1	Relevance of Transport in the Agenda for Sustainable Development	94
2	Synergies between the BIMSTEC Master Plan for Transport Connectivity and Other Selected Connectivity Frameworks	96
3	Major Routes/Corridors in the BIMSTEC Region	98
4	Schematic Map of Development of Bay of Bengal Initiative for Multi-Sectoral Technical and Economic Cooperation Road Corridors	100
5	Long List of Master Plan Projects	103
6	Existing and Proposed Multimodal and Intermodal Transport Corridors in the BIMSTEC Region	135
7	Resources to Implement the Projects in the Master Plan, 2018, ($ billion)	136
8	Monitoring Formats for the Master Plan Flagship Projects and Initiatives	139

Tables, Figures, and Boxes

Tables

1	Planned Flagship Projects to Enhance Arterial Links to Ports and Borders	18
2	Planned Flagship Projects to Upgrade Border Roads	24
3	Planned Projects to Upgrade Port Access Roads	28
4	Planned Flagship Project for the Development of Buddhist and Temple Tourism Circuits by Road	31
5	Planned Flagship Project for the Sharing of Road Planning Data among Bay of Bengal Initiative for Multi-Sectoral Technical and Economic Cooperation Member States	32
6	Preliminary Draft Format for a Bay of Bengal Initiative for Multi-Sectoral Technical and Economic Cooperation Road Planning Database	33
7	Planned Flagship Projects for Through-Transport Agreements	35
8	Planned Flagship Projects to Enhance Rail Connectivity between Ports, Dry Ports, and Borders, and Their Hinterlands	39
9	Planned Flagship Projects to Provide Rail Connectivity for Landlocked Member States	41
10	Planned Flagship Project for the Development of Buddhist and Temple Tourism Circuits by Road	42
11	Planned Flagship Project for the Sharing of Railway Planning Data among Bay of Bengal Initiative for Multi-Sectoral Technical and Economic Cooperation Member States	43
12	Planned Flagship Projects to Develop Deeper Water Ports	47
13	Planned Flagship Project for the Development of Coastal Shipping	51
14	Planned Flagship Projects to Develop International Inland Water Transport	55
15	Planned Flagship Projects for Expansion of Airport Capacity	58
16	Planned Flagship Projects for Multimodal and Intermodal Transport Development	65
17	Planned Flagship Projects to Develop Border Infrastructure	70
18	Planned Flagship Projects to Develop Inland Clearance or Inland Container Depots	73
19	Planned Flagship Project to Simplify and Harmonize Import–Export Documentation in the Bay of Bengal Initiative for Multi-Sectoral Technical and Economic Cooperation Region	75
20	Planned Flagship Project for Further Development of Automated Systems	79
21	Project for the Development of Advanced Logistics	80
22	Flagship Capacity Building Projects in the Transport and Related Sectors	82
23	Planned Flagship Project for Training in Trade Facilitation	84
24	Planned Flagship Project for Training in Border Management	85
A1	Relevance of Transport to Selected Sustainable Development Goals	94
A7.1	Long List Projects (Including Ongoing Projects, as of 2018), 2018–2028	136
A7.2	Long List Projects (Excluding Ongoing Projects, as of 2018), 2018–2028	137
A7.3	Flagship Projects (Including Ongoing Projects, as of 2018), 2018–2028	137
A7.4	Flagship Projects (Excluding Ongoing Projects, as of 2018), 2018–2028	138
A8.1	Overall Status Report	139
A8.2	(Flagship) Project Profile Format	143
A8.3	Simplified Time-Based Implementation Monitoring Spreadsheet for Each Flagship Project	144

Figures

1	The Centrality of the Bay of Bengal Initiative for Multi-Sectoral Technical and Economic Cooperation	2
2	Building Blocks of the Master Plan	5
3	Logic of the Flow of the Text in the Sector Sections	7
4	Potential Cross-Border Value Chains in the Bay of Bengal Initiative for Multi-Sectoral Technical and Economic Cooperation Region	10
5	Proposed New Coastal Shipping Routes from Ranong	51
6	Indo–Bangladesh Protocol Routes	54
7	The Proposed Mekong–India Economic Corridor	67
8	Schematic of the Application of Business Process Analysis	76
9	Schematic of an Electronic Single Window	78

Boxes

1	Brief Profiles of Bay of Bengal Initiative for Multi-Sectoral Technical and Economic Cooperation Member States	8
2	Development of the India-Myanmar–Thailand Trilateral Highway	21
3	Development of the Kathmandu–Terai Fast Track Road Project	22
4	How to Achieve the Strategy to Develop Key Border Link Roads	24
5	Improvement of Road Connectivity between Thilawa and Yangon	29
6	Illustrative Tourism Circuits in the Bay of Bengal Initiative for Multi-Sectoral Technical and Economic Cooperation Region	30
7	The Objective of Coordinating Road Programs in Bay of Bengal Initiative for Multi-Sectoral Technical and Economic Cooperation	32
8	Estimates of the Benefits of Through-Transport in the Bay of Bengal Initiative for Multi-Sectoral Technical and Economic Cooperation Region	36
9	Development of a Bridge Parallel to the Bangabandhu (Jamuna) Bridge with Twin Dual-Gauge Rail Lines	40
10	The Scope for Regional Cooperation in the Ports and Maritime Sector	45
11	Assessing the Need for Deep Water Ports	46
12	Provision of Additional Port Capacity in Bangladesh through the Development of Deeper Ports	48
13	The Benefits of Investing in Container Handling Equipment: The Case of Chattogram Port	49
14	India's Sagarmala Programme	50
15	Expansion of Hazrat Shahjalal International Airport, Dhaka, 2019–2022	60
16	Development of Bandaranaike International Airport, Colombo, 2017–2020	61
17	The Desirability of Developing Multiple Airports in One Metropolitan Area	61
18	The Kaladan Multimodal Transit Transport Project	66
19	The Scope for Private Sector Participation in the Development of Border Infrastructure	69
20	Economic Impacts of Bottlenecks in Trade Business Processes	74
21	The Potential of Public–Private Partnerships for Financing Transport Connectivity Infrastructure in the Bay of Bengal Initiative for Multi-Sectoral Technical and Economic Cooperation Region	88

Foreword

Transport connectivity is the most fundamental requirement of any regional integration process. A well-established transport network is a prerequisite for reaping the benefits of a free trade area, including the promotion of trade and investment, as well as progress in other areas of cooperation such as tourism, people-to-people contact, and cultural exchange. For this reason, transport and communications was included as one of the initial areas of cooperation when the Bay of Bengal Initiative for Multi-Sectoral Technical and Economic Cooperation (BIMSTEC) was established more than 20 years ago.

Convinced that connectivity is vital to promote regional integration, the leaders of the BIMSTEC member states during their Goa Retreat in October 2016 directed preparation of a master plan for BIMSTEC connectivity. The 15th Ministerial Meeting held at Kathmandu, Nepal, on 11 August 2017, tasked the BIMSTEC Transport Connectivity Working Group (BTCWG) to develop the draft Master Plan. Accordingly, the process of drafting the Master Plan was initiated in the Second BTCWG Meeting held at Bangkok, Thailand, on 13–14 November 2017 with the technical assistance of the Asian Development Bank (ADB).

During the Fourth BIMSTEC Summit held at Kathmandu, Nepal, on 30–31 August 2018, the leaders underlined the importance of multidimensional connectivity, which promotes synergy among connectivity frameworks in our region, as a key enabler to economic integration for shared prosperity. The leaders noted with satisfaction the preparation of the draft BIMSTEC Master Plan for Transport Connectivity and called for its early adoption and thanked ADB for providing support for preparation of the Master Plan. They tasked BTCWG to work out the modalities for its implementation, giving due attention to the special circumstances and needs of the member states. The leaders agreed that the Master Plan would serve as a strategic document that guides actions and promotes synergy among various connectivity frameworks, such as the Association of Southeast Asian Nations (ASEAN) Master Plan on Connectivity 2025 (MPAC 2025) and the Ayeyawady–Chao Phraya–Mekong Economic Cooperation Strategy (ACMECS), to achieve enhanced connectivity and sustainable development in our region.

It is pertinent to recall that ADB carried out a study known as the BIMSTEC Transport Infrastructure and Logistic Study (BTILS) in 2007, which was updated and enhanced in 2014. Many of the projects identified in the BTILS have either been completed or are in the process of completion. The present Master Plan was considered necessary since various other initiatives with overlapping domains have been initiated in the region. In addition, many of the projects in the BTILS had already been completed or were nearly completed. As directed by the leaders of the BIMSTEC member states during their Goa Retreat and as emphasized by the leaders during the Fourth BIMSTEC Summit, the Master Plan took note of these factors and addressed various other missing infrastructure requirements links in the region, producing a long-term development program, to 2028.

The current Master Plan identifies 141 "flagship" projects to enhance connectivity in the Bay of Bengal region at an estimated cost of $47.0 billion.[1]

The implementation of this Master Plan will not be an easy task. It will require commitment from the member states and international development partners. Support will be required from donors, as well as efforts from the respective governments to carry out necessary reforms and capacity development.

Finally, the Secretariat is thankful to India, the lead member state in BIMSTEC for the transport sector, and to all the BIMSTEC member states, for their active participation in the preparation of the Master Plan, and to ADB for supporting the effort.

Tenzin Lekphell
Secretary General of BIMSTEC

---

[1] The BIMSTEC Transport Connectivity Working Group in its 3rd meeting held virtually on 8 December 2020 in New Delhi, India, approved text referring to 137 "flagship" projects at a cost of $48.7 billion, but these numbers were adjusted to reflect changes in project data made by the member states during and shortly after the meeting.

Preface

The Asian Development Bank (ADB) is pleased to support the Bay of Bengal Initiative for Multi-Sectoral Technical and Economic Cooperation (BIMSTEC) Secretariat in preparing the BIMSTEC Master Plan for Transport Connectivity. As a regional development bank mandated to promote regional cooperation among its member states, ADB values its partnership with BIMSTEC, which is a platform to harness shared and accelerated growth through mutual cooperation in areas of common interests, including transport and trade.

ADB has been cooperating with BIMSTEC since 2005. Through regional technical assistance, ADB supported the preparation of the BIMSTEC Transport Infrastructure and Logistics Study (BTILS), as well as the Updating and Enhancement of the BTILS. ADB has assisted the preparation and implementation of many projects identified in the BTILS, the Updating and Enhancement of the BTILS, and the Master Plan through its loan and/or grant, and technical assistance programs. ADB has also supported the strengthening of the BIMSTEC Secretariat, which was established in September 2014.

The Master Plan presents a comprehensive 10-year strategy and action plan for improving the subregion's transport linkages covering roads and road transport, railways and rail transport, ports and maritime transport, inland water transport, civil aviation and airports, multimodal and intermodal transport, trade facilitation, and human resource development in the sector.

It recommends strategies and actions to enhance transport connectivity between and across BIMSTEC's member states. It sets out a vision, a mission, and a policy framework to promote the development of international transport linkages and services. In addition, it articulates the implementation strategies to be adopted and the goals to be achieved founded on those policies, and it includes proposed measures to monitor the realization of these goals.

The resources required to achieve the Master Plan's goals are substantial, with an estimated investment of about $22.0 billion over the 10-year period (2018–2028) for the "flagship" or "signature" projects, excluding ongoing ones. Continued and coordinated support of the governments of the member states and international development partners is necessary to meet the region's needs for improved transport connectivity. ADB remains committed to assisting the member states in the BIMSTEC region's transport development.

The Master Plan has benefited from the contribution of many individuals, including officials of the ministries concerned on foreign affairs, trade, and transport sectors of the member states, staff of the BIMSTEC Secretariat, staff and consultants of ADB, representatives from international development partners, and other stakeholders. All their contributions are gratefully acknowledged.

Kenichi Yokoyama
Director General
South Asia Department
Asian Development Bank

Abbreviations

ADB	Asian Development Bank
ACMECS	Ayeyawaddy–Chao Phrya–Mekong Economic Cooperation Strategy
AH	Asian Highway
APEC	Asia-Pacific Economic Cooperation
ASEAN	Association of Southeast Asian Nations
ASYCUDA	Automated System for Customs Data
BIMSTEC	Bay of Bengal Initiative for Multi-Sectoral Technical and Economic Cooperation
BPA	business process analysis
BTCWG	BIMSTEC Transport Connectivity Working Group
BTILS	BIMSTEC Transport Infrastructure and Logistics Study
CBM	coordinated border management
China Exim Bank	Export-Import Bank of China
GDP	gross domestic product
GVC	global value chain
IBM	integrated border management
ICD	inland clearance depot or inland container depot
ICP	integrated check post
ICT	information and communication technology
ILOC	Indian Line of Credit
JICA	Japan International Cooperation Agency
JPY	Japanese yen
km	kilometer
Lao PDR	Lao People's Democratic Republic
LCC	low-cost carrier
LCL	less than container load
NEDA	Neighbouring Countries Economic Development Cooperation Agency (Thailand)
OFID	OPEC Fund for International Development
OPEC	Organization of Petroleum Exporting Countries
PPP	public–private partnership
PRC	People's Republic of China
REG	Regional
SAARC	South Asian Association for Regional Cooperation
SDG	Sustainable Development Goal
SHC	SAARC Highway Corridor
SIWC	SAARC Inland Waterways Corridor
SPS	sanitary-phytosanitary
SPV	special purpose vehicle
SRC	SAARC Railway Corridor
TA	technical assistance

TAR	Trans-Asian Railway
TBT	technical barrier to trade
TCD	target completion date
U	Underway
UNESCAP	United Nations Economic and Social Commission for Asia and the Pacific
WCO	World Customs Organization
WTO	World Trade Organization

Executive Summary

As directed by the leaders of the Bay of Bengal Initiative for Multi-Sectoral Technical and Economic Cooperation (BIMSTEC) member states, the BIMSTEC Master Plan for Transport Connectivity (the Master Plan) was prepared as a strategic document to guide actions and promote synergies among various connectivity frameworks, to achieve enhanced connectivity and sustainable development of the region. A previous BIMSTEC Transport Infrastructure and Logistics Study (BTILS) was completed in November 2007 and updated and enhanced between May 2013 and May 2014, but many of the projects in the BTILS have already been completed or are nearly completed. Therefore, as directed by the leaders of the BIMSTEC member states, this Master Plan took note of these factors and addressed various other missing connectivity requirements in the region, producing a long-term development program, to 2028.

The Master Plan provides a specific framework for organizing a set of policies, strategies, and projects toward realizing a shared vision of peace, prosperity, and sustainability. Because of BIMSTEC's unique geographic position as a bridge linking South and Southeast Asia, the Master Plan is strategically relevant not only for BIMSTEC, but also for its neighboring regions. Leveraging its unique position for strengthening regional connectivity can help BIMSTEC tap into economic opportunities for developing South and Southeast Asia. By establishing better transport links and faster border crossings throughout the region, transformational connections can be built between the two subregions through Myanmar and Thailand and beyond, with BIMSTEC serving as a bridge between South and Southeast Asia and reinforcing relations between and among these regions and countries.

The Master Plan adopts a holistic approach, covering both hard infrastructure, including physical roads, railways, ports, inland waterways, and airports, and soft infrastructure, including the services using that infrastructure for international transport. Thus, it includes capacity building, transport access agreements, and the harmonization of rules, regulations, policies, and measures related to transport between and among BIMSTEC countries with a view to facilitating the cross-border movement of BIMSTEC trade in support of the proposed BIMSTEC Free Trade Area.

The building blocks of the Master Plan, including the overarching regional vision as articulated by the leaders of the member states, the strategic objectives, the vision of the Master Plan, the various operational areas (i.e., subsectors), cross-cutting concerns, and implementation, are summarized in the following figure.

Key principles of the Master Plan include the following:

(i) In view of BIMSTEC's position as a key partner in regional cooperation and integration, a key function of the Master Plan is to demonstrate the organization's role and relevance in promoting improvements in intraregional transport connectivity, including connectivity between South and Southeast Asia.

(ii) Connectivity initiatives must be based on universally recognized international norms, good governance, the rule of law, openness, transparency, and financial responsibility, and must be pursued in a manner that respects the sovereignty, equality, and territorial integrity of nations.

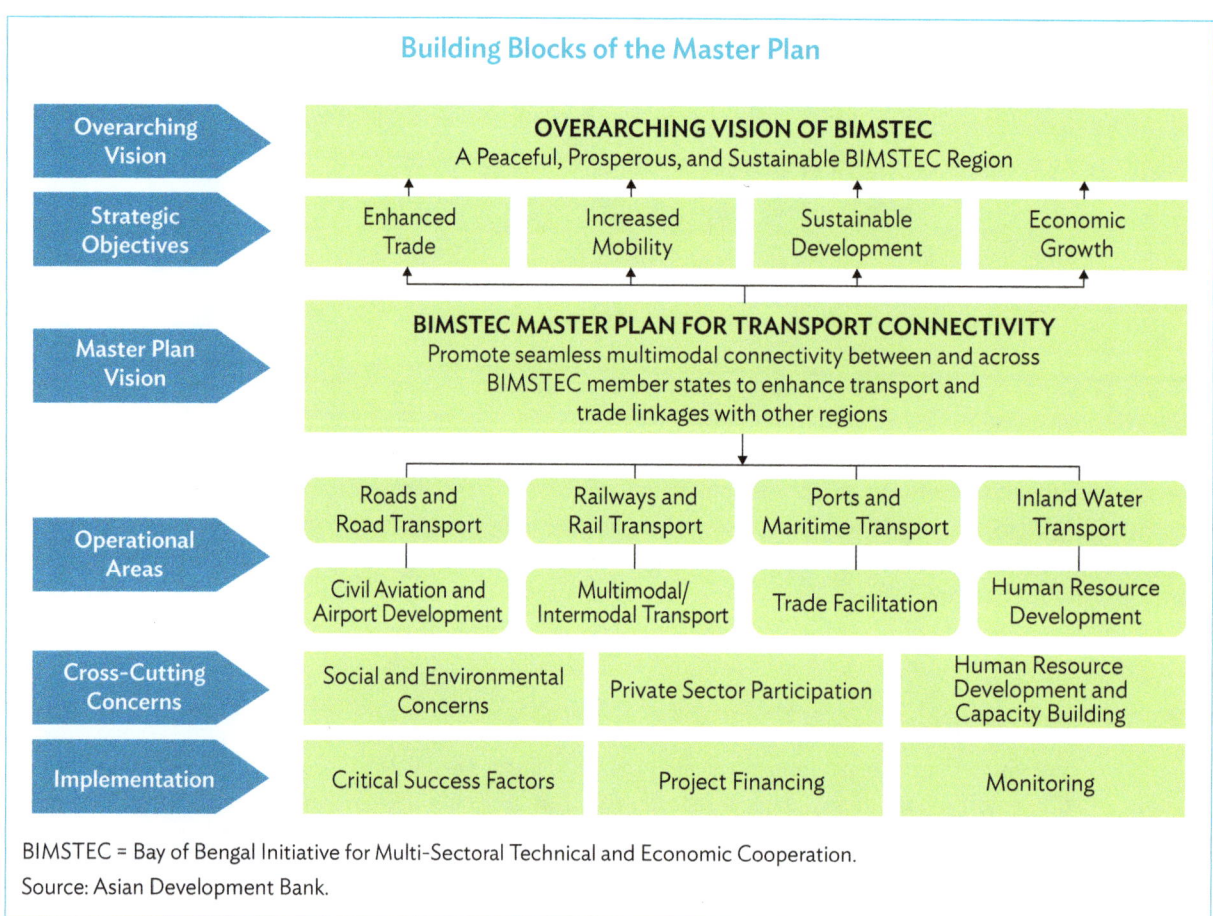

BIMSTEC = Bay of Bengal Initiative for Multi-Sectoral Technical and Economic Cooperation.
Source: Asian Development Bank.

(iii) Since the Master Plan is not a negotiated document, but was developed and finalized based only on consultations, it is nonbinding on member states. The Master Plan should be flexible in its structure and recommendations to respond to emerging trends and priorities.

(iv) Projects listed in the Master Plan may only be for the information of member states. Deliberations upon of adoption of the Master Plan may not be treated as endorsement or approval of the projects listed in the Master Plan.

(v) Projects recommended or listed in the Master Plan will be executed keeping in mind each member state's procedures, practices, and relevant national laws.

(vi) It is critical to differentiate between BIMSTEC and other regional initiatives, to demonstrate BIMSTEC's unique position in the regional cooperation environment (consider, e.g., BIMSTEC's support for the India–Myanmar–Thailand Trilateral Highway initiative, which spans South and Southeast Asia).

(vii) As called for by the leaders of the BIMSTEC member states at their Fourth Summit, the Master Plan complements the transport and/or other plans of other regional organizations or groupings with overlapping geographical territory, such as those of the Association of Southeast Asian Nations (ASEAN), the Ayeyawaddy–Chao Phrya–Mekong Economic Cooperation Strategy (ACMECS), the Indian Ocean Rim Association (IORA), and the Mekong–Ganga Cooperation (MGC) program (see Appendix 2 for discussion specifically of the synergies with related ASEAN and ACMECS plans).

(viii) This Master Plan is identifiable as an individual master plan rather than as a replica of other regional master plans, which is achieved with different structure and substance, while maintaining compatibility and creating synergies with the other plans in terms of content.

(ix) The overall process for developing the Master Plan included the formulation of policies and strategies in each sector and subsector to achieve the plan's vision, and based on these policies and strategies, formulation of projects, both hard and soft.
(x) The Master Plan takes into account the specific circumstances and requirements of the respective member states, with differing geographic areas and features, population, level of economic activities, and other unique circumstances, while considering the requirement for seamless cross-border movement of people, goods, and vehicles.
(xi) The proposed projects benefit more than one member state (rather than being purely national undertakings) to qualify as BIMSTEC initiatives. That said, there is no need for unanimous concurrence (i.e., the "2+x" principle may be applied).
(xii) This document is a master plan, which incorporates as many considerations as possible, but it is not a convention or an international agreement; implementation must be undertaken individually and bilaterally, based on multilateral principles.
(xiii) The recommended high-capital infrastructure projects should be reconfirmed in each case by feasibility studies. Infrastructure should be designed in such a way as to allow future development if and when such developments are justified by demand and covered by funding sources.
(xiv) Expertise available within the region in terms of planning, construction, execution, and operationalization may be optimally utilized in the interest of the master plan.
(xv) Maintenance plans for all infrastructure projects should also be drawn up at the time of planning so that infrastructure facilities do not suffer after completion of the project liability period.
(xvi) Finally, the Master Plan was produced at a point in time based upon the best information available. Inevitably, changes will occur that will affect the costs and benefits of each proposed project (e.g., changes in the timetables for implementation of other projects, improved information from project-specific studies, and external factors such as national and regional macroeconomic performance). Therefore, the Master Plan is a "live document" providing a robust platform for improving regional transport connectivity, but which requires review(s) over time to respond to emerging trends and priorities.

Key strategies—all with associated projects—were developed as follows:[2]

(i) Road and Road Transport

- Prioritization of road development along the key national arterial routes that represent the region's main existing and potential trade corridors.
- Progressive upgrading of key border link roads between crossings and the national road network along BIMSTEC corridors, with coordinated development on both sides of the border.
- Upgrading or construction of dedicated port access roads in situations where there is congestion on the existing access roads or where new ports are being developed.
- Development of road-based Buddhist and temple tourism circuits.
- Exchange of information on national road development programs and establishment of a mechanism for the effective exchange of relevant road planning data to facilitate future coordination of road investments.
- Implementation of transport access agreements and regional through-transport arrangements.

---

[2] BIMSTEC and Asian Development Bank. 2018. *Updating and Enhancement of the BIMSTEC Transport Infrastructure and Logistics Study, Final Report*. Dhaka.

(ii) Railways and Rail Transport

- Prioritization of rail access to ports, especially for the movement of bulk and semi-bulk cargo and the movement of container traffic between the ports, land borders, and inland clearance/container depots.
- Development of rail links between India and the landlocked member states of Bhutan and Nepal.
- Development of rail-based Buddhist and temple tourism circuits.
- Exchange of information on national railway development programs and establishment of a mechanism for the effective exchange of relevant road planning data to facilitate future coordination of railway investments.

(iii) Ports and Maritime Transport

- Development of new ports and expansion of existing harbor infrastructure to increase the capacity of the region's ports to handle growth in container traffic.
- Investment in additional container handling equipment, commensurate with demand and the need to improve handling performance consistent with global good and best practice.
- Development of coastal or short-sea shipping.

(iv) Inland Water Transport

- Development of sustainable, economically viable inland water transport between member states, e.g., by providing multimodal and intermodal connectivity.

(v) Civil Aviation and Airport Development

- Demand-based development of airport facilities.
- Investment in cargo infrastructure and equipment at major airports with prioritization for this purpose wherever possible.
- Development of additional infrastructure at the region's main airports to facilitate the handling of low-cost carrier services, without compromising the infrastructure needed for legacy (full-service) carriers.

(vi) Multimodal and Intermodal Transport

- To establish seamless multimodal and intermodal transport linkages, pursuit of initiatives that efficiently combine the use of different modes of transport, including inland clearance/container depots (ICDs) and dry ports as well as multimodal transport corridors.

(vii) Trade Facilitation

- Development of border infrastructure at the main BIMSTEC land border crossings.
- Development of inland clearance/container depots at appropriate locations.
- Review and rationalization of documentation requirements in relation to import and export clearance and promotion of the development of mutual recognition agreements.
- Upgrading of existing information and communication technology (ICT) systems within national customs administrations and establishment of national single windows.
- Adoption of advanced logistical systems as an approach for reducing the high level of distribution costs and transport time.

(viii) Human Resource Development

- Provision of training designed to enhance the capacity and skill of personnel engaged in the transport and related sectors.
- Enhanced training of public and private sector personnel in trade facilitation.
- Enhanced training of border personnel in good and best practices in modern border management.

(ix) Implementation

- Facilitation of overall and closer coordination with its development partners on financing and technical assistance.
- Leadership in monitoring implementation of Master Plan projects.

Critical success factors for the Master Plan include:

(i) political will and commitment by the member states, which may be demonstrated by cooperation between and among participating states, budgeting for identified projects, and including projects in national development plans;
(ii) creation of an appropriate policy and regulatory framework for implementation, e.g., with through-transport agreements, access agreements for developing coastal shipping services between and among member states;
(iii) development of a pipeline of bankable projects, with economic and financial viability, to accelerate the implementation of infrastructure projects;
(iv) addressing of social and environmental concerns;
(v) development of human resources and associated capacity;
(vi) partnership with the private sector in infrastructure, in view of budget constraints and the needs in other socioeconomic sectors; and
(vii) robust monitoring.

The resources to implement the "flagship" (or "signature") projects in the Master Plan have been estimated at $47.0 billion (141 projects, including ongoing projects, as of 2018) and $22.0 billion (73 projects, excluding ongoing projects) in 2018 values.[3] Half or more of these amounts would be in the roads and road transport (sub) sector. The Master Plan does not provide detailed financing proposals since these depend on considerations that will become clearer during the implementation period. However, given the breadth and magnitude of funding requirements, it will be critical to ensure that full funding potentials are mobilized. A separate study on financing for BIMSTEC transport connectivity was initiated with the support of ADB.

---

[3] The BIMSTEC Transport Connectivity Working Group in its 3rd meeting held virtually on 8 December 2020 in New Delhi, India, approved text referring to 137 "flagship" projects at a cost of $47.0 billion, but these numbers were adjusted to reflect changes in project data made by the member states during and shortly after the meeting.

I. Introduction and Background

Background

The Bay of Bengal Initiative for Multi-Sectoral Technical and Economic Cooperation (BIMSTEC) was established as a regional organization in June 1997 to promote free trade within the region, increase cross-border investment and tourism, and promote technical cooperation. Bangladesh, Bhutan, India, Myanmar, Nepal, Sri Lanka, and Thailand are members. BIMSTEC connects South and Southeast Asia, a region with a population of about 1.5 billion and a gross domestic product (GDP) of $2.7 trillion. The need to enhance transport connectivity[1] in this "triangular basin"[2] is necessary for BIMSTEC to achieve its core objectives. Since its establishment in September 2014, the BIMSTEC Secretariat has been responsible for the overall coordination and monitoring of activities of the regional grouping, including activities related to the development of intraregional transport linkages.[3]

A BIMSTEC Transport Infrastructure and Logistics Study (BTILS) was completed in November 2007 with support from the Asian Development Bank (ADB). The final report and its recommendations were then endorsed at the 12th BIMSTEC Ministerial Meeting. At the request of the BIMSTEC Working Group (the predecessor to the BIMSTEC Secretariat), ADB updated and enhanced the BTILS, reflecting changes since its completion and extending the planning timeframe to 2020, including assessment of the effect of various trade-related initiatives in the region. The study—conducted between May 2013 and May 2014—prepared (i) a profile of the transport and logistics environment of the member states, focusing on international connectivity, both inside and outside of the BIMSTEC region; (ii) recommendations for future BIMSTEC policies and strategies to enhance connectivity and promote intra-BIMSTEC trade; (iii) a list of relevant hard and soft infrastructure projects to enhance BIMSTEC connectivity and trade; and (iv) recommendations on the implementation of the agreed BIMSTEC policies and strategies. The updating and enhancement report was completed in June 2014 and issued formally in July 2018. On 16 October 2016, the leaders of the BIMSTEC member states during the Goa Retreat in India in their Agenda for Action, directed "development of a Master Plan on Connectivity within the Transport and Communication Sector." The 15th BIMSTEC Ministerial Meeting, held in Kathmandu, Nepal, on 11 August 2017, endorsed the updating and enhancement report and tasked a BIMSTEC Transport Connectivity Working Group (BTCWG) to formulate a draft BIMSTEC Master Plan for Transport Connectivity, to identify the strategic goals for enhancing the international transport sector in the region, both in the short and long term. At the 2nd Meeting of the BTCWG, held in Bangkok, Thailand, on 13–14 November 2017, it was agreed on to entrust ADB with the drafting of the Master Plan for Transport Connectivity as part of its technical assistance (TA) for BIMSTEC. A Workshop on the

---

[1] Transport connectivity may be defined as the "availability of transport that enables people and goods to reach a range of destinations at a reasonable generalized cost." Oxera, *Understanding the Theory of International Connectivity*, prepared for the (United Kingdom) Department of Transport. April 2010, Section 2.1. p. 3. Generalized cost is a concept that represents the entire cost of a given trip, including financial cost, the value of travel time, frequency, wait time, interchange time, access time, and reliability of a service.

[2] The term is from C. Xavier. 2018. *Bridging the Bay of Bengal: Toward a Stronger BIMSTEC*. Carnegie India. February. p. 5.

[3] It is committed to becoming a "dynamic, effective and result-oriented regional organization for promoting a peaceful, prosperous and sustainable Bay of Bengal Region through meaningful cooperation and deeper integration." Bay of Bengal Initiative for Multi-Sectoral Technical and Economic Cooperation. *Fourth Summit Declaration*, 30–31 August 2018, Kathmandu, Nepal. p. 2.

BIMSTEC Master Plan for Transport Connectivity, held in Bangkok on 17–18 September 2018, refined the Second Draft, and the 3rd Meeting of the BTCWG, held virtually from New Delhi, India, on 8 December 2020, finalized the BIMSTEC Master Plan for Transport Connectivity.

Objective

The BIMSTEC Master Plan for Transport Connectivity (the Master Plan) provides the framework for organizing a set of policies, strategies, and projects toward realizing a shared vision of peace, prosperity, and sustainability. Because of BIMSTEC's unique geographic position as a bridge linking South and Southeast Asia, the Master Plan is strategically relevant not only for BIMSTEC, but also for its neighboring regions. Leveraging its unique position for strengthening regional connectivity can help BIMSTEC tap into economic opportunities for developing the region. By establishing better transport links and faster border crossings throughout South and Southeast Asia, transformational connections can be built between the two subregions through Myanmar and Thailand and beyond, with BIMSTEC serving as a bridge between South and Southeast Asia and reinforcing relations between and among these regions and countries.[4] Figure 1 presents a schematic image showing the centrality of BIMSTEC in the region and the vital role it can serve in unifying various (sub)regional cooperation initiatives.

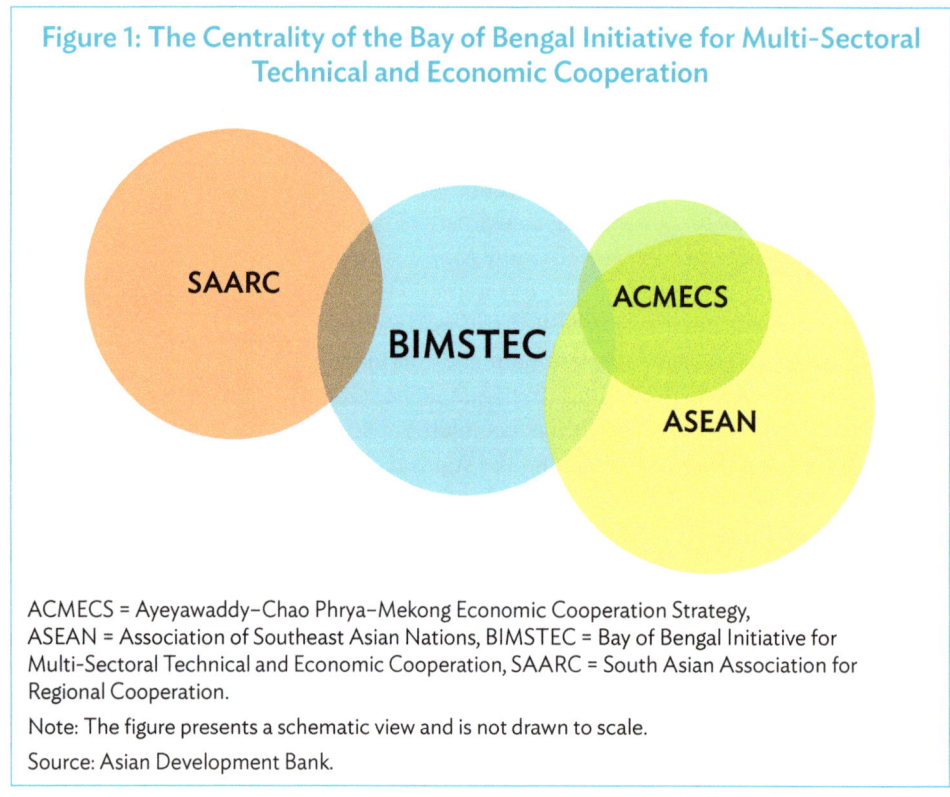

Figure 1: The Centrality of the Bay of Bengal Initiative for Multi-Sectoral Technical and Economic Cooperation

ACMECS = Ayeyawaddy–Chao Phrya–Mekong Economic Cooperation Strategy, ASEAN = Association of Southeast Asian Nations, BIMSTEC = Bay of Bengal Initiative for Multi-Sectoral Technical and Economic Cooperation, SAARC = South Asian Association for Regional Cooperation.
Note: The figure presents a schematic view and is not drawn to scale.
Source: Asian Development Bank.

---

[4] M. M. Rahman and C. Kim. 2016. Prospects for Economic Integration of BIMSTEC: Trade and Investment Scenario. *International Journal of u- and e- Service, Science and Technology*, Vol. 9, No. 4, 2016. pp. 235–248. http://dx.doi.org/10.14257/ijunesst.2016.9.4.24.

Vision and Mission

At the Fourth BIMSTEC Summit held in Kathmandu, Nepal, on 30–31 August 2018, the leaders of the seven BIMSTEC member states, in their Joint Summit Declaration, resolved to consolidate and deepen cooperation among them to make BIMSTEC an effective platform for promoting peace, prosperity, and sustainability. The leaders agreed on the role of transport connectivity in serving as a key enabler to achieve these shared aspirations. Accordingly, they envisaged a seamless multimodal/intermodal[5] transport system across the region with efficient transit facilities to enhance the mobility of goods and people, which in turn will stimulate trade and investment, to thereby generate (inclusive) economic growth in the region.[6]

Following the direction of the leaders of the BIMSTEC member states, the vision of the BIMSTEC Master Plan for Transport Connectivity is a seamlessly connected Bay of Bengal region to achieve peace, prosperity, and sustainability. The mission of the Master Plan is to strengthen connectivity between and within BIMSTEC member states through improved multimodal and intermodal transport.[7]

Importantly, as demonstrated in Appendix 1, the BIMSTEC Master Plan for Transport Connectivity will contribute to the Sustainable Development Goals (SDGs) embodied in the 2030 Agenda for Sustainable Development.[8]

Scope

The Master Plan focuses on the following key areas to achieve its vision:[9]

(i) Roads and road transport. The development of physical infrastructure and services along the primary road corridors handling or having the potential to carry volumes of trade or passengers between member states or to primary maritime gateways, and the international road transport sector plying these corridors.

(ii) Railways and rail transport. The development of rail infrastructure and services connecting member states or to relevant primary maritime gateways and the construction of missing links within the region's international rail network.

(iii) Ports and maritime transport. The development of the region's main ports and maritime gateways to facilitate intra-BIMSTEC trade and enhance maritime connectivity and access to global markets.

(iv) Inland water transport. The development of key waterways to help transport some intraregional road traffic via a more environmentally friendly transport mode.

---

[5] Strictly speaking, while both multimodal and intermodal transport refer to the movement of cargo from origin to destination by multiple modes of transport with different transport carriers, multimodal transport is done under a single contract or bill of lading, while intermodal transport is done under independent contracts. http://logisticsportal.org/community/blogs/-/blogs/difference-between-intermodal-shipping-and-multimodal-shipping.
[6] Bay of Bengal Initiative for Multi-Sectoral Technical and Economic Cooperation. *Fourth Summit Declaration, 30-31 August 2018, Kathmandu, Nepal.*
[7] As understood in this Master Plan, "the mission is the journey, while the vision is the destination."
[8] Consider, for example, with accessible air connectivity especially low-cost carriers, many nationals from BIMSTEC member states are able to work in the Middle East and other regions and send remittances regularly to their home countries. M. Ozaki. 2012. *Worker Migration and Remittances in South Asia.* Asian Development Bank, South Asia Working Paper Series, No. 12, May 2012.
[9] Bay of Bengal Initiative for Multi-Sectoral Technical and Economic Cooperation. 2017. Concept Paper for Master Plan on BIMSTEC Transport Connectivity. 2nd Meeting of the BTCWG, Bangkok, Thailand, 13–14 November 2017.

(v) Civil aviation and airport development. The development of international standard airports and aviation services enabling increased passenger and cargo choices and more services between airports in the member states.

(vi) Multimodal and intermodal transport. The development of multimodal and intermodal transport regimes and services using more than one mode of transport in an international movement.

(vii) Trade facilitation. The harmonization and simplification of border and customs clearance processes relating to the movement of freight and passengers among member states, as well as the development of advanced logistics systems to reduce the costs and time of international transport.

(viii) Human resource development. Training to enhance the capacity and skill of personnel of member states engaged in the above transport and related sectors.[10]

The Master Plan adopts a holistic approach, covering both hard infrastructure, including roads, railways, ports, inland waterways, and airports, and soft infrastructure, including the services using that infrastructure for international transport. Thus, it includes capacity building, transport access agreements, and the harmonization of rules, regulations, policies, and measures related to transport between and among BIMSTEC countries with a view to facilitating the cross-border movement of BIMSTEC trade in support of the proposed BIMSTEC Free Trade Area.

Figure 2 summarizes the building blocks of the Master Plan, including the overarching regional vision as articulated by the leaders of the member states at the Fourth Summit, the strategic objectives, the vision of the Master Plan, the various operational areas (i.e., subsectors), cross-cutting concerns, and implementation.

Key Principles of the Master Plan

Key principles of the Master Plan include the following:

(i) In view of BIMSTEC's position as a key partner in regional cooperation and integration, a key function of the Master Plan is to demonstrate the organization's role and relevance in promoting improvements in intraregional transport connectivity, including connectivity between South and Southeast Asia.

(ii) Connectivity initiatives must be based on universally recognized international norms, good governance, the rule of law, openness, transparency, and financial responsibility, and must be pursued in a manner that respects the sovereignty, equality, and territorial integrity of nations.

(iii) Since the Master Plan is not a negotiated document, but was developed and finalized based only on consultations, it is nonbinding on member states. The Master Plan should be flexible in its structure and recommendations to respond to emerging trends and priorities.

---

[10] Following the direction of the leaders of the BIMSTEC member states, it was agreed during the 2nd Meeting of the BTCWG that the Master Plan will focus on transport connectivity while addressing soft aspects only to the extent that the core focus on physical aspects is not diluted. Report of the Second Meeting of the BIMSTEC Transport Connectivity Working Group. 13–14 November 2017, Bangkok, Thailand. p. 4, para. 11.

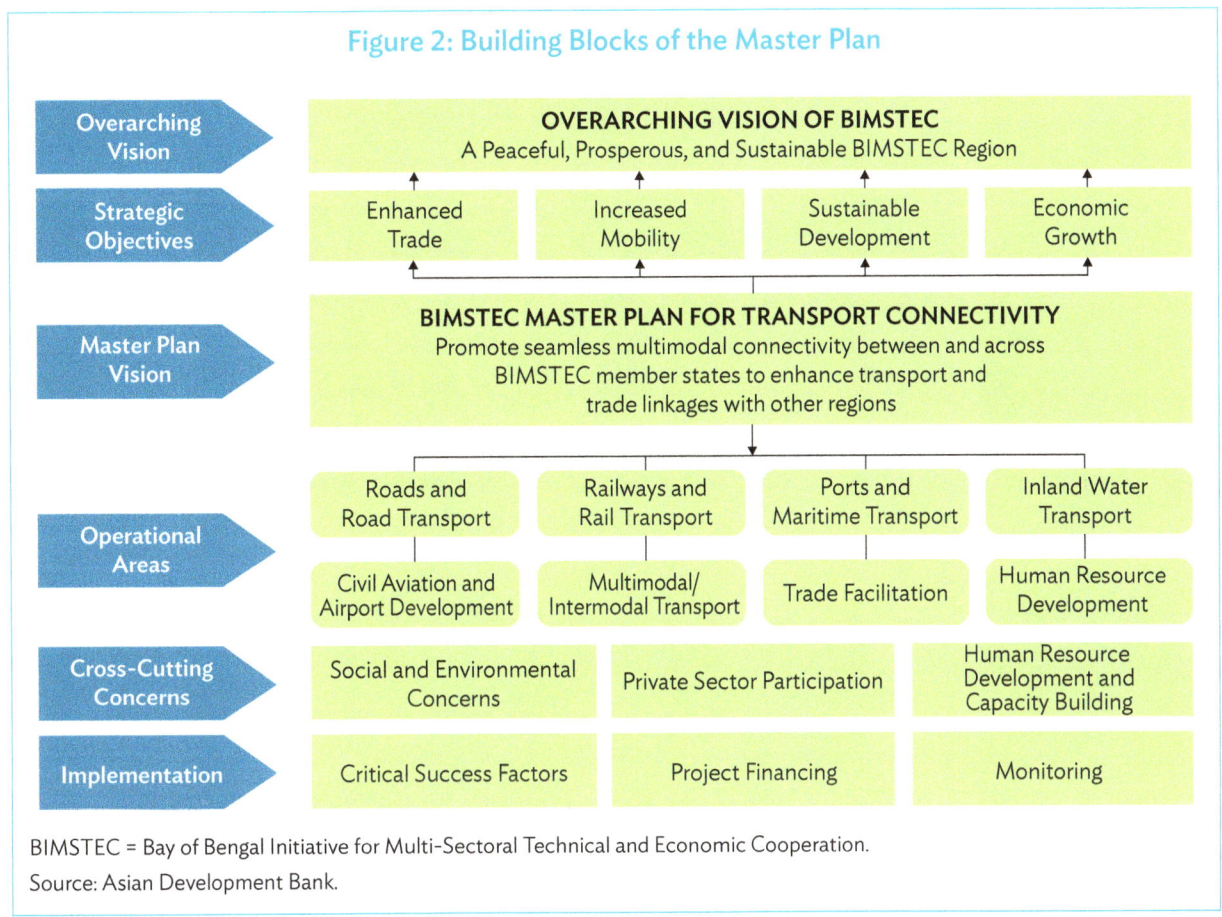

Figure 2: Building Blocks of the Master Plan

BIMSTEC = Bay of Bengal Initiative for Multi-Sectoral Technical and Economic Cooperation.
Source: Asian Development Bank.

(iv) Projects listed in the Master Plan may only be for the information of member states. Deliberations upon of adoption of the Master Plan may not be treated as endorsement or approval of the projects listed in the Master Plan.

(v) Projects recommended or listed in the Master Plan will be executed keeping in mind each member state's procedures, practices, and relevant national laws.

(vi) It is critical to differentiate between BIMSTEC and other regional initiatives, to demonstrate BIMSTEC's unique position in the regional cooperation environment (consider, e.g., BIMSTEC's support for the India–Myanmar–Thailand Trilateral Highway initiative, which spans South and Southeast Asia).[11]

(vii) As called for by the leaders of the BIMSTEC member states at their Fourth Summit,[12] the Master Plan complements the transport and/or other plans of other regional organizations or groupings with

---

[11] Accordingly, the Master Plan study does not constitute an endorsement of connectivity initiatives undertaken in the region by other organizations or of their funding mechanism(s).
[12] Bay of Bengal Initiative for Multi-Sectoral Technical and Economic Cooperation. *Fourth Summit Declaration, 30–31 August 2018, Kathmandu, Nepal.* p. 5: "the Master Plan would serve as a strategic document that guides actions and promotes synergy among various connectivity frameworks, such as the ASEAN Master Plan on Connectivity 2025 (MPAC 2025), the Ayeyawady–Chao Phraya–Mekong Economic Cooperation Strategy (ACMECS), to achieve enhanced connectivity and sustainable development in our region".

overlapping geographical territory, such as those of the Association of Southeast Nations (ASEAN), the Ayeyawaddy–Chao Phrya–Mekong Economic Cooperation Strategy (ACMECS), the Indian Ocean Rim Association (IORA), and the Mekong–Ganga Cooperation (MGC) program (see Appendix 2 for discussion specifically of the synergies with related ASEAN and ACMECS plans).[13]

(viii) This Master Plan is identifiable as an individual master plan rather than as a replica of other regional master plans, which is achieved with different structure and substance, while maintaining compatibility and creating synergies with the other plans in terms of content.

(ix) The overall process for developing the Master Plan included the formulation of policies and strategies in each sector and subsector to achieve the plan's vision, and based on these policies and strategies, formulation of projects, both hard and soft.

(x) The Master Plan takes into account the specific circumstances and requirements of the respective member states, with differing geographic areas and features, population, level of economic activities, and other unique circumstances, while considering the requirement for seamless cross-border movement of people, goods, and vehicles.[14]

(xi) The proposed projects benefit more than one member state (rather than being purely national undertakings) to qualify as BIMSTEC initiatives. That said, there is no need for unanimous concurrence (i.e., the "2+x" principle may be applied).

(xii) This document is a master plan, which incorporates as many considerations as possible, but it is not a convention or an international agreement; implementation must be undertaken individually and bilaterally, based on multilateral principles.

(xiii) The recommended high-capital infrastructure projects should be reconfirmed in each case by feasibility studies. Infrastructure should be designed in such a way as to allow future development if and when such developments are justified by demand and covered by funding sources.

(xiv) Expertise available within the region in terms of planning, construction, execution, and operationalization may be optimally utilized to further the master plan.

(xv) Maintenance plans for all infrastructure projects should also be drawn up at the time of planning so that infrastructure facilities do not suffer after completion of the project liability period.

(xvi) Finally, the Master Plan was produced at a point in time based upon the best information available. Inevitably, changes will occur that will affect the costs and benefits of each proposed project (e.g., changes in the timetables for implementation of other projects, improved information from project-specific studies, and external factors such as national and regional macroeconomic performance). Therefore, the Master Plan is a "live document" providing a robust platform for improving regional transport connectivity, but which requires reviews over time to respond to emerging trends and priorities.

---

[13] One of BIMSTEC's core objectives is "to maintain close and beneficial cooperation with existing international and regional organizations with similar aims and purposes."

[14] BIMSTEC recognizes "the special needs and circumstances of the least developed and land-locked developing countries in the region" and "the necessity to provide meaningful support to their development process." Bay of Bengal Initiative for Multi-Sectoral Technical and Economic Cooperation. *Fourth Summit Declaration, 30–31 August 2018, Kathmandu, Nepal.* p. 2.

Structure of the Master Plan

The section immediately following presents the (overall) Master Plan framework, including an overview of the BIMSTEC region, the transport and trade environment of BIMSTEC (including the development of cross-border value chains), key regional transport issues, and cross-cutting issues.

The document then proceeds by operational area (i.e., sector by sector) rather than scattering the discussion of the various operational areas or sectors across different sections, with subsections on sector overview, policies, and strategies presented together with proposed priority ("flagship" or "signature") projects, including BIMSTEC development logic (i.e., rationale) and timeframes for implementation, since the projects flow directly from these subsections. However, the sector-focused structure is not meant to imply a series of "silos"; as stated in Section 8.2, wherever possible, an integrated approach to the development of transport infrastructure is recommended rather than developing each of the transport modes independently.

The logic of the flow of the text in the sector-by-sector sections is shown in Figure 3. The subsections on issues include highlights of recent progress in the member states in improving regional connectivity. The planning horizon (i.e., implementation period) has been assumed to be 2018 to 2028, i.e.,10 years[15] (and beyond); focusing on short-term projects ("low-hanging fruit") may enable a showing of "quick wins" and early successes, but it would not reflect the need for continued successes throughout the timescale of the Master Plan. The flagship projects[16] were selected mainly based on relevance to BIMSTEC intraregional connectivity, including reference to major routes and corridors in the BIMSTEC region identified in prior initiatives, which are set out in Appendix 3, and to corridors developed during preparation of this Master Plan, which are schematically mapped in Appendix 4.[17] Appendix 5 presents a long list of projects in each category. To enliven the text, the Master Plan includes a number of textboxes, e.g., to highlight notable ongoing and planned projects, or to discuss relevant topics in more depth (such as the benefits of through-transport agreements or arrangements, the scope for regional cooperation in the ports and maritime [sub]sector, the desirability of developing multiple airports in one city).

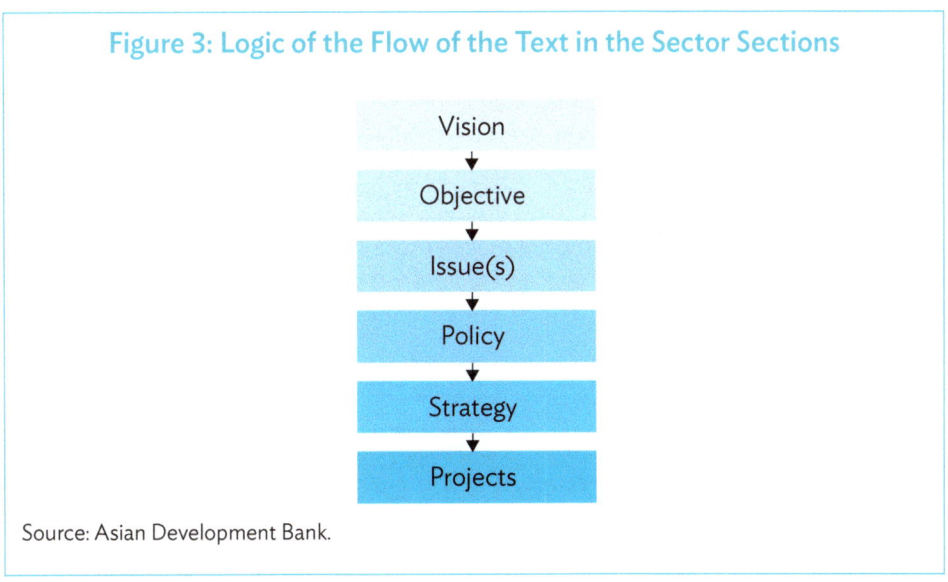

Figure 3: Logic of the Flow of the Text in the Sector Sections

Source: Asian Development Bank.

---

[15] The BTILS adopted a shorter timescale of 2014–2020.
[16] Overambitious action plans that lead to unnecessarily high expectations that, if not fulfilled, can lead to a loss of commitment and momentum.
[17] During the master plan period, the member states may consider selecting additional flagship projects.

II. Overall Master Plan Framework

Overview of the Bay of Bengal Initiative for Multi-Sectoral Technical and Economic Cooperation Region

The Bay of Bengal is the largest bay in the world, creating a "triangular basin" stretching from Sri Lanka and India in the west, to Bangladesh in the center, and to Southeast Asia in the east. It has a combined population of about 1.5 billion (21% of the global total) and a gross domestic product (GDP) of $2.7 trillion, with annual average economic growth rates of between 3.4% and 7.5% between 2012 and 2016. India has the largest regional economy, followed by Thailand and Bangladesh. One-quarter of the world's traded goods cross the Bay of Bengal. But while the region is of vital strategic importance, the BIMSTEC member states are not closely integrated.[18]

The member states are briefly profiled in Box 1.

> **Box 1: Brief Profiles of Bay of Bengal Initiative for Multi-Sectoral Technical and Economic Cooperation Member States**
>
> (i) **Bangladesh,** with direct borders with India and Myanmar and in close proximity to both Bhutan and Nepal situated to the north, occupies a central position in BIMSTEC. Bangladesh is keen to provide access to the seaports of Mongla and Chattogram for the landlocked member states (Bhutan and Nepal) and the northeastern states of India. In addition, it is working for the development of road connectivity to Myanmar with a view to promoting future transit between and among Bangladesh, Bhutan, India, Myanmar, Nepal, and Thailand. In South Asia, Bangladesh, Bhutan, India, and Nepal signed a Motor Vehicles Agreement in June 2015 for cross-border transport facilitation between and among these countries in an accelerated fashion; once in force, this agreement will open a number of routes for international road transport in South Asia. Most of the trade coming across Bangladesh's land borders is bilateral with India, supplemented by small volumes to and from Nepal and Bhutan. The country has a comprehensive highway network of 21,302 km.
>
> (ii) **Bhutan** is a mountainous landlocked country sharing borders with India in the east, west, and south and the People's Republic of China (PRC) in the north. With a population of about 800,000, Bhutan is the smallest of the BIMSTEC countries. The transport of goods and people in Bhutan is mainly by road, despite some limited domestic air services introduced relatively recently. Thus, improving the road and air connectivity of Bhutan is vital to facilitate its future trade.
>
> *continued on next page*

---

[18] C. Xavier. 2018. *Bridging the Bay of Bengal: Toward a Stronger BIMSTEC.* Carnegie India. February. p. 5.

Box 1 continued

(iii) **India** is the largest BIMSTEC member state in its geographic area, economy, and population, and it is the key player in the region. The overall concept of enhancing BIMSTEC connectivity is compatible with India's Act East policy, which has gained new momentum from the recent opening up of Myanmar to the east. The country has the largest physical infrastructure of any country within the BIMSTEC region with over 5.89 million km of roads including 132,500 km of national highways; 67,300 km of railways, of which 20,000 km are electrified; 12 major seaports; and 4 major international airports.

(iv) **Myanmar** is in the center of the BIMSTEC region and borders three other BIMSTEC member states. It has a key role as a potential land bridge connecting South and Southeast Asia. As a result, Myanmar is in the process of enhancing its international infrastructure linkages, in collaboration with neighboring countries. Of all the transport modes in Myanmar, road transport is the most dominant in terms of domestic transport and distribution, but the maritime and aviation modes are becoming more significant in international connectivity.

(v) **Nepal** is a landlocked mountainous country with a population of about 29 million. It is surrounded by India to the east, west, and south, and by the PRC to the north. Transport is dominated by the road sector and, to a lesser extent, by the aviation sector, with plans to develop significant rail coverage. Establishing a modern road network is difficult and costly due to the mountainous terrain covering most of the country. Enhancement of the transport infrastructure has relied heavily on external funding.

(vi) **Sri Lanka** is an island nation state in the Indian Ocean located off the southern tip of India. It has a population of about 21 million. The country's transport infrastructure includes a road network of about 116,000 km, a rail network of 1,640 route-km, 2 international airports, and a major port at Colombo.

(vii) Of the BIMSTEC member states, **Thailand** is the most advanced in transport infrastructure, logistics, and trade facilitation. The transport sector contributes about 7% to its national economy and underpins its important export activities. In terms of physical infrastructure, the road network dominates with a total length of about 202,000 km, of which 51,500 km are classified as highways and 450 km as controlled-access expressways and motorways. Thailand's rail network extends nearly 4,130 km, implying a relatively low density for a country of its size. The country has two major ports, Laem Chabang and Bangkok, and the world's 20th busiest airport, Suvarnabhumi in Bangkok.

BIMSTEC = Bay of Bengal Initiative for Multi-Sectoral Technical and Economic Cooperation. km = kilometer.
Source: Bay of Bengal Initiative for Multi-Sectoral Technical and Economic Cooperation. Updating and Enhancement of the BIMSTEC Transport Infrastructure and Logistics Study, Phase I Final Report. March 2014. Executive Summary.

The Transport and Trade Environment of the Bay of Bengal Initiative for Multi-Sectoral Technical and Economic Cooperation Region

While BIMSTEC's member states account for 3.8% of global trade and about 60% of BIMSTEC's combined GDP comes from trade, trade within BIMSTEC is relatively limited in importance except for the landlocked member states (Bhutan and Nepal). Although the BIMSTEC region has been one of the fastest-growing economic regions in the world, intraregional trade accounts for only about 5% of total trade in the region, compared to 26% of the total trade within ASEAN, 52% of the total trade in the countries of the United States-Mexico-Canada Agreement, and 58% of the total trade within the European Union.[19] Similarity in export products among BIMSTEC member

---

[19] Japan International Cooperation Agency and PADECO Co., Ltd. 2014. Data Collection Survey on Transport Infrastructure Development for Regional Connectivity in and around South Asia. March 2014.

states suggests that in many cases, they are competitors, and not providers of raw materials required by other member states. Accordingly, most member states rely on trading with distant markets, in both imports and exports, and this is reflected in the low tonnages crossing the land borders, relative to those passing through the seaports. Strengthening of infrastructure linkages can help unlock the region's economic potential. Indeed, dramatic growth in the regional flow of goods has been forecasted—by almost 350% by 2030 in constant value terms—with the development of cross-border value chains[20] (Figure 4) and the reduction of physical and nonphysical barriers to

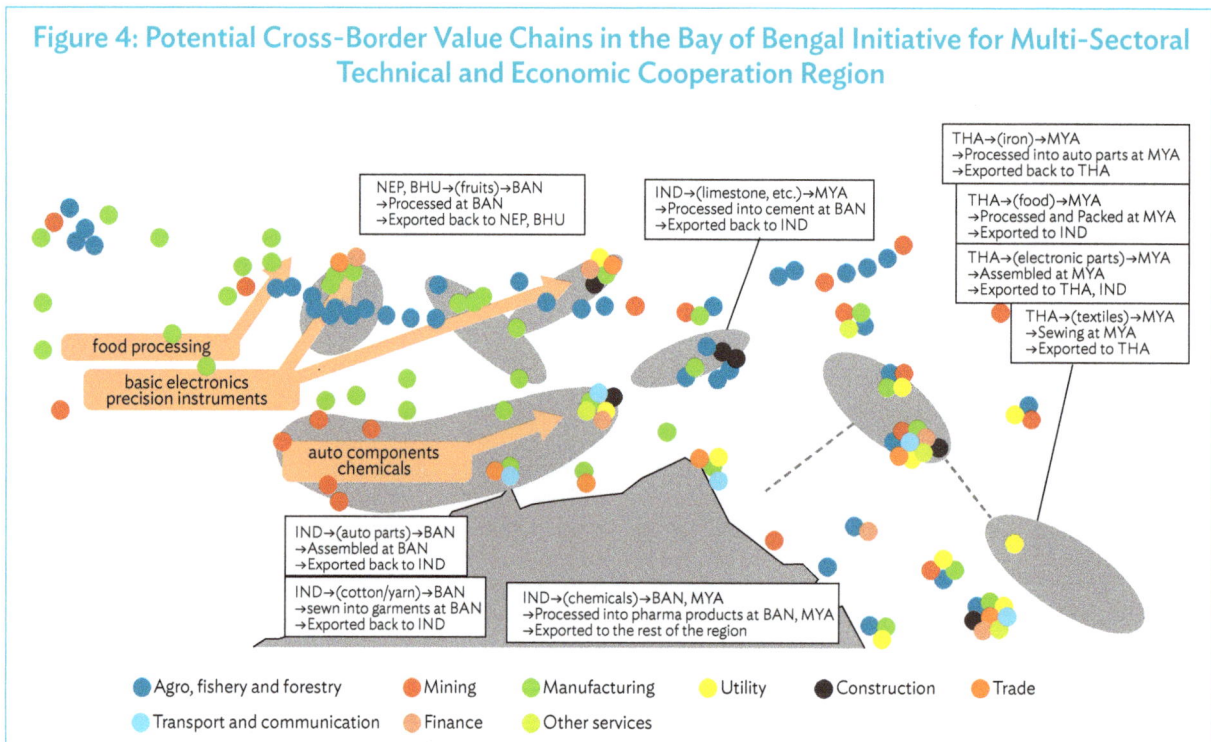

Figure 4: Potential Cross-Border Value Chains in the Bay of Bengal Initiative for Multi-Sectoral Technical and Economic Cooperation Region

BAN = Bangladesh, BHU = Bhutan, IND = India, MYA = Myanmar, NEP = Nepal, THA = Thailand.

Note: Existing clusters of industries are notionally shown in different colors, and those with potential linkages are circled with shaded areas with relevant descriptions. The potential shift of some industries (i.e., food processing, basic electronics, precision instruments, auto components, and chemicals) is shown with the pink arrows. As seen, the potential for the regional value chains can be identified in various locations, although the potential has not been explored much yet, as a huge amount of labor and domestic demand still needs to be absorbed within India.

Source: Japan International Cooperation Agency and PADECO Co., Ltd. 2014. Data Collection Survey on Transport Infrastructure Development for Regional Connectivity in and around South Asia. March 2014. p. ES–iii.

---

[20] Potential sectors for regional value chains include (i) textiles (India→Bangladesh→India: Bangladesh can process cotton imported from India, for exporting garment products back to India), (ii) wood products (Myanmar→Bangladesh→India: Bangladesh can process timber imported from Myanmar, for exporting wood products such as furniture to the larger market in India), and (iii) pharmaceuticals (India→Bangladesh, Myanmar: Bangladesh and Myanmar can import chemicals and other raw materials from India, for processing into medicines and medical instruments to be exported to third countries). Sectors that can be shifted from India to the rest of the region include food processing (→Nepal, with a view to adding value to the agricultural products), basic (semi-high technology), electronics and precision instruments (→Nepal, Bhutan, to take advantage of the good access to utilities such as power and water), auto components (→Bangladesh, to take advantage of the substantially lower labor cost and emerging peripheral subsectors), and chemicals such as liquid fertilizers (→Bangladesh, to maximize the geographical advantage between India as a supplier of raw materials and the rest of the region as potential consumers). Expectations of Myanmar are growing regarding sectors such as textiles, food processing, and medical appliances; the relatively low labor costs in Myanmar can drive such value chain development.

trade. That said, external trade will remain significant over the next decade and, therefore, port connectivity will still be as important as land border connectivity, even for intra-BIMSTEC trade.[21]

Key Regional Transport Issues

Road transport accounts for about 70% of the freight movement within the BIMSTEC region and dominates the overall regional transport system. BIMSTEC has one of the largest railway networks in the world, extending over 77,000 route-km, with systems in Bangladesh, India, Myanmar, Sri Lanka, and Thailand. The region is also interconnected by both mainline and deep-sea container and feeder ships distributing containers throughout the region from hub ports. There are regional waterways between Bangladesh and India. In addition, there are over 350 flights linking regional destinations.[22]

While much has been achieved in recent years to enhance transport connectivity between and across member states, significant gaps remain, underscoring the need for this Master Plan. Specific indications of status and key issues are set out below:

(i) Roads are the dominant transport infrastructure used in all member states. Only India and Thailand have major Asian Highway Class I highway networks, although such highways in northeastern India are still under development. Bangladesh, Nepal, and Sri Lanka have plans to develop Class I roads or networks, but Bhutan and Myanmar will generally rely on Class II and III roads, especially in relation to connectivity with their neighbors. Key residual issues that need to be addressed include (a) the enhancement of arterial road links carrying significant volumes of intra-BIMSTEC trade; (b) the upgrading of border links, including access to maritime borders (i.e., ports); and (c) coordination of the scheduling of road programs to assist in enhancing connectivity between and among the member states. Regarding road transport, the need to transship cargo at international borders results in higher transaction costs, particularly for the importing country; the development of through transport would increase transport efficiency and reduce trade costs.

(ii) Railways have generally become less important for intra-BIMSTEC transport, and each of the railway networks operates independently. While development of a regional dimension in railway infrastructure is difficult, there is a need to (a) enhance rail connectivity between ports, dry ports, and borders, and their hinterlands; and (b) provide rail connectivity for landlocked member states.

(iii) Ports and maritime transport play an important role in trade in all BIMSTEC member states directly or indirectly (the latter in the case of the landlocked member states). Most of each member state's international trade, except for Bhutan and Nepal, is carried by sea. In addition, most intra-BIMSTEC trade in tonnage terms is currently carried by sea due to physical constraints on land connectivity, the lower unit costs of maritime transport compared with those of long-distance road transport, the types of goods traded, and the concentration of supply and demand along seaboards. Areas of concern with a regional dimension include the need for (a) access to deeper water to enable larger vessels to call, (b) improved

---

[21] Bay of Bengal Initiative for Multi-Sectoral Technical and Economic Cooperation. *Updating and Enhancement of the BIMSTEC Transport Infrastructure and Logistics Study, Phase I Final Report.* March 2014. Executive Summary; Asian Development Bank. 2010. *Regional Transport Development in South Asia, Technical Assistance Report.* October 2010; Egis International and Egis India. *2013. ADB TA-7650 (REG): Regional Transport Development in Asia, Final Report.*; and Japan International Cooperation Agency and PADECO Co., Ltd. 2014. *Data Collection Survey on Transport Infrastructure Development for Regional Connectivity in and around South Asia.* March.

[22] Asian Development Bank. 2010. *Regional Transport Development in South Asia, Technical Assistance Report.* October 2010 (updated in text).

(iii) container handling performance at key ports, and (c) use of information technology in the handling of cargo and containers.[23]

(iv) At present, inland water transport is primarily used for domestic rather than international transport; it mainly serves specific markets and is constrained by network geography. That said, the development of a sustainable and economically viable inland waterways (sub)sector in the region can contribute to the achievement of Sustainable Development Goals through poverty reduction and job creation.

(v) Multimodal and intermodal transport is increasingly being recognized in the region as a way of achieving the seamless movement of freight and passengers using multiple modes of transport, resulting in lower transport costs, e.g., through dry ports, or inland clearance/container depots (ICDs), or more ambitious schemes such as the development of multinational, multimodal transit transport corridors, such as the one linking "mainland" India, Myanmar, and North East India.

(vi) Regarding civil aviation and airport development, the member states have a wide range of air connectivity. Aviation has been the most dynamic of the transport modes in the region in recent years and has the highest profile internationally. This situation has to a large extent been driven by the rapid growth in low-cost carrier (LCC) operations and the increasing numbers of such carriers. The most critical issue at present is the need for continued expansion of airport capacity for passengers and freight.

(vii) Trade facilitation is a continuing requirement, both in terms of infrastructure and facilities (i.e., border infrastructure and facilities, and the development of ICDs), and improved practices and procedures, e.g., through the simplification and harmonization of import–export and transit documentation, further development of automated clearance systems, and advanced logistics.

A major constraint in regional connectivity in the BIMSTEC region has been inadequate coordination between and among transport (sub)sectors and intermodal connectivity. While addressing constraints by mode, an optimal multimodal mix should be pursued to ensure economic and energy efficiency, which requires coordination between and among both transport and non-transport agencies. Over the longer term, an optimal modal mix should mitigate climate change impacts.

The BIMSTEC regional transport connectivity Master Plan will support regional development by focusing on external regional and ultimately global linkages. Recently, various regional development strategies have been prepared and the member states have begun to reflect the importance of external and global linkages in their national development plans. However, further integration is required, and the development of national transport projects of regional significance through this Master Plan will contribute to achieving this aim.

---

[23] Asian Development Bank. 2018. *Updating and Enhancement of the BIMSTEC Transport Infrastructure and Logistics Study, Final Report.* Manila.

Key Strategies

Key strategies for the BIMSTEC Master Plan for Transport Connectivity include the following in the various sectors or subsectors:[24]

(i) Road and Road Transport

- Prioritization of road development along the key national arterial routes that represent the region's main existing and potential trade corridors.

- Progressive upgrading of key border link roads between crossings and the national road network along BIMSTEC corridors, with coordinated development on both sides of the border.

- Upgrading or construction of dedicated port access roads in situations where there is congestion on the existing access roads or where new ports are being developed.

- Development of road-based Buddhist and temple tourism circuits.

- Exchange of information on national road development programs and establishment of a mechanism for the effective exchange of relevant road planning data to facilitate future coordination of road investments.

- Implementation of transport access agreements and regional through-transport arrangements.

(ii) Railways and Rail Transport

- Prioritization of rail access to ports, especially for the movement of bulk and semi-bulk cargo and the movement of container traffic between the ports, land borders, and ICDs.

- Development of rail links between India and the landlocked member states of Bhutan and Nepal.

- Development of rail-based Buddhist and temple tourism circuits.

- Exchange of information on national railway development programs and establishment of a mechanism for the effective exchange of relevant road planning data to facilitate future coordination of railway investments.

(iii) Ports and Maritime Transport

- Development of new ports and expansion of existing harbor infrastructure to increase the capacity of the region's ports to handle growth in container traffic.

- Investment in additional container handling equipment, commensurate with demand and the need to improve handling performance consistent with global good and best practice.

- Development of coastal or short-sea shipping.

---

[24] Asian Development Bank. 2018. *Updating and Enhancement of the BIMSTEC Transport Infrastructure and Logistics Study, Final Report*. Manila.

(iv) Inland Water Transport

- Development of sustainable, economically viable inland water transport between member states, e.g., by providing multimodal and intermodal connectivity.

(v) Civil Aviation and Airport Development

- Demand-based development of airport facilities.

- Investment in cargo infrastructure and equipment at major airports with prioritization for this purpose wherever possible.

- Development of additional infrastructure at the region's main airports to facilitate the handling of LCC services, without compromising the infrastructure needed for legacy (full-service) carriers.

(vi) Multimodal and Intermodal Transport

- To establish seamless multimodal and intermodal transport linkages, pursuit of initiatives that efficiently combine the use of different modes of transport, including ICDs and dry ports as well as multimodal transport corridors.

(vii) Trade Facilitation

- Development of border infrastructure at the main BIMSTEC land border crossings.

- Development of ICDs at appropriate locations.

- Review and rationalization of documentation requirements in relation to import and export clearance and promotion of the development of mutual recognition agreements.

- Upgrading of existing information and communication technology (ICT) systems within national customs administrations and establishment of national single windows.

- Adoption of advanced logistical systems as an approach for reducing the high level of distribution costs and transport time.

(viii) Human Resource Development

- Provision of training designed to enhance the capacity and skill of personnel engaged in the transport and related sectors.

- Enhanced training of public and private sector personnel in trade facilitation.

- Enhanced training of border personnel in good and best practices in modern border management.

(ix) Implementation

- Facilitation of overall and closer coordination with its development partners on financing and technical assistance.

- Leadership in monitoring implementation of Master Plan projects.

Cross-Cutting Issues

Social and Environmental Concerns

Although strengthening transport connectivity in BIMSTEC will bring net benefits, possible negative consequences will need to be addressed, including environmental impacts (e.g., air and noise pollution, waste disposal), increased land prices, increased road traffic accidents, the transborder spread of communicable human and animal diseases, and deforestation. Such concerns may result from the negative impacts of specific projects, but there may be larger overall effects, especially regarding climate change which, in turn, can affect the condition and operation of various transport facilities.

Private Sector Participation

Private sector participation is essential for transport development. Public funds can only cover a fraction of infrastructure projects, and the potential contributions from international development partners are limited, indicating a need for substantial private sector investment. Public–private partnerships (PPPs) provide an important source of funds for infrastructure funding as, for example, demonstrated by the experience of India. Improving transparency, the regulatory framework, and governance of PPP projects can increase the effectiveness of this approach. Details are presented in Section XI.

Human Resource Development and Capacity Building

The planning and implementation of transport sector connectivity initiatives in the BIMSTEC region has been constrained in some cases by a need for human resource development and capacity building. Specific training is required in (i) the transport and related sectors, (ii) trade facilitation, and (iii) border management. The programs should be tailored to meet the specific requirements of the subsector or field of operation. Coordination between and among member states in the planning and implementation of these programs will be beneficial since it will enable a pooling of expertise and resources as well as a cross-fertilization of approaches. Details are presented in Section X.

III. Roads and Road Transport

Sector Overview

Roads are the dominant transport infrastructure used in all of the BIMSTEC member states. They are not only the main means of domestic connectivity, but they are also the main conduit for the movement of intra-BIMSTEC trade, either directly across land borders or via their connectivity to seaports. While all countries participate in the Asian Highway Initiative, as stated in Section II on Key Regional Transport Issues, only India and Thailand currently have major Asian Highway Class I highway networks, although such highways in the northeastern states of India are still under development. Bangladesh, Nepal, and Sri Lanka have plans to develop Class I roads or networks, but Bhutan and Myanmar will generally rely on Class II and III roads during the planning period, especially for connectivity with their neighbors.

While there is an overall need to upgrade the road network throughout the region, the Master Plan focuses on BIMSTEC's role. Its key aims and implications for road development are as follows:

(i) creating an enabling environment for rapid economic development by enhancing the quality of road connectivity between member states;
(ii) accelerating social progress in the subregion by improving accessibility to regional trading opportunities;
(iii) promoting active collaboration and mutual assistance on matters of common interest through joint development of the key trade routes; and
(iv) cooperating more effectively in joint efforts that support, and are complementary to, the national development plans of member states by promoting the linking of the planning and scheduling of road development projects on routes directly or indirectly connecting member states.

These roles suggest the need for:

(i) enhancement of arterial road links carrying significant volumes of intra-BIMSTEC trade;
(ii) upgrading of border linkages, including access to the maritime borders (i.e., ports); and
(iii) coordination in the scheduling of road programs to assist in connecting member states.

In addition, there have been calls for:

(i) developing Buddhist and temple circuit road connectivity;[25] and
(ii) having through-transport agreements between and among BIMSTEC member states, as necessary to reduce transport costs and facilitate intraregional trade for the overall benefit of member states.

---

[25] Bay of Bengal Initiative for Multi-Sectoral Technical and Economic Cooperation. *Fourth Summit Declaration, 30–31 August 2018, Kathmandu, Nepal*. p. 9: "commitment to developing and promoting Buddhist Tourist Circuit, Temple Tourist Circuit, ancient cities trail….".

Enhancement of Arterial Links to Borders and Ports

Issues

Most of the distance in a trade movement is along arterial road linkages along national road networks. These arterial roads are critical to promoting further development of trade between member states, especially between the maritime and mountain economies of the region, providing opportunities for development of the landlocked (and potentially "landlinked") member states. Examples of such arterial links include the India–Myanmar–Thailand Trilateral Highway, the Kolkata–Birgunj and Kolkata–Kathmandu links, the Dhaka–Chattogram[26] Corridor, the Kolkata–Siliguri–Guwahati–Imphal link, the Kolkata–Siliguri–Phuentsholing link, and the Kandy–Colombo link. All of these highways are either currently or in the future will be essential to the development of trade connectivity within the region.

While most national road development plans are mainly oriented toward satisfying growing domestic traffic demand in each country and enhancing internal connectivity,[27] it is important that these particular arterial trade routes are prioritized because of their trade development potential. In most cases, these links are scheduled for development and, therefore, the issue relates more to prioritization than identification. Enhancement of these arterial links is considered as important or more important than even border links since they often have a greater impact on overall transport rates and, therefore, trade competitiveness.

Recent progress in the BIMSTEC region in enhancing arterial links to borders and ports—an important part of improving transport connectivity in BIMSTEC—include (i) four-laning of the Dhaka–Chattogram highway (191 km, $414 million, 2009–2017), which has developed Bangladesh's main arterial trade link between Chattogram Port and Dhaka; (ii) construction of the Chukkha–Damchu bypass on the Thimphu–Phuentsholing Highway in Bhutan, reducing 29 km along the country's primary trade route linking the country's capital and its main border crossing (2014–2018); (iii) improvement of a number of regionally significant roads in India, e.g., the Motihari–Raxaul Highway, the missing highway link near Siliguri (NH 31D), upgrading of the Siliguri–Guwahati (NH 31C), Guwahati–Shillong (NH 31C), and Siliguri–Kolkata links (NH 34), and upgrading as well as improvement of other highway links in West Bengal and Bihar (various years), all improving roadway capacity linking India with other BIMSTEC member states; (iv) improvement of sections of the Trilateral Highway in Myanmar (various years) and improvement of the Mandalay–Monywa link (2016–2018), which can handle traffic to and from Thailand and potentially through to India; and (v) upgrading of the Narayanghat–Mugling Road (33 km, completed in 2018) in Nepal, to improve roadway capacity to facilitate smooth transportation and international trade. While these projects have developed key transport corridors in the region, transforming them into economic corridors will take time.[28]

The most critical physical barriers to cross-regional transport may be those in Myanmar, which provides the only land bridge between South and Southeast Asia. Actively participating in the development of regional connectivity between and among member states, to date, Myanmar has prioritized road upgrading projects to border crossings as provided for in its national transport master plan and subject to funding constraints.

In addition, a key feature of a number of roads in this and the following section is provision of access to the sea for the landlocked member states (Bhutan and Nepal), consistent with Article 125 of the United Nations

---

[26] Chattogram is the new official name for what was called Chittagong; the new name, which is closer to the Bangla pronunciation, is used in this Master Plan. Other changes made in 2018 (and reflected in this Master Plan) include Barishal replacing Barisal, Bogura replacing Bogra, Cumilla replacing Comilla, and Jashore replacing Jessore.

[27] A vision of large volumes of "end-to-end" traffic is not likely and does not even occur on expressway systems in Europe or North America. Asian Development Bank and Asian Development Bank Institute. 2015. *Connecting South Asia and Southeast Asia*. p. 55.

[28] J.-F. Gautrin. Land-Based Cross-Border Infrastructure. In M. G. Plummer, P. J. Morgan, and G. Wignaraja. 2016. *Connecting Asia: Infrastructure for Integrating South and Southeast Asia*. Asian Development Bank Institute. p. 64.

Convention on Law of the Sea (1982), which provides a right of access to and from the sea and freedom of transit for landlocked states.

Policy

Road linkages between the BIMSTEC concentrations of trade supply and demand and the land and sea borders should be accorded high priority in national road transport plans, thus, expediting intra-BIMSTEC trade movements and reducing transaction costs.[29]

Strategy

BIMSTEC will encourage member states to prioritize road development along the key national arterial routes that represent the region's main existing and potential trade corridors.[30]

Projects

Appendix 5 includes a long list of planned projects to enhance arterial links to borders and ports, while Table 1 highlights planned flagship projects in this category selected mainly based on relevance to BIMSTEC intraregional connectivity, including reference to major routes and corridors in the BIMSTEC region that were previously defined, which are set out in Appendix 3, and to corridors developed during the preparation of this Master Plan, which are schematically mapped in Appendix 4.

Table 1: Planned Flagship Projects to Enhance Arterial Links to Ports and Borders

Code	Project Description	BIMSTEC Development Logic	Estimated Cost, 2018 ($ million)	(Possible) Funding Sources	Timescale
BAN-RD-001	Improvement of the Jatrabari intersection (Mawa) on the Dhaka–Khulna Highway and the Pantchchar–Bhanga road section to four lanes	Enhancing and accommodating future traffic flow between Dhaka and Kolkata along AH 1 and BIMSTEC Road Corridor 1 as well as connecting southwestern parts of Bangladesh (especially Greater Faridpur, Barishal, and Khulna) with the capital, resulting in significant reductions in transport times and costs between and among BIMSTEC member states	1,295	Government	2016–2020
BAN-RD-004	Construction of the Padma Multipurpose Bridge at Mawa	Linking of Dhaka and the Indian border near Kolkata, as well as connecting southern parts of the country, resulting in significant reductions in transport times and costs between and among BIMSTEC member states	3,706	Government	2009–2019

continued on next page

---

[29] Asian Development Bank. 2018. *Updating and Enhancement of the BIMSTEC Transport Infrastructure and Logistics Study, Final Report.* Manila.
[30] Ibid.

Table 1 continued

Code	Project Description	BIMSTEC Development Logic	Estimated Cost, 2018 ($ million)	(Possible) Funding Sources	Timescale
BAN-RD-008	Road Connectivity Project Joydevpur–Chandra–Tangail–Elenga to four-lane highway	Connection of northwestern Bangladesh with northeastern India, Bhutan, and Nepal	682	ADB, OFID, ADFD	2013–2018
BAN-RD-009	Road Connectivity Project II (four-laning Elenga–Hatikamrul–Rangpur, 190.4 km)	Connection of northwestern Bangladesh with northeastern India, Bhutan, and Nepal	1,494	ADB	2016–2020
BAN-RD-010	Construction of the second Katchpur, Meghna, and Gomti Bridges and rehabilitation of existing bridges (total bridge length of 2,736 m)	Development of the country's main arterial trade link between Chattogram Port and Dhaka	1,035	Government and JICA	2013–2021
BAN-RD-011	Construction of the Dhaka–Chattogram Expressway (217 km)	Provision of faster access between the capital and the main port of Bangladesh	3,701	PPP, with proposal for ADB viability gap financing under process of approval	2019–2023
BAN-RD-014	Four-laning of the Dhaka (Katchpur)–Sylhet Highway (226 km, NH 2)	Provision of connectivity down the eastern side of Bangladesh for traffic from India's northeastern states to Dhaka and Chattogram	1,800	Government and other funding sources to be identified	2019–2023
BHU-RD-021	Upgrading of the Gelephu–Trongsa National Highway (before 244 km, but shortened to 201 km), including four bridges	Improved north–south connection to NH 31 in India and also to Gelephu Airport in Bhutan	82	Funding sources to be identified	2018–2023
IND-RD-023	Upgrading of Imphal–Moreh NH39	Improved connectivity between India and Myanmar along AH 1 and AH 2	180	Government (National Highways and Infrastructure Development Corporation) and ADB	2018–2023
MYA-RD-029	Improvement (two-laning) of the Yagyi–Kalewa road (139 km)	Reconstruction of a key section of the India–Myanmar–Thailand Trilateral Highway	174 (INR 11.7 billion)	India (grant)	2015–2021

continued on next page

Table 1 continued

Code	Project Description	BIMSTEC Development Logic	Estimated Cost, 2018 ($ million)	(Possible) Funding Sources	Timescale
MYA-RD-030	Construction of Kawkareik–Eindu Road	Enhancing access to a primary BIMSTEC east–west trade corridor along the India–Myanmar–Thailand Trilateral Highway	131.8 (including 110 from ADB, 20 from AIF, and 1.8 from Government)	ADB, AIF, and government	2015–2021
MYA-RD-031	Provision of 69 new bridges along the Kalewa–Tamu Road	Development of the northern section of the India–Myanmar–Thailand Trilateral Highway	54	India (grant)	2014–2024
MYA-RD-034	Gyaing (580 m), Kawkareik (796 m), and Zathapyin (480 m) bridges	As above	308 (JPY 33.86 billion)	JICA Loan	2016–2024
MYA-RD-037	Development of new Htee Kee (Myanmar)–Baan Phu Nam Ron (Thailand) border crossing road	Provision of a new east–west connection, linking with a new Dawei Port	142 (THB 4.5 billion)	Thailand (NEDA)	2018–2024 (feasibility study under discussion between Ministry of Construction and NEDA, Thailand)
NEP-RD-038	Kathmandu–Terai Fast Track Road, including construction of a new four-lane expressway between Kathmandu and Nijgadh (76.2 km) and upgrading of Nijgadh–Pathlaiya segment from two to four lanes (18 km)	Provision of an arterial trade link between Kathmandu and the main border crossing with India; also enabling the development of a new airport for the Kathmandu region	2,000	Government (and Nijgadh–Pathalaiya section by the World Bank)	2016–2024
NEP-RD-041	Upgrading of Narayanghat–Mungling–Kathmandu road (146 km) and studies on axle load control and road safety measures	Improvement of a critical section of an existing trade corridor	700	World Bank and government	2013–2024 (Narayanghat–Mungling completed in 2018; Mungling–Kathmandu to be undertaken in 2020–2024)
NEP-RD-042	Upgrading of East-West Highway (1,028 km)	Improvement of an important section of AH 2, serving international trade and traffic	2,010	ADB, World Bank, and the government	2016–2025

continued on next page

Table 1 continued

Code	Project Description	BIMSTEC Development Logic	Estimated Cost, 2018 ($ million)	(Possible) Funding Sources	Timescale
SRL-RD-044	Central Expressway, Phases I–IV, including Kadawata, Mirigama, Kurunagala, and Dambulla	Improved connectivity between Colombo port and the northern part of the country	800–1,000	PRC (China Exim Bank) and others	2017–2025
THA-RD-046	Four-laning of the Mae Sot–Tak Highway (51 km, Route 12 mountain section)	Expedited trade between Thailand and Myanmar	90	Government	2015–2019

ADB = Asian Development Bank, ADFD = Abu Dhabi Fund for Development, AH = Asian Highway, AIF = Association of Southeast Asian Nations Infrastructure Fund, BAN = Bangladesh, BHU = Bhutan, BIMSTEC = Bay of Bengal Initiative for Multi-Sectoral Technical and Economic Cooperation, China Exim Bank = Export-Import Bank of China, IND = India, INR = Indian rupee, JICA = Japan International Cooperation Agency, JPY = Japanese yen, km = kilometer, m = meter, MYA = Myanmar, NEDA = Neighbouring Countries Economic Development Cooperation Agency, NEP = Nepal, NH= National Highway, OFID = Organization of Petroleum Exporting Countries Fund for International Development, PPP = public–private partnership, PRC = People's Republic of China, SRL= Sri Lanka, THA = Thailand, THB = Thai baht.

Source: Asian Development Bank.

Box 2 and Box 3 feature the development of two notable arterial road projects to link borders, the India–Myanmar–Thailand Trilateral Highway and the Kathmandu–Terai Fast Track Road Project in Nepal.

Box 2: Development of the India-Myanmar-Thailand Trilateral Highway

The India–Myanmar–Thailand Trilateral Highway—first proposed at a trilateral ministerial meeting on transport linkages held in Yangon, Myanmar, in April 2002—will eventually be a four-lane highway, extending about 1,300 km, which will connect Moreh, India with Mae Sot, Thailand, via Myanmar (see the map below). Segments include (i) Moreh–Tamu–Kalewa (150 km, completed in 2017), (ii) Kalewa–Yagyi (121 km, to be upgraded by 2020), (iii) Yagyi–Chaungma–Monywa (64 km, completed), (iv) Monywa–Mandalay (136 km, completed), (v) Mandalay–Meiktila bypass (123 km, completed in 2010), (vi) Mektila bypass–Taungoo–Oktwin–Payagyi (Pyay) (238 km, completed in 2010), (vii) Payagyi–Theinzayat (Thein Za Yat–Thaton) (140 km, completed in 2017), (viii) Thaton–Mawlamyine–Kawkareik (134 km, to be upgraded by 2020), (ix) Kawkareik–Myawaddy (26 km, completed in 2017), and (x) Myawaddy–Mae Sot (20 km, to be completed in 2019). As of March 2018, 48% of the road was Class III, 30% was Class I, 20% was Class II, and less than 2% was below Class III.

The highway is expected to increase trade in the ASEAN–India Free Trade Area. For this purpose, India has proposed extending the road to Cambodia, the Lao People's Democratic Republic, and Viet Nam, along the 3,200-km East–West Corridor of the ACMECS. In December 2017, India offered a $1 billion line of credit for India–ASEAN connectivity projects.

continued on next page

Box 2 continued

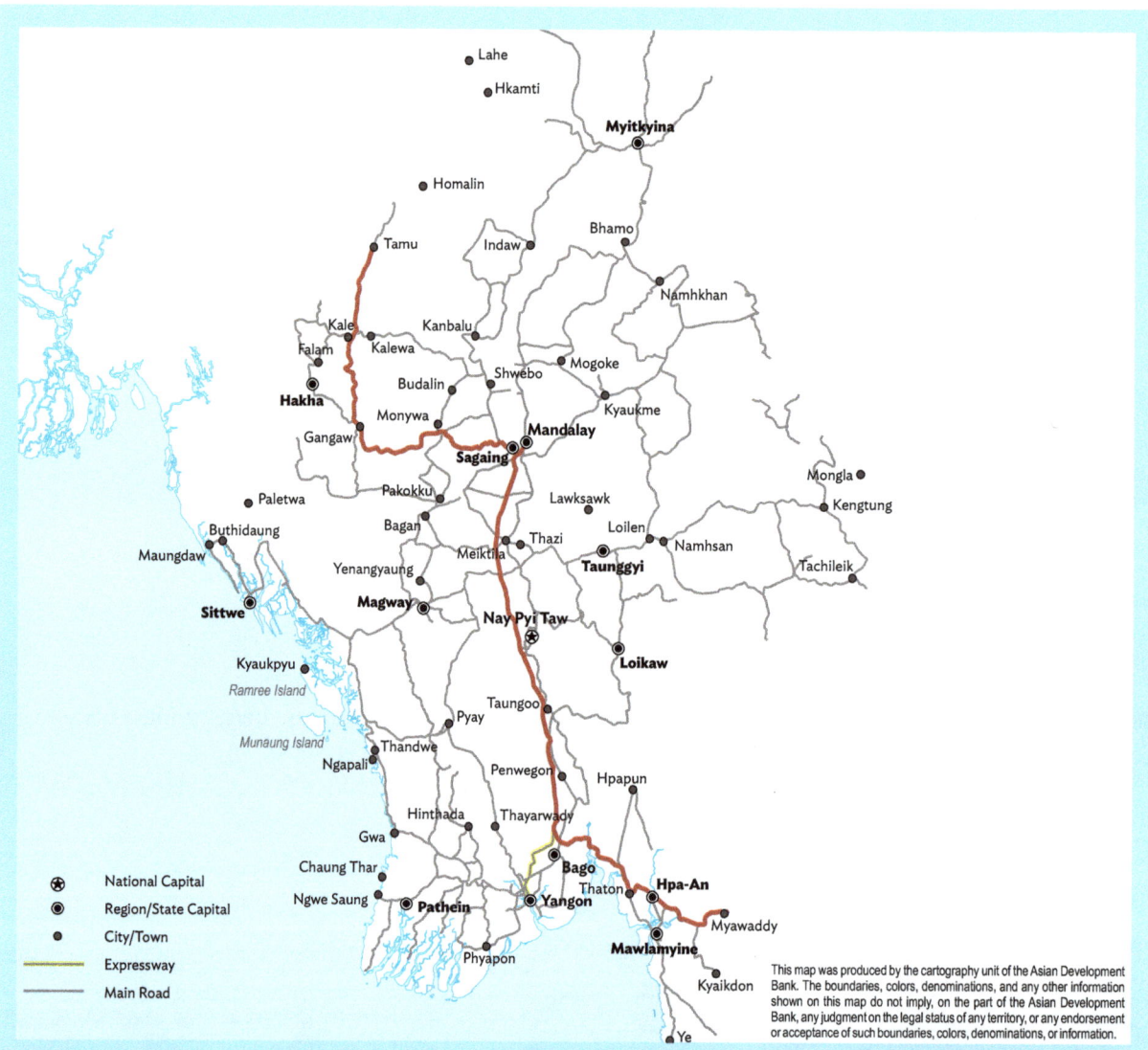

ACMECS = Ayeyawaddy–Chao Phrya–Mekong Economic Cooperation Strategy, ASEAN = Association of Southeast Asian Nations, km = kilometer.

Sources: N. Bana and K. Yhome. 2017. The Road to Mekong: The India–Myanmar–Thailand Trilateral Highway Project. *ORF [Observer Researcher Foundation] Issue Brief*, Issue No. 171, February 2017; http://www.knowmadicnews.com/2015/09/04/thailand-myanmar-india-road-trip/ (map).

Box 3: Development of the Kathmandu–Terai Fast Track Road Project

The Kathmandu–Terai Fast Track Road Project—a "transformational intervention"—will develop a 76-kilometer expressway that will substantially reduce the distance, time, and cost between Kathmandu and the Terai–Indian border. The existing routes are indirect and long. A more direct route will save about 150 kilometers and reduce travel time by up to 5 hours. Also, the road will increase reliability since the existing road is subject to frequent disruptions and closures during the monsoon season, which increases transport costs.

Sources: C. B. Shrestha. 2014. Kathmandu-Terai Fast Track: From Non-Starter to National Project, *Spotlight Nepal*, Vol. 8, No. 12, December 2014; World Bank. 2014. *A Vision for Nepal, Policy Notes for the Government, Synthesis Report*. p. xi.

Upgrading of Border Roads

Issues

Border roads in the region were seldom designed for current border activities and traffic flows and are often unsuitable for modern transport vehicles. An additional problem is the encroachment of local retail and pedestrian activities onto main roads passing through rural and urban settlements causing delays, congestion, and accidents.

Traditionally, the member states have focused their road development programs on internal connectivity between domestic centers of population and economic activity. In each of the BIMSTEC member states, the national capital is located in the approximate center of the country, often distant from its main land borders. The second feature of the region is there are no major urban areas at the borders, although in the case of the two landlocked member states (Bhutan and Nepal), large towns have developed based mainly on cross-border trading activities.

The main function of border crossings has been to process bilateral or short-distance transit trade, with relatively low traffic levels compared to the core national road networks. Except for the landlocked member states, trade across the land borders represents only a relatively small percentage of the overall international trade of the countries. In many cases, these roads to the frontiers were not designed as border roads, but they became so with independence. Therefore, they are often on the periphery of the national road network and have typically been accorded low investment priority within national road programs.

To enable BIMSTEC to become a more integrated development and trading community, it is critical that the member states become more effectively interconnected. Except for Sri Lanka (an island country), it is important that efficient road connections be established to serve intra-BIMSTEC trading opportunities. The border roads physically link the more important border crossings with the arterial road routes in the respective member states on either side of the border.

There is a relationship between the cost of developing a particular road in a border area and the traffic likely to travel along that border route. Such linkages between capacity and demand are normally assessed by estimating economic rates of return in feasibility studies, but at the planning stage these rates of return are unknown. Nevertheless, this cost-traffic demand relationship should be taken into account, particularly considering the major differences in the development costs and traffic levels at the various BIMSTEC border crossings. Projects at borders, where higher levels of traffic can potentially be generated, are more likely to attract funding and be implemented than projects at borders, where trade activity is significantly less.

There may be some overlapping between arterial roads and border roads when arterial roads approach border areas. It may (somewhat arbitrarily) be considered that border link roads are (mainly) within, say, 50 km of the borders.

Recent examples of progress in the BIMSTEC region in upgrading border links include (i) upgrading of the Balukhali–Gundum border road between Bangladesh and Myanmar ($10 million, 2 km, completed in 2018); (ii) the Panitanki–Naxalbari–Shivmandir–Fulbari road improvement along Asian Highway 2 in West Bengal, improving connectivity between India and Bangladesh, Bhutan, and Nepal ($100 million, completed in 2018), assisted by ADB; (iii) the Jaigaon–Hashimara–Telipara–Mainaguri–Changrabandha road improvement along Asian Highway 48, also in West Bengal, improving connectivity between Bangladesh and Bhutan ($152 million, completed in 2018), assisted by ADB; (iv) improvement of the Kohalpur–Nepalgunj border link road in western Nepal ($9 million, 2013–2017), assisted by ADB; and (v) improvement of the road between Myawaddy and Kawkareik, in Myanmar ($35 million, 46 km, 2013–2017), assisted by Thailand.

Policy

BIMSTEC member states should upgrade link road connectivity between their core national road network and the border crossings, to handle modern transport and to facilitate bilateral trade and passenger traffic.

Strategy

BIMSTEC will encourage progressive upgrading of key border link roads between crossings and the national road network along BIMSTEC corridors, with coordinated development on both sides of the border. Box 4 presents suggestions on how this strategy can be achieved.

Box 4: How to Achieve the Strategy to Develop Key Border Link Roads

This strategy to develop border roads can be achieved through the adoption of two substrategies depending on the volume of through traffic: (i) the construction of more limited-access roads designed to separate the line-haul and access functions of the road network (e.g., bypasses, as included in this Master Plan), and (ii) the development of local road management plans for small towns and villages.

These two issues—improving or upgrading the design of roads linking to border crossings, and the intrusion of local retail and pedestrian activities onto main roads—are, to a certain extent, related in that both cause congestion and prevent the free flow of traffic to and from border crossings, although the ability to implement an effective policy or strategy to address these issues is different. Upgrading the design and construction of roads to accommodate modern transport vehicles is a relatively straightforward endeavor, requiring only appropriate transport planning and designs, plus budget availability. Some progress has been achieved on this over the last decade, although the presence of local retail shops and other businesses, such as vehicle and tire repair, which occupy roadways, is a cultural reality in many BIMSTEC member states, and this issue is compounded by the difficulty of enforcing traffic and parking regulations.

Source: Asian Development Bank. 2014. *Updating and Enhancement of the BIMSTEC Transport Infrastructure and Logistics Study, Phase II Report.* May 2014. p. 14.

Projects

Appendix 5 includes a long list of planned projects to upgrade border roads, while Table 2 highlights planned flagship projects in this category, selected mainly based on relevance to BIMSTEC intraregional connectivity.

Table 2: Planned Flagship Projects to Upgrade Border Roads

Code	Project Description	BIMSTEC Development Logic	Estimated Cost, 2018 ($ million)	(Possible) Funding Sources	Timescale
BAN-RD-051	Four-laning of the Bhanga-Bhatiapara-Kalna-Lohagora-Narail-Jashore-Benapole Highway (135 km)	Upgrading of the main border corridor linking Bangladesh and India, a key trade link	1,100	ILOC	2019–2024
BAN-RD-052	Four-laning of the Chattogram-Cox's Bazar-Teknaf Highway	Connecting Chattogram Port and Myanmar	1,270	Government-to-government PPP with Japan, ADB, and government	2018–2023

continued on next page

Table 2 continued

Code	Project Description	BIMSTEC Development Logic	Estimated Cost, 2018 ($ million)	(Possible) Funding Sources	Timescale
BAN-RD-054	Four-laning of the Rangpur to Burimari Highway (128 km)	Connection with Changrabandha (India) and Bhutan	960	ADB	2019–2023
BHU-RD-057	Construction of Samrang-Jomotsangkha section (58 km)	Improved accessibility along the southern Bhutan border with India	21 (roads and 19 bridges)	Government of India	2023
BHU-RD-058	Construction of the Lhamoizhingkha-Sarpang section of the SEWH (75 km, including about 14 bridges)	As above	52	Funding source not yet confirmed	2018–2028
IND-RD-063	Upgrading of NH 44 Silchar–Agartala–Sabroom in Assam and Tripura (NH 53 and NH 44) with Karimganj–Sutrakhandispur of NH 151 to the India-Bangladesh border	Improved connectivity between India and Bangladesh	610	Government (National Highways and Infrastructure Development Corporation) and JICA	2019–2023
IND-RD-064	Two-laning from the Assam–Meghalaya border, Dudhanai to Dalu, via Bagmara, NH 62	As above	227	JICA	2021–2022
IND-RD-065	Improvement of NH 208 between Teliamura and Harina (158 km) in Tripura	As above	285	JICA	2021–2022
IND-RD-066	Upgrading road between Kolkata and Bongaon near Petrapole on the India-Bangladesh border	As above	130	Government and ADB	2021–2022
IND-RD-067	Two-laning of alternate route between Barak Valley (Silchar) to Guwahati via Harangajao-Turuk in Assam	As above	452	Government	2021–2022
IND-RD-068	Development of link roads between Srirampu–Dhubri and Phulbari to Tura with a new bridge across the Brahamputra River on NH 127B	As above	530	JICA	2019–2023
IND-RD-069	Improvement of Manu-Simlung, NH 44 in Tripura	As above	170	As above	2021–2022
IND-RD-070	Improvement of NH 51 between Tura and Dalu connecting with the India-Bangladesh border	As above	79	As above	2018–2020
IND-RD-071	Shillong-Dawki including rehabilitation of the Dawki bridge on the India-Bangladesh border	As above	31	As above	2019–2023
IND-RD-072	Construction of a new extradosed bridge over the Feni River at Sabroom in southern Tripura, connecting India and Bangladesh	As above	13	Government	2017–2020

continued on next page

Table 2 continued

Code	Project Description	BIMSTEC Development Logic	Estimated Cost, 2018 ($ million)	(Possible) Funding Sources	Timescale
IND-RD-073	Khowai–Agartala link road	As above	85	Government	2019–2023
IND-RD-074	Improvement of NH 512 between km 82.4 and km 99.5, and between km 104.2 and km 106.6 in Dakshin Dinajpur, West Bengal	As above	21	Government	2017–2022
IND-RD-075	Maram–Peren–Dimapur road in Manipur and Nagaland	Improved connectivity between India and Myanmar	360	As above	2021–2022
IND-RD-076	Four-laning of Imphal–Moirang, NH-150 in Manipur	As above	180	ADB	2021–2022
IND-RD-078	Divided four-lane road linking the Kohima and Kedima, Kromg, and Imphal section of NH 39 in Manipur	As above	280	As above	2021–2022
IND-RD-079	Ukhrul–Tolloi–Tadubi in Manipur	As above	230	As above	2021–2022
IND-RD-080	Ukhrul–Jessami, NH 202 in Manipur	As above	230	As above	2019–2023
IND-RD-081	Jiribam–Tipaimukh in Manipur	As above	210	As above	2019–2023
IND-RD-082	Aizawl–Tuipang connecting with the Kaladan multimodal transport corridor	As above	946	JICA	2021–2022
IND-RD-083	Improvement of Imphal–Kangchup–Tamenglong–Tousem–Haflong	As above	184	Government and ADB	2021–2022
IND-RD-084	Construction and upgrading of alternate highway to Gangtok from Bagrakot to Kafer	Improved connectivity between India, Bhutan, and Nepal	48	Government	2018–2020
IND-RD-086	Development of the Siliguri–Mirik–Darjeeling link road	Improved connectivity between India and Nepal	150	ADB	2020–2021
IND-RD-087	Gelephu (Bhutan) to Samthaibari (near Hapachara in Assam)	As above	117	Government	2019–2021
IND-RD-088	Additional approach roads to ICPs or land ports (ICP Raxual, Bihar approach road [7 km], ICP Bihar; Jogbani, Bihar approach road [1 km]; ICP Rupaidiha, Uttar Pradesh approach road [1.5 km]; ICP Sunaulli approach road [0.5 km], ICP Moreh approach road [3 km])	Links to border crossings through ICPs	To be specified	Government	2018–2020
NEP-RD-091	Connection between the ICP and the ICD bypass road at Birgunj	Linking of main border development with national road network	12	Government, and Birgunj Municipality	2018–2020
NEP-RD-093	Construction of Mahakali Bridge border link to India	Reduction in transport costs for bilateral traffic	36	Government	2016–2020

continued on next page

Table 2 continued

Code	Project Description	BIMSTEC Development Logic	Estimated Cost, 2018 ($ million)	(Possible) Funding Sources	Timescale
NEP-RD-095	Widening of the Birgunj bypass to four lanes	Provision of extra capacity for traffic generated by ICD volumes	47	ADB and government	2016–2021
REG-RD-097(IND and NEP)	Construction of Mechi Bridge	Improved connectivity between India and Nepal	25	ADB and India	2016–2021
REG-RD-098 (MYA and THA)	Border link project between Mae Sot (Thailand) and Myawaddy (Myanmar), including a bypass road and new border checkpoints	Expediting trade between Thailand and Myanmar	122	Government of Thailand	2015–2019

ADB = Asian Development Bank, AIIB = Asian Infrastructure Investment Bank, BAN = Bangladesh, BHU = Bhutan, BIMSTEC = Bay of Bengal Initiative for Multi-Sectoral Technical and Economic Cooperation, China Exim Bank = Export-Import Bank of China, ICD = inland clearance/inland container depot, ICP = integrated check post, ILOC = Indian Line of Credit, IND = India, km = kilometer, MYA = Myanmar, NEP = Nepal, NH = national highway, PPP = public–private partnership, REG = regional, SEWH = Southern East–West Highway (Bhutan), THA = Thailand.

Source: Asian Development Bank.

Upgrading of Port Access Roads

Issues

Ports are only as effective as their ability to connect with their hinterlands and, therefore, good road connectivity to a port is critical for its overall performance as a multimodal and intermodal transfer facility. Much of the trade between BIMSTEC member states passes through the main ports and this is expected to continue in the foreseeable future. This situation arises from a combination of factors including physical constraints on land connectivity, the lower unit costs of maritime transport compared with long-distance road transport, the types of goods that are traded, and the concentrations of supply and demand along seaboards. In addition, since many BIMSTEC member states depend on trade with distant countries, maritime trade is the only medium for the transport of imports and exports, other than for high-value goods carried by air.

In most cases, the larger BIMSTEC ports are located in or close to major metropolitan areas, which tends to lead to road traffic congestion, especially when the freight vehicles serving the port have to directly interface with domestic and commuter flows within an urban environment near the port gates. There is a need for some form of traffic separation, such as dedicated port access roads designed to move the point of interface further away from the port gate and business areas of the city, thus, optimizing the flow of traffic to and from the port. In cases in which the port is in the city center, solutions such as overhead access roads are complex and expensive. Nevertheless, such congestion will only increase unless remedial action is undertaken. Several key BIMSTEC ports either have such access roads or have them are under construction or at the planning stage, such as at Chennai, Colombo, and Kolkata, and that completed at Chattogram.

In some cases, the solution adopted to address such congestion has been to physically transfer the port to an alternate location outside the city center, when such a strategy is feasible. Examples of this approach are the development of Laem Chabang about 125 km southeast of Bangkok, and Thilawa, about 25 km south of Yangon.

This strategy will only be effective if the access to the new port is significantly better than access to the existing port. In effect, the greater travel distance costs between the points of supply and demand and the new port must be offset by faster transit times compared with those at the old port. Thus, the second element of enhancing port access roads is the development of new highways to serve these new port locations to make them competitive.

As with border roads, there may be some overlapping between arterial roads and port access roads when arterial roads approach ports—again, it may (somewhat arbitrarily) be considered that port access roads are (mainly) within, say, 50 km of the ports.

An example of recent progress in the BIMSTEC region in upgrading port access roads is the completion of the Nong Kham interchange, which has reduced congestion on approaches to Laem Chabang Port ($17 million, Government of Thailand, 2011–2015).

Policy

Road connectivity at the main BIMSTEC ports should be enhanced between the port gate and the main road networks to eliminate congestion on port access roads, thus, reducing transaction costs associated with trade, including for intra-BIMSTEC traffic.

Strategy

BIMSTEC will encourage member states to include the upgrading or construction of dedicated port access roads in their national road development plans in situations where there is congestion on the existing access roads or where new ports are being developed.

Projects

Appendix 5 includes a long list of planned port access road projects, while Table 3 highlights planned flagship projects in this category selected mainly based on relevance to BIMSTEC intraregional connectivity.

Box 5 features the development of a notable port access road project to improve road connectivity between Yangon and the Thilawa Special Economic Zone.

Table 3: Planned Projects to Upgrade Port Access Roads

Code	Project Description	BIMSTEC Development Logic	Estimated Cost, 2018 ($ million)	(Possible) Funding Sources	Timescale
BAN-RD-099	Chattogram Port Access Road (13 km)	Link to Chattogram Port, a major BIMSTEC gateway	150	ADB	2021–2023
MYA-RD-101	Improvement of Thilawa–East Dagon Road (8.7 km, two lanes)	Linking the port and SEZ with Yangon and the national road network	42 (JPY 4.613 billion)	JICA loan	2015–2019

continued on next page

Table 3 continued

Code	Project Description	BIMSTEC Development Logic	Estimated Cost, 2018 ($ million)	(Possible) Funding Sources	Timescale
SRL-RD-102	Southerly extension of Colombo–Katunayake Expressway with a new six-lane Kelani Bridge at Peliyagoda, plus elevated port access road	Linking of the Colombo Port to the expressway network	700 (400 for the bridge and approach roads and 300 for the elevated port access road)	JICA (bridge and approach roads) and ADB (elevated port access road)	2018–2021 (bridge) and 2019–2021 (elevated port access road)

ADB = Asian Development Bank, BAN = Bangladesh, BIMSTEC = Bay of Bengal Initiative for Multi-Sectoral Technical and Economic Cooperation, km = kilometer, JICA = Japan International Cooperation Agency, MYA = Myanmar, SEZ = special economic zone, SRL = Sri Lanka.
Source: Asian Development Bank.

Box 5: Improvement of Road Connectivity between Thilawa and Yangon

Road connectivity between Thilawa Port and Yangon is a challenge, which has constrained the development of the Thilawa Special Economic Zone (SEZ), the only SEZ currently operating in Myanmar. The Thilawa–East Dagon Road Project includes a 32.8-km, four-lane divided roadway connecting the Thilawa port area with Highway No. 2. The components of the project include (i) the reconstruction of 5.5 km of the currently partially improved four-lane divided road; (ii) widening of 16.5 km of a recently constructed two-lane road into a four-lane divided typical section, along with the construction of additional two-lane bridges; (iii) resurfacing and minor repairs of the 1.4-km Thanlyin Bridge, including a verification of the original bridge design and as-built drawings, and a complete detailed bridge-condition survey; and (iv) the reconstruction and widening of a northerly 9.4 km section of the two-lane road connection with Highway No. 2. In addition, with a JICA loan of JPY31.051 billion ($285 million equivalent), a new proposed Bago River Bridge is expected to meet the increasing traffic demand between Yangon and the SEZ.

JPY = Japanese yen, km = kilometer.
Sources: Ministry of Construction, Myanmar; Japan International Cooperation Agency. 2014. *The Preparatory Survey for The Project for Construction of Bago River Bridge.* March 2014.

Road-Based Buddhist and Temple Tourism Circuits

Issues

At the Fourth BIMSTEC Summit held in Kathmandu, Nepal, on 30–31 August 2018, the leaders of the seven BIMSTEC member states, in their Joint Summit Declaration, underscoring the importance of Buddhism in the region, called for the development of Buddhist and temple tourism circuits.[31] Box 6 lists illustrative religious tourism circuits in the region.

---

[31] Bay of Bengal Initiative for Multi-Sectoral Technical and Economic Cooperation. *Fourth Summit Declaration, 30-31 August 2018, Kathmandu, Nepal.* paras. 25 and 27.

> **Box 6: Illustrative Tourism Circuits in the Bay of Bengal Initiative for Multi-Sectoral Technical and Economic Cooperation Region**
>
> Ayodhya (IND)–Chitrakoot (IND) –Varanasi (IND)–Buxar (IND)–Patna (IND)–Darbhanga (IND)–Sitamarhi (IND)–Janakpur (NEP–Kathmandu (NEP)–Colombo (SRL)–Negombo (SRL)–Chilaw (SRL)–Matale(SRL)–Kotuwa (SRL)–Nuwara Eliya (SRL)–Bandarawela (SRL)–Kataragama (SRL)–Ussangoda (SRL)–Colombo (SRL)
>
> Kathmandu (NEP)–Pokhara (NEP)–Butwal (NEP)–Tanakpur (IND)–Jageshwar Dham (IND)–Haridwar (IND)–Rishikesh (IND)–Char Dham (IND) (Gangotri, Yamunotri, Kedarnath, Badrinath)
>
> Kapilavastu (NEP)–Lumbini (NEP)–Kathmandu (NEP)–Paro (BHU)–Thimphu (BHU)–Punakha (BHU)–Bumthang (BHU)–Trashigang (BHU)–Paro (BHU)–Amaravathi (IND)–Chandavaram (IND)–Guntupallli (IND)–Bhattiprolu (IND)–Colombo (SRL)–Kataragama (SRL)–areas around Monaragala (SRL)–areas around Badulla (SRL)–Kandy (SRL)–Anuradhapura (SRL)–Colombo (SRL)
>
> BHU = Bhutan, IND = India, NEP = Nepal, SRL = Sri Lanka.
>
> Notes:
> 1. Other similar tourist sites or circuits are located throughout the region (e.g., some important Buddhist sites are found in Bangladesh, including Paharpur in Naogaon, Mahasthangarh in Bagura, Mainamati in Cumilla, and Bikrampur in Dhaka district). See also Asian Development Bank. 2009. *Proposed Loans, Asian Development Fund Grant, and Administration of Loan, People's Republic of Bangladesh, India, and Nepal: South Asia Tourism Infrastructure Development Project, Report and Recommendation of the President to the Board of Directors*. October 2009. Appendix 2 (South Asia Tourism Circuits and Infrastructure Vision and Sector Analysis). pp. 31–40.
> 2. Some circuits require air travel in addition to road travel.
>
> Source: South Asian Subregional Economic Cooperation and Asian Development Bank. 2017. *SASEC Powering Asia in the 21st Century*. p. 32. https://www.adb.org/sites/default/files/publication/233646/sasec-powering-asia.pdf.

Policy

Recognizing the importance of Buddhism in the region, BIMSTEC will seek to develop road-based religious tourism circuits, to promote intra-BIMSTEC tourism and cultural exchange(s) based on historical cultural ties.

Strategy

BIMSTEC will encourage member states to develop road-based Buddhist and temple tourism circuits.

Projects

Table 4 presents a flagship regional project for the development of road-based Buddhist and temple tourism circuits. A corresponding project has been identified to develop rail-based Buddhist and temple tourism circuits by road.

Coordination of Road Programs

Issues

Most road planning in the BIMSTEC region is undertaken at the national level and is often presented in the form of time-based national road development plans or equivalents. Such national road plans include a combination of ongoing projects, reflecting development demands identified at the national or state, province, or division level,

Table 4: Planned Flagship Project for the Development of Buddhist and Temple Tourism Circuits by Road

Code	Project Description	BIMSTEC Development Logic	Estimated Cost, 2018 ($ million)	(Possible) Funding Sources	Timescale
REG-RD-109	Technical assistance to identify road-based Buddhist and temple tourism circuits	Promotion of intra-BIMSTEC tourism and cultural exchange(s) based on historical cultural ties	0.5	Not yet identified	2019

BIMSTEC = Bay of Bengal Initiative for Multi-Sectoral Technical and Economic Cooperation, REG = regional.
Source: Asian Development Bank.

and projected availability of funding. Generally, they do not include specific reference to or relationship with the plans of neighboring countries. Indeed, there is usually little or no coordination of efforts to develop long-distance, intraregional trade, or tourist routes. Road planning and development remains a national—rather than a bilateral, multilateral, or regional—activity.

That said, there have been some coordinated road projects in the BIMSTEC, such as the India–Myanmar–Thailand Trilateral Highway, but even in such cases the coordination tends to be in terms of joint understandings in relation to the end goal, rather than coordinated implementation. Various regional initiatives promote an element of cooperation in road planning with the provision of funding support to develop particular transport corridors. However, even in these cases, the funding is nationally based and the member state either may not require any funding or may have different funding priorities.

At this stage, there is no coordinated regional road development program covering the BIMSTEC member states or even a methodology to keep members advised of ongoing or projected developments in neighboring member states that might affect their planning or scheduling of road improvements. While an integrated BIMSTEC road development plan is probably unrealistic, given the diversity of the region, there is a case for raising awareness of ongoing and proposed road development plans and projects. Coordination between and among member states on road development can be greatly facilitated if a mechanism is developed by which relevant planning data are exchanged regularly between member states.

Policy

For BIMSTEC to become more physically integrated, it is important that member states as part of their national planning mechanisms coordinate their road planning to enhance the region's connectivity, thus, supporting joint efforts to develop complementary road planning. Box 7 elaborates on the objective of coordinating road programs in BIMSTEC.

Strategy

BIMSTEC will encourage member states to exchange information on their national road development programs and establish a mechanism for the effective exchange of relevant road planning data to facilitate future coordination of road investments.

> **Box 7: The Objective of Coordinating Road Programs in Bay of Bengal Initiative for Multi-Sectoral Technical and Economic Cooperation**
>
> The objective of coordinating road programs would be to enable decision makers involved in national road planning to be aware of road development projects taking place in the region as a whole, so they can feed that information as appropriate into their own national planning mechanisms. To enhance the potential for regional cooperation in road planning, it will also be important to include national and regional initiatives of the various international development partners. This would assist in enabling the development of a comprehensive road planning database that could be made available to national planners as a mechanism to coordinate road investments.
>
> Source: Asian Development Bank. 2014. *Updating and Enhancement of the BIMSTEC Transport Infrastructure and Logistics Study, Phase II Report.* 2014. pp. 67.

Projects

As noted, the development of the Trilateral Highway linking India, Myanmar, and Thailand—conceived at a trilateral ministerial meeting on transport linkages held in Yangon, Myanmar, in April 2002—is an example of coordination in the scheduling of road programs to assist in enhancing connectivity between and among member states. This includes the new border link between Mae Sot (Thailand) and Myawaddy (Myanmar), which is a more specific example of such coordination.

Over the period from 2019–2028, with initial development in 2019–2020, it is planned that the BTCWG will establish a database mechanism whereby the member states can exchange road planning data (e.g., development timeframe, network characteristics such as traffic and road condition) to facilitate the coordination of investments in roads of regional significance (Table 5). Table 6 presents a preliminary draft format for a BIMSTEC road database, which could be established on a shared information technology platform and completed by the member states.

Table 5: Planned Flagship Project for the Sharing of Road Planning Data among Bay of Bengal Initiative for Multi-Sectoral Technical and Economic Cooperation Member States

Code	Project Description	BIMSTEC Development Logic	Estimated Cost, 2018 ($ million)	(Possible) Funding Sources	Timescale
REG-RD-110	Sharing of relevant road planning data through a BIMSTEC database	Increasing efficiency of road investments by ensuring availability of data on road projects and conditions in neighboring member states	0.5	Not yet identified	2019–2020 (initial development)

BIMSTEC = Bay of Bengal Initiative for Multi-Sectoral Technical and Economic Cooperation, REG = regional.
Source: Asian Development Bank.

Table 6: Preliminary Draft Format for a Bay of Bengal Initiative for Multi-Sectoral Technical and Economic Cooperation Road Planning Database

Member State	Roads of Regional Significance	Development Timeframe	Traffic (AADT)	Road Condition (e.g., IRI)
BAN				
BHU				
IND				
MYA				
NEP				
SRL				
THA				

AADT = average annual daily traffic, BAN = Bangladesh, BHU = Bhutan, IND = India, MYA = Myanmar, NEP = Nepal, IRI = international roughness index, SRL = Sri Lanka, THA = Thailand.
Source: Asian Development Bank.

Through-Transport Agreements

Issues

International transport in the BIMSTEC region mainly consists of domestic transport operations that interface with, or are adjacent to, international borders. Thailand is the only BIMSTEC country with an identifiable international road transport sector, with specific international licenses required to allow Thai trucks to enter Cambodia and the Lao People's Democratic Republic while engaged in an international transport operation. Indian transporters can carry goods to and from inland Bhutan[32] and Nepal, and Bhutanese and Nepali transporters can collect or deliver goods in India or to and from Indian ports under bilateral arrangements. Foreign transporters are not permitted to

---

[32] In the case of Bhutan, Indian transporters can only carry into Bhutan those goods that cannot be dismantled or transshipped at the border points, or goods destined to the Pasakha Industrial Estate.

enter Bangladesh or Myanmar, other than at border transfer points, and Sri Lanka as an island has no international road transport requirements.

The transport operations in most BIMSTEC member states are mainly undertaken by owner-drivers using older rigid units, often operating as part of a cooperative. Only in Thailand are there large numbers of fleet operators with modern articulated transport vehicles, although there are growing numbers of such vehicles in Bangladesh, India, Myanmar, and Sri Lanka, especially around the ports, since 40-foot containers can only be transported on articulated vehicles. These 40-foot containers tend to be in demand in the BIMSTEC region, especially for the carriage of exports, since they have a high volume-to-weight ratio. While there is still a need to modernize the fleet, the potential influence of BIMSTEC as a regional development forum on this particular issue is likely to be limited. The problem will only be resolved by increased investment by the private sector, although factors such as the removal of foreign direct investment restrictions and enhanced roads could encourage such investment. Given the situation, it is proposed that BIMSTEC focus on transport facilitation in the form of encouraging through-transport agreements where the national governments are the key players in agreeing to such arrangements.

The inability of road transporters to travel into neighboring countries may be considered a trade restriction, since it directly increases transport and transaction costs. Current restrictions constrain the potential to develop a competitive and vibrant international road transport sector. The need to transship cargo at border crossings directly increases trade costs through additional border handling charges, as well as increasing the risk of damage and pilferage. In addition, the cost of hiring two separate transporters with shorter journeys is likely to be higher than the total cost of hiring a single carrier to convey the goods from origin to destination.

That said, the development and implementation of through-transport agreements faces significant hurdles. From the transporter's perspective, the major barrier is the potential adverse impact on the domestic trucking industry in one member state or the other. At almost all BIMSTEC land borders, there is a major imbalance between imports and exports. This situation means that the routing control of the major cargo flow lies with the larger exporting country, since exporters tend to use their own national carriers. This demand imbalance results in those countries with the smaller export flow fearing domination by their neighbor's transport operators. This suggests that in an open market situation, countries such as India and Thailand would potentially dominate international transport to and from their neighbors. Consequently, there is understandable resistance to through transport from the domestic transport sector in some member states because domestic transport operators would potentially lose the revenue earned on the import movement.

There is also possible resistance from the trading organizations until through transport becomes more widely established. Much of the intra-BIMSTEC trade is currently based on trading terms whereby the responsibility for transport costs changes at the border (e.g., "free-delivered border" terms). The main benefits of through transport tend to accrue to the importers, rather than the exporter, and thus, the party with the routing control may be less enthusiastic in pushing for development of through transport.[33]

These challenges notwithstanding, through transport is inherently more efficient and cost-effective, and thus, would help promote intra-BIMSTEC trade in particular. This approach has been pursued in various initiatives involving some of the member states (e.g., the Bangladesh–Bhutan–India–Nepal [BBIN] Motor Vehicles Agreement, various ASEAN transport facilitation agreements). Within BIMSTEC, there is an effort to negotiate a Motor Vehicles Agreement for the Regulation of Passenger, Personal and Cargo Vehicular Traffic between and among

---

[33] Other challenges are underdeveloped road networks and other associated infrastructure, environmental impacts, and possible law and order issues.

BIMSTEC member states, with calls for negotiation first of a framework agreement on transit, transshipment, and the movement of vehicular traffic.

Policy

BIMSTEC recognizes the need to implement through-transport agreements between BIMSTEC member states and their neighbors to reduce transport costs and to facilitate and promote intraregional trade for the overall benefit of member states.

Strategy

BIMSTEC will encourage member states to implement transport access agreements with their neighbors, based on either limited or unlimited access, taking into account the unique circumstances encountered by smaller countries, and will support regional initiatives designed to encourage such through-transport arrangements. ICT may be used to integrate vehicle permit, driving license, insurance, vehicle standards and inspection certificate, environmental, and road safety requirements.

Projects

Building on the various initiatives pursued by the member states, the flagship project in this category will be to formulate and implement[34] a regional through-transport agreement in the BIMSTEC region,[35] with completion targeted for 2020. Phased implementation of through-transport agreements and arrangements (multilateral, quadrilateral, trilateral, and bilateral, as needed), will take place from 2021 to 2028.[36] Table 7 summarizes the (flagship) projects.

Table 7: Planned Flagship Projects for Through-Transport Agreements

Code	Project Description	BIMSTEC Development Logic	Estimated Cost, 2018 ($ million)	(Possible) Funding Sources	Timescale
REG-RD-111	Formulation of a regional through-transport agreement among BIMSTEC member states	Increasing efficiency of international road transport by avoiding the need for transshipment at border crossings	1	Member states	2019–2020 (negotiations and finalization)
REG-RD-112	Phased implementation of through-transport agreements	As above	3	As above	2021–2028 (phased implementation)

BIMSTEC = Bay of Bengal Initiative for Multi-Sectoral Technical and Economic Cooperation, REG = regional.
Source: Asian Development Bank.

---

[34] Experience has shown that the signing and ratification of agreements does not automatically lead to implementation; institutional and capacity gaps must be identified and addressed.
[35] It may be useful to take cognizance of some of the existing bilateral transport agreements or protocols in this context and see how they could be expanded to multi-country agreements.
[36] In developing such agreements, particularly multilateral ones, it will be important to take into consideration the asymmetry among member states and other unique challenges faced by member states. Concept Paper for Master Plan on BIMSTEC Transport Connectivity, discussed and agreed on during the 2nd Meeting of the BTCWG, Bangkok, Thailand, 13–14 November 2017 (updated in March 2018). para. 61.

Box 8 suggests the benefits of through-transport agreements or arrangements in quantitative terms.

> **Box 8: Estimates of the Benefits of Through-Transport in the Bay of Bengal Initiative for Multi-Sectoral Technical and Economic Cooperation Region**
>
> A 2014 JICA study estimated the benefits of through-transport including transport cost reductions for Bhutan, India, and Nepal from developing functional corridors for transit traffic through Bangladesh and the gains of Bangladesh from transport business opportunities. This exercise was undertaken based on the unit transport cost per distance by mode by country and transport volume by route developed in ADB TA-7650: Regional Transport Development in South Asia (2013). Transshipment time at some border crossings was assumed to be zero in this estimation because it was assumed that an optimal situation regarding through transport would be realized. Based on calculations of benefits from cost savings by route, total benefits of $156.7 million were estimated for Bhutan, India, and Nepal; also, based on the estimated income of Bangladesh from port charges, benefits of $50.2 million were estimated (all totals were in 2014 values and based on 2011 traffic volumes). The study authors noted that these results "should be considered indicative rather than definitive." An earlier (2010) study by distinguished Bangladeshi authors (Muhammad Yunus and Mohammad Rahmatullah) found significantly higher benefits for Bangladesh than did this conservative JICA estimation.
>
> JICA = Japan International Cooperation Agency, TA = technical assistance.
> Source: Japan International Cooperation Agency and PADECO Co., Ltd. 2014. *Data Collection Survey on Transport Infrastructure Development for Regional Connectivity in and around South Asia*. March. Appendix 4. pp. A-41 to A-46.

IV. Railways and Rail Transport

Sector Overview

BIMSTEC's key objectives in the railway (sub)sector are similar to those for roads:

(i) create an enabling environment for rapid economic development by enhancing rail connectivity between member states;
(ii) promote active collaboration and mutual assistance on matters of common interest through joint development of rail networks; and
(iii) cooperate more effectively in joint efforts that are supportive of, and complementary to, the national development plans of member states by promoting the linking of the planning and scheduling of rail developments directly or indirectly connecting member states.

The BTILS identified five railway sector issues. While there has been some progress in capacity development in Bangladesh arising from line improvements and new rolling stock, there has been limited progress regarding the other issues. The railway sector is becoming less important for intra-BIMSTEC transport, and environmental factors favoring the use of rail are unlikely to appreciably change this trend. Therefore, a cautious approach has been adopted in selecting future BIMSTEC policies, strategies, and projects since the chances of successful implementation appear less certain.

A key consideration is that each of the rail networks in the region operates independently. There is limited commonality of issues regarding international services, and, therefore, development of a regional dimension to railway infrastructure is difficult.

The approach to identifying common themes was to examine a long list of projects identified in the 2014 reports, supplemented by new projects put forward by the member states in 2017 and 2018, which indicate the future plans of the various national railway organizations. Two areas of commonality are rail connectivity to key seaports and with landlocked member states. In addition, there have been recent calls to develop Buddhist and temple circuit rail connectivity. Therefore, the recommended policies, strategies, and strategies in the railway sector were focused on these specific issues.

Enhanced Rail Connectivity between Ports, Dry Ports, and Borders, and Their Hinterlands

Issues

A common theme regarding the railway sector is the importance of rail connectivity between ports and dry ports, and borders, and their hinterlands. For example, Bangladesh has been upgrading the line between Chattogram and Dhaka to handle more container traffic at the Dhaka ICDs, India has been developing dedicated freight corridors connecting to key ports in a manner to separate passenger and freight flows on busy passenger lines, Myanmar is considering possible upgrading of rail links to Thilawa as that port expands, Sri Lanka has been extending railway lines to attract more port traffic and to develop connections between the port and an ICD or cargo village, and Thailand has proposed further enhancement of the Bangkok–Laem Chabang connection to handle more container traffic.

While these situations vary by member state and the priority accorded the development of these port linkages differs substantially, there is an underlying commonality of objectives in the enhancement of rail accessibility between the major ports and their respective hinterlands. Considering the major problems in connecting the rail networks internationally, the importance of rail connectivity with the seaports may be considered more significant, especially for the movement of bulk and semi-bulk cargo, as well as for handling container traffic.

Recent progress in the BIMSTEC region in enhancing rail connectivity between ports, dry ports, and borders, and their hinterlands includes (i) construction of double track between Tongi and Bhairab Bazar including signaling ($267 million, with ADB support, 2006–2018), construction of second bridges for mainline upgrading (e.g., as at Bhairab Bazaar and Titas) with approach rail lines (Indian Line of Credit [ILOC], $117 million, 2010–2018), in Bangladesh; (ii) gauge conversion of Maynaguri–Changrabandha, linking India with Bangladesh (2016), and restoration of the Radikapur–Birol line connecting India with Bangladesh (2017); (iii) upgrading of the Trincomalee rail line ($50 million, with support of ADB, the China Exim Bank, and the Government of India), in Sri Lanka; and (iv) development of a new rail terminal (Single Rail Transfer Operator Development Project) at Laem Chabang ($63 million, State Railways of Thailand and Port Authority of Thailand, 2016–2018), in Thailand.

Policy

BIMSTEC member states require enhanced rail accessibility to their main ports, dry ports, and land borders to support the growth in intraregional trade and to encourage economic and social development at inland locations.

Strategy

BIMSTEC will encourage member states to prioritize rail access to ports, especially for the movement of bulk and semi-bulk cargo and the movement of container traffic between the ports, land borders, and ICDs.

Projects

Appendix 5 includes a long list of projects to enhance rail connectivity between ports, dry ports, and borders, and their hinterlands, while Table 8 highlights planned flagship projects in this category selected mainly based on relevance to BIMSTEC intraregional connectivity. Several of the projects relate to and are supportive of the Trans-Asian Railway (TAR) of United Nations Economic and Social Commission for Asia and the Pacific (UNESCAP), as mentioned in Appendix 3.

Table 8: Planned Flagship Projects to Enhance Rail Connectivity between Ports, Dry Ports, and Borders, and Their Hinterlands

Code	Project Description	BIMSTEC Development Logic	Estimated Cost 2018 ($ million)	(Possible) Funding Sources	Timescale
BAN-RW-002	Construction of dual-gauge, double rail line and conversion of existing rail line into dual gauge between Akhaura and Laksham	Mainline upgrading to increase freight and passenger capacity between the largest port and capital of Bangladesh; potential link to North East India	784	ADB and EIB	2014–2020
BAN-RW-003	Construction of Sheikh Mujib Railway Bridge (parallel to the Jamuna Bridge) with twin dual-gauge lines	Improved rail connectivity with India by removing current restrictions	1,173	JICA	2016–2023 (including project preparation)
BAN-RW-004	Padma Bridge Rail Link	Improved rail connectivity between Bangladesh and India	4,216	PRC	2016–2022
BAN-RW-010	Construction of dual gauge railway between Bogura and Shahid M. Monsur Ali	Improved rail connectivity between Bangladesh and India	796	ILOC	2018–2022
IND-RW-020	New Belonia–Feni line connecting with the India–Bangladesh border	Improved rail connectivity between Bangladesh and India	Not yet estimated	As above	Timing not yet specified, but survey completed
IND-RW-021	Radhikapur–Birol rail link	Improved rail connectivity between Bangladesh and India	Not yet estimated	India	Timing not yet specified, but survey ongoing
SRL-RW-026	Matara to Kataragama Railway Extension Project (120 km)	Enhanced rail connectivity with sea and airports in southern Sri Lanka, including Hambantota seaport and Mattala Rajapaksa Airport	278	PRC (China Exim Bank) for Phase 1 (Matara–Beliatta, 26 km)	2014–2028
REG-RW-031(BAN and IND)	Akhaura–Agartala rail link (new 12-km line)	Improved rail connectivity between Bangladesh and India	144	India	2016–2021
REG-RW-032 (BAN and IND)	New line linking Haldibari–Chilahati (3 km)	Improved rail connectivity between Bangladesh and India, and with Bhutan	12 (for segment in IND)	India	2019–2021
REG-RW-033 (IND and MYA)	New lines linking Jiribam–Imphal (125 km) in Manipur, Imphal–Moreh (111 km) connecting with the India–Myanmar border, and a new line linking Moreh–Tamu–Kalay (128 km) onward to Mandalay	Linking of India and Myanmar by rail	Not yet estimated (1,000 for Jiribam–Imphal)	As above	2017–2028 (to be confirmed)

ADB = Asian Development Bank, BAN = Bangladesh, BIMSTEC = Bay of Bengal Initiative for Multi-Sectoral Technical and Economic Cooperation, EIB = European Investment Bank, ILOC = Indian Line of Credit, IND = India, JICA = Japan International Cooperation Agency, MYA = Myanmar, PRC = People's Republic of China, REG = regional, SRL = Sri Lanka, THA = Thailand.

Source: Asian Development Bank.

Box 9 features the development of a notable project in Bangladesh to enhance rail connectivity to main ports (broadly defined).

> ### Box 9: Development of a Bridge Parallel to the Bangabandhu (Jamuna) Bridge with Twin Dual-Gauge Rail Lines
>
> The existing Jamuna Multipurpose (Bangabandhu) Bridge—co-financed by ADB, the Japan International Cooperation Agency, and the World Bank—is situated on the Joydevpur–Ishurdi section of the Bangladesh Railway network, which is an important part of the national railway network as well as an important part of the Bay of Bengal Initiative for Multi-Sectoral Technical and Economic Cooperation railway network. However, the existing bridge has a single-track, dual-gauge line—it was originally designed for four-lane highway traffic with a meter-gauge single rail track and was later modified to carry dual-gauge trains, but with restrictions (e.g., the wagon load is not to exceed a nominal uniform distributed load of 43.7 kilonewtons per meter, locomotives are to have an empty wagon behind them,[a] there is to be only one locomotive per train, bridge speed is not to exceed 20 kilometers per hour, and effective means for enforcing the loading and clearance provisions are to be adopted).
>
> Although this railway line has great potential to serve heavy traffic (especially freight traffic) with neighboring countries, it has been limited due to these restrictions. Therefore, to meet increasing national and (sub)regional traffic demand, the Government of Bangladesh plans to build a 4.8-kilometer dedicated railway bridge 300 meters upstream of the existing Bangabandhu (Jamuna) Bridge. Construction of this megaproject is to be completed by 2023.
>
> [a] To comply with the requirement that the axle of the wagon trailing the locomotive is to be at least 6.5 meters from the near-axle of the locomotive.
>
> Source: Ministry of Railways, Bangladesh.

Rail Connectivity for Landlocked Member States

Issues

The issue of rail connectivity for landlocked member states was included in the BTILS and remains although there have been positive developments (e.g., feasibility studies have been undertaken on the development of new links to Bhutan and Nepal and construction of two links to Nepal has commenced). If the landlocked member states (Bhutan and Nepal) have greater access to lower-cost rail services, they may be able to increase their trade of lower-value products for which road transport is cost-prohibitive. However, there is potential implementation risk in developing a new mode in a country.

Policy

BIMSTEC recognizes the specific connectivity requirements of the landlocked member states and supports their need for modal alternatives where viable to promote intra-BIMSTEC trade and social development along the borders of the respective member states.[37]

Strategy

BIMSTEC will encourage the development of rail links between India and the landlocked member states of Bhutan and Nepal.[38]

---

[37] Asian Development Bank. 2018. *Updating and Enhancement of the BIMSTEC Transport Infrastructure and Logistics Study, Final Report.* Manila.
[38] Ibid.

Projects

There has been recent progress regarding rail connectivity with Nepal. The Government of India has approved and commenced development of two potential links—(i) Jaynagar–Bardibas (69 km) and (ii) Jogbani–Biratnagar (19 km)—and has sanctioned surveys for links between (iii) Nepalganj and Nepalganj Road (12 km), (iv) Nautanwa and Bhairahawa (15 km), and (v) New Jalpaiguri and Kakarbitta (46 km). The India–Nepal Joint Working Group has been meeting regularly to identify requirements for operating railway services along these cross-border links and finalize the necessary bilateral modalities expeditiously.[39]

Development of rail links to Bhutan may take longer to realize than the development of rail links to Nepal. However, feasibility studies to extend rail connectivity to Bhutan through development of Kokhrajhar (Assam)–Gelephu (Bhutan) (57 km), Pathsala (Assam)–Nanglam (Bhutan) (51 km), Rangiya (Assam)–Samdrupjongkhar (Bhutan) (48 km), Banarhat (West Bengal)–Samtse (Bhutan) (23 km), and Hasimara (West Bengal)–Phuentsholing (Bhutan) (18 km) rail links have been undertaken.

Table 9 presents planned flagship projects to provide rail connectivity for landlocked member states.

Table 9: Planned Flagship Projects to Provide Rail Connectivity for Landlocked Member States

Code	Project Description	BIMSTEC Development Logic	Estimated Cost, 2018 ($ million)	(Possible) Funding Sources	Timescale
REG-RW-035 (IND and BHU)	Development of Kokhrajhar (Assam)–Gelephu (Bhutan) (57 km), Pathsala (Assam)–Nanglam (Bhutan) (51 km), Rangiya (Assam)–Samdrupjongkhar (Bhutan) (48 km), Banarhat (West Bengal)–Samtse (Bhutan) (23 km), and Hasimara (West Bengal)–Phuentsholing (Bhutan) (18 km)	Project to provide Bhutan with intermodal transport options	To be estimated	India	2019–2028 and beyond
REG-RW-036 (IND and NEP)	Development of (i) Jaynagar–Bardibas (69 km, including 3 km in India and 66 km in Nepal), (ii) Jogbani–Biratnagar (19 km), (iii) Nepalganj–Nepalganj Road (12 km), (iv) Nautanwa–Bhairahawa (15 km), and (v) New Jalpaiguri–Kakarbitta (46 km)	Project to provide Nepal with multimodal and intermodal transport options on more routes to Kolkata (and onward to other BIMSTEC countries)	900+	India	2018–2025; the first two (sub)projects are ongoing

BHU = Bhutan, BIMSTEC = Bay of Bengal Initiative for Multi-Sectoral Technical and Economic Cooperation, IND = India, NEP = Nepal, REG = regional.
Source: Asian Development Bank.

---

[39] Ministry of External Affairs, India. India–Nepal Statement on Expanding Rail Linkages: Connecting Raxaul in India to Kathmandu in Nepal. New Delhi, 7 April 2018. On 31 August 2018, the respective governments signed a memorandum of understanding for a preliminary engineering and traffic study on a broad gauge line between Raxaul, India, and Kathmandu, Nepal; the costs of the proposed Raxaul–Kathmandu link would be high, considering the heavy tunneling requirements.

Rail-Based Buddhist and Temple Tourism Circuits

Issues

As noted in Section III, Road-Based Buddhist and Temple Tourism Circuits at the Fourth BIMSTEC Summit held in Kathmandu, Nepal, on 30-31 August 2018, the leaders of the seven BIMSTEC member states, in their Joint Summit Declaration, underscoring the importance of Buddhism in the region, called for the development of Buddhist and temple tourism circuits.[40] Consider, for example, that recently the Government of India introduced a Buddhist Circuit Tourist Train and Ramayan Express Train, and a Sri Lankan leg will connect Kandy, Nuwara Eliya, Colombo, and Negombo.

Policy

Recognizing the importance of Buddhism in the region, BIMSTEC will seek to develop rail-based religious tourism circuits, to promote intra-BIMSTEC tourism and cultural exchange(s) based on historical cultural ties.

Strategy

BIMSTEC will encourage member states to develop rail-based Buddhist and temple tourism circuits.

Projects

Table 10 presents a flagship regional project for the development of rail-based Buddhist and temple tourism circuits by rail. A corresponding project has been identified to develop road-based Buddhist and temple tourism circuits.

Table 10: Planned Flagship Project for the Development of Buddhist and Temple Tourism Circuits by Road

Code	Project Description	BIMSTEC Development Logic	Estimated Cost, 2018 ($ million)	(Possible) Funding Sources	Timescale
REG-RW-037	Technical assistance to identify rail-based Buddhist and temple tourism circuits	Promotion of intra-BIMSTEC tourism and cultural exchange(s) based on historical cultural ties	0.5	Not yet identified	2019

BIMSTEC = Bay of Bengal Initiative for Multi-Sectoral Technical and Economic Cooperation, REG = regional.
Source: Asian Development Bank.

Coordination of Railway Programs

Issues

Similar to road programs (as mentioned in Section III, Coordination of Road Programs), railway planning in the BIMSTEC region is undertaken at the national level and is often presented in the form of time-based national

---

[40] Bay of Bengal Initiative for Multi-Sectoral Technical and Economic Cooperation. *Fourth Summit Declaration, 30-31 August 2018, Kathmandu, Nepal.* paras. 25 and 27.

railway development plans or equivalents. Such national railway plans include a combination of ongoing projects, reflecting development demands identified at the national or state, province, or division level, and projected availability of funding, but generally they do not include specific reference to or relationship with the plans of neighboring countries. As with road planning, railway planning and development remains a national—rather than a bilateral, multilateral, or regional—activity.

At this stage there is no coordinated regional railway development program covering the BIMSTEC member states or even a methodology to keep members advised of ongoing or projected developments in neighboring member states that might affect their planning or scheduling of railway improvements. Accordingly, there is a case for raising awareness of ongoing and proposed railway development plans and projects. Coordination between member states on railway development can be greatly facilitated if a mechanism is developed by which relevant planning data are exchanged regularly between member states. The logic is the same as for the coordination of road programs, discussed in Section III, Coordination of Road Programs.

Policy

For BIMSTEC to become more physically integrated, it is important that member states as part of their national planning mechanisms coordinate their railway planning to enhance the region's connectivity, thus, supporting joint efforts to develop complementary railway planning.

Strategy

BIMSTEC will encourage member states to exchange information on their national railway development programs and establish a mechanism for the effective exchange of relevant road planning data to facilitate future coordination of road investments.

Projects

From 2019 to 2028, with initial development in 2019–2020, it is planned that the BTCWG will establish a database mechanism whereby the member states can exchange railway planning data (e.g., development timeframe, network characteristics such as traffic and track condition) to facilitate the coordination of investments in railways of regional significance (Table 11).

Table 11: Planned Flagship Project for the Sharing of Railway Planning Data among Bay of Bengal Initiative for Multi-Sectoral Technical and Economic Cooperation Member States

Code	Project Description	BIMSTEC Development Logic	Estimated Cost, 2018 ($ million)	(Possible) Funding Sources	Timescale
REG-RW-038	Sharing of relevant railway planning data through a BIMSTEC database	Increasing efficiency of railway investments by ensuring availability of data on railway projects and conditions in neighboring member states	0.3	Not yet identified	2019–2020 (initial development)

BIMSTEC = Bay of Bengal Initiative for Multi-Sectoral Technical and Economic Cooperation, REG = regional.
Source: Asian Development Bank.

V. Ports and Maritime Transport

Sector Overview

Maritime transport plays an important role in trade in all BIMSTEC member states directly or indirectly (in the case of the landlocked member states). Most of each member state's international trade, except for Bhutan and Nepal, is carried by sea. In addition, most intra-BIMSTEC trade in tonnage terms is currently carried by sea due to physical constraints to land connectivity, the lower unit costs of maritime transport compared with those of long-distance road transport, the types of goods traded, and the concentration of supply and demand along seaboards. Even the trade between India and the landlocked member states often includes significant re-exports of goods that originally came through Indian ports. Therefore, maritime transport and seaports will have an important role in the future transport development of the BIMSTEC region.[41]

An analysis of the region's port environment in the BTILS suggested there were two key areas of concern that are common to several member states and, therefore, could be considered as having a regional dimension: (i) access to deeper water to enable larger vessels to call, and (ii) the container handling performance at some of the key ports in the Bay of Bengal.[42] Therefore, the recommended policies, strategies, and strategies in the ports and maritime sector were designed to address these specific issues. However, it is important to recognize that ports by their nature tend to be unique, differing in terms of physical infrastructure, layouts, cargo handled, services provided, and handling performance, and thus there are limitations in the scope for regional cooperation in the (sub)sector (Box 10).

---

[41] It has been suggested that improving ports (and port access) has the greatest potential for improving connectivity between South Asia and Southeast Asia, more than improving land connectivity across remote border crossings. Asian Development Bank and Asian Development Bank Institute. 2015. *Connecting South Asia and Southeast Asia*. p. 84. Citing D. Wignall and M. Wignall. 2014. Seaborne Trade between South Asia and Southeast Asia, Asian Development Bank Institute (ADBI) Working Paper Series, No. 508. December 2014. Consider, for example, that land-based trade between India and Myanmar accounts for only about 3.5% of bilateral trade. C. Xavier, *Bridging the Bay of Bengal: Toward a Stronger BIMSTEC*. Carnegie India. February 2018. p. 25. Citing Export-Import Bank of India. 2017. *India's Engagements with CLMV [Cambodia–Lao PDR–Myanmar–Viet Nam]: Gateway to ASEAN Markets*. February 2017. That said, it is expected that with improved infrastructure and easier border crossing procedures, the volume of goods and passenger traffic will increase. J.-F. Gautrin. Land-Based Cross-Border Infrastructure. In M. G. Plummer, P. J. Morgan, and G. Wignaraja. 2016. *Connecting Asia: Infrastructure for Integrating South and Southeast Asia*. Asian Development Bank Institute. p. 37.

[42] Issues related to development of port interfaces mainly concern road and rail connectivity into individual ports, and were addressed in preceding sections. In considering issues to be addressed, operational issues related to port performance and ICT systems, which would be difficult for a regional cooperation body to monitor, were not included.

> **Box 10: The Scope for Regional Cooperation in the Ports and Maritime Sector**
>
> While their overall function as a multimodal and intermodal transfer facility is common, the profiles of different ports usually vary and therefore their synergy within a regional development context is more difficult to identify than is the case in the road and rail modes. In relation to BIMSTEC aims, the services they provide help create an enabling environment for rapid economic development and accelerate social progress, but conversely, their level of collaboration and mutual assistance is limited, especially if they are competing with each other for traffic. Each port tends to be focused on serving the particular needs of its immediate hinterland, and as the distance from the port increases, so does the potential competition from other ports. The presence of land borders presents a barrier that can artificially extend or constrain a port's hinterland and consequently have an impact on competition. For example, western Bangladesh is closer to Kolkata than Chattogram, but Bangladesh importers route their traffic through Chattogram, rather than transiting via a third country. Similarly, Chattogram is closer to many of the northeastern states of India than is Kolkata, but exporters there go through Kolkata even though the distance is greater. Thus, the nature and size of a port's hinterland varies as much as the ports themselves. The reality is that most ports operate almost in isolation from each other and consequently do not see regional collaboration and cooperation as being critical.
>
> BIMSTEC = Bay of Bengal Initiative for Multi-Sectoral Technical and Economic Cooperation.
> Source: Asian Development Bank. 2014. *Updating and Enhancement of the BIMSTEC Transport Infrastructure and Logistics Study, Phase II Report*. May. p. 73.

Development of Deeper Water Ports

Issues

The trend in container shipping has been toward increased reliance on hub-and-spoke operations, with the larger vessels or mother ships connecting the hubs and the feeder vessels serving the subsidiary ports. Only Colombo with its strategic hub position is likely to attract the larger container vessels, while all of the other BIMSTEC ports will continue to rely mainly on feeder connectivity. The size of these feeder ships will depend on demand, as well as draft availability at the ports of call. The larger ports with higher demand, such as Laem Chabang and Chennai, will attract larger feeder vessels and even the occasional direct services covering lower-volume routes. Chattogram, Kolkata, Yangon, and Thilawa are realistically expected to attract only smaller container vessels, not only because of draft restrictions, but also due to the relatively limited traffic demand. (See Box 11 for further discussion.)

Nevertheless, increased trade has led to a greater requirement for larger vessels than before. Consequently, "deeper water" was needed rather than deepwater per se. Thilawa exemplified such a situation where despite its having 1.5 m more draft than Yangon, it was unable to attract significant container traffic. This proved that there was no demand for larger and deeper draft vessels in Yangon due to the trade restrictions at that time. The Government of Myanmar recently established new port facilities at Thilawa to accommodate larger feeder vessels that can handle increased traffic demand. The Myanmar Port Authority also contracted a third-party dredging company to improve the navigation channel to Yangon Port along the Yangon River by making it deeper and safe.

Examples of progress in the BIMSTEC region in port development include (i) major port development projects in India between 2016 and 2018, including at Kolkata ($21 million, for dry cargo transloading facilities), Ennore ($116 million, for a container terminal, 24 km north of Chennai Port), Vishakapatnam in Andhra Pradesh ($42 million, for dredging), and Tuticorin in Tamil Nadu ($67 million, for dredging and berths); (ii) development of a deepwater port at Sittwe, Myanmar ($120 million, with support from India), as part of the Kaladan Multimodal Transit Transport Project (see Box 18); (iii) a national ports master plan in Sri Lanka, with ADB support (2016–2018); and (iv) development of a new coastal terminal at Laem Chabang (Terminal A) to reduce road traffic ($65 million, Port Authority of Thailand, 2016–2018), in Thailand. Especially worth noting is Bangladesh in 2015 allowing India to use Chattogram and Mongla Ports for cargo to and from its northeastern region,[43] and the opening of Visakhapatnam Port in 2016 for Nepal's trade with third countries.

There are projects planned and underway that will accommodate larger feeder vessels at Bay of Bengal and Andaman Sea ports. These should help stabilize freight rates because larger vessels are more efficient due to economies of scale. Thus, these developments should be beneficial to the BIMSTEC member states, including the landlocked member states that rely on ports in the littoral member states.

> ### Box 11: Assessing the Need for Deep Water Ports
>
> There has been some confusion in public discourse regarding the need to develop deep water ports. The recent emergence of mega container vessels requiring 16-meter draft is cited as a reason for developing new deep water ports, irrespective of demand and commercial factors. However, for most ports in the region, volumes are relatively small in global terms. Considering that even Laem Chabang has difficulty in attracting the larger container vessels and Colombo only has such vessels calling because of its hub role and immediate proximity to the Southern Ocean Corridor, it is considered that there will be insufficient demand in either the Bay of Bengal or the Andaman Sea for large container vessels for many years to come. In reality, the demand for deep water ports relates exclusively to the handling of bulk cargo such as oil, fuel, liquefied petroleum gas, grain, rice, steel, and the like that moves in large volumes per shipment and where economies of scale are more pronounced.
>
> Source: Asian Development Bank. 2014. *Updating and Enhancement of the BIMSTEC Transport Infrastructure and Logistics Study, Phase II Report*. May. p. 74.

Policy

BIMSTEC recognizes the need for deeper water ports in the northern parts of the Bay of Bengal and the Andaman Sea to accommodate larger container feeder vessels, to facilitate trade and promote economic development in the vicinity of port complexes.

Strategy

BIMSTEC will actively promote the development of new ports in the member states and the expansion of existing harbor infrastructure to increase the capacity of the region's ports to handle growth in container traffic.

Projects

Appendix 5 includes a long list of planned projects to develop deeper water ports on the Bay of Bengal and Andaman Sea, while Table 12 highlights planned flagship projects in this category selected mainly based on relevance to BIMSTEC intraregional connectivity. In some cases, project components may be (re)defined to facilitate transit cargo for landlocked member states, including, for example, dedicated container park yards and warehousing

---

[43] See the Bangladesh–India Memorandum of Understanding Relating to the use of Chittagong and Mongla Ports, 2015. Considering congestion and other challenges at Chattogram Port at present, improvement of Mongla Port in the short term is recommended.

facilities for less than container load (LCL) cargo. For example, for Nepal, dedicated container parking yards in the Ports of Kolkata and Visakhapatnam in India, and Chattogram and Mongla Ports in Bangladesh, may be developed, along with warehousing facilities for LCL cargo for onward movement.

Table 12: Planned Flagship Projects to Develop Deeper Water Ports

Code	Project Description	BIMSTEC Development Logic	Estimated Cost 2018 ($ million)	(Possible) Funding Sources	Timescale
BAN-PM-002	Karnaphuli Container Terminal at Chattogram	New container facilities in congested port handling BIMSTEC traffic	200	Government (Port Authority)	2022–2026
BAN-PM-006	Payra Port Development Project (first terminal, connecting road, bridge over the Andermanik River and related facilities)	New seaport to serve southern Bangladesh and possibly Bhutan and Nepal	474	Government	2018–2021
BAN-PM-007	Upgrading of Mongla Port (e.g., construction of container terminals including cargo handling equipment, tower, and container delivery yard)	Improvement of Bangladesh's second port, which serves Bhutan, India, and Nepal	656	Government and ILOC	2018–2021
IND-PM-014	Augmentation of capacity of Haldia Dock Complex, Kolkata Port Trust (new lock gate in existing dock or basin and modification of existing lock gate)	Increased capacity at major BIMSTEC gateway	200	Government and ADB	To be progammed
MYA-PM-016	New port facilities at Thilawa Special Economic Zone	New port complex to handle intra-BIMSTEC trade	175 (JPY 19.087 billion)	Government, JICA, and PPP	2016–2019
MYA-PM-017	New port facilities at Dawei	Potential new maritime link between South and Southeast Asia	3,050	Investor	Not yet programmed
SRL-PM-020	Extension of East Terminal at Colombo	Facilitation of the handling of international cargo, including transshipment and bilateral traffic with other BIMSTEC members states	430–1,150	Government (Sri Lanka Ports Authority; 400 meters of container yard), and BOT	2014–2022
SRL-PM-021	Construction of West Terminal at Colombo	Provision of additional capacity to handle mega container ships	840	BOT	2023–2026
THA-PM-023	Development of Phase III at Laem Chabang	Provision of additional capacity, including for handling of BIMSTEC traffic	1,500	Port Authority of Thailand and others	2019–2022 (feasibility study now under review)

ADB = Asian Development Bank, BAN = Bangladesh, BIMSTEC = Bay of Bengal Initiative for Multi-Sectoral Technical and Economic Cooperation, BOT = build–operate–transfer, China Exim Bank = Export-Import Bank of China, EPC = engineering, procurement, and construction, ILOC = Indian Line of Credit, IND = India, JICA = Japan International Cooperation Agency, JPY = Japanese yen, MYA = Myanmar, PPP = public–private partnership, PRC = People's Republic of China, SPV = special purpose vehicle, SRL = Sri Lanka, THA = Thailand.

Source: Asian Development Bank.

As a case in point, Box 12 presents the need for the provision of additional port capacity in Bangladesh through the development of deeper ports.

> **Box 12: Provision of Additional Port Capacity in Bangladesh through the Development of Deeper Ports**
>
> On Goldman Sachs' List of the Next 11 emerging economies of the 21st century, Bangladesh has a rapidly increasing export sector that requires additional port capacity through the development of deeper ports. The country's two current ports—Chattogram and Mongla (with the former handling 92% of the country's port throughputs)—lack sufficient draft for large container ships and require transshipment to smaller vessels. Accordingly, the country has ambitious plans for expanding its port capacity, including not only the development of the Patenga and Karnaphuli container terminals at Chattogram (to transform Chattogram into the "region's Rotterdam"), but also the development of the Payra deep sea port and the Matarbari port development project.
>
> Sources: Ministry of Shipping, Bangladesh; W. Shepard. Bangladesh's Deep Sea Port Problem. *The Diplomat*, 7 June 2016; Goldman Sachs. *How Solid are the BRICS?* Global Economics Paper No. 134, 1 December 2005; and C. S. Kasturi. *Bangladesh Bets on Connectivity for Its Next Economic Leap*, 4 May 2018.

Improvement of Container Handling Performance at Bay of Bengal and Andaman Sea Ports

Issues

The original BTILS report in 2007 highlighted low container handling performance at some of the Bay of Bengal ports, especially at Kolkata and Chattogram, but there has been some improvement since then. One reason for the improvement has been a change in scheduling by carriers, which has resulted in a decrease in the use of feeder vessels on circuits in favor of more direct calls connecting with hub ports; this change makes cargo handling easier because of the reduced need for re-stowing and faster unloading with larger dedicated vessels. Another reason is that the ports have invested more in container handling equipment, including additional ship-to-shore gantry cranes, which reduces reliance on self-handling geared feeder ships, which are inherently more difficult and slower to work. Additional terminal equipment also means better servicing between the container yard and the ship-to-shore crane.

Even with improvement in container handling performance at Bay of Bengal and Andaman Sea ports in recent years, further improvement is required, based on investment in new container handling equipment, to respond to increased demand. Box 13 discusses the benefits of such investments, drawing on the case of Chattogram Port. Another example of recent progress in improving container handling performance at Bay of Bengal ports is the provision of additional harbor cranes and transloading facilities for dry cargo at Kolkata (2013–2016, $37 million).

Policy

BIMSTEC recognizes the importance of container shipping and the need for ports to continue investing in modern container handling equipment to ensure improved terminal handling performance to support the enabling environment for rapid economic development.

> **Box 13: The Benefits of Investing in Container Handling Equipment:
> The Case of Chattogram Port**
>
> The relationship between investment in container handling equipment and enhanced performance is demonstrated by Chattogram Port. In 2007, the port handled 290 TEUs per hour and equipment availability was only 45%, but by 2012 these performance indicators had increased to 442 TEUs per hour with 74% equipment availability, mainly due to the delivery of additional handling equipment. Based on this successful experience, additional container handling equipment was procured by the Chittagong Port Authority for the New Mooring Container Terminal Port (2014–2016, $172 million).
>
> Source: Asian Development Bank. 2014. *Updating and Enhancement of the BIMSTEC Transport Infrastructure and Logistics Study, Phase II Report*. May. p. 76.

Strategy

BIMSTEC will encourage the port (sub)sector to invest in additional container handling equipment, commensurate with demand and the need to improve handling performance consistent with global good and best practice.

Projects

The projects in the previous subsection will generally improve container handling performance by upgrading existing terminals and developing new terminals. Featured in the previous subsection on the development of deeper ports in the Bay of Bengal and the Andaman Sea was the development of new port facilities at the Thilawa Special Economic Zone, which may also be considered as a specific example of a project to improve container handling performance through the development of a new port complex to handle intra-BIMSTEC trade. The project will include a new container terminal operation system, based on best practices in Japan.[44] Other projects to develop deeper ports will include modern container handling equipment.

Development of Coastal/Short-Sea Shipping

Issues

Coastal (or short-sea) shipping refers to the movement of cargo and passengers mainly by sea along a coast, without crossing an ocean. The requirements for the movement of vessels in this part of the sea are different from international standards and, therefore, involve lower costs.[45]

Within the BIMSTEC region, there is a significant opportunity to leverage coastal shipping for regional trade between and among India, Bangladesh, Myanmar, Sri Lanka, and Thailand, as well as Nepal and Bhutan, considering the geographic contiguity of these countries; however, this opportunity has not been fully exploited to date. India alone has a coastline of about 7,500 km and, as set out in Box 14, has launched the Sagarmala Programme to spearhead national, port-led development and harness the prospects of country's coastline and river network.

---

[44] Japan International Cooperation Agency, Kamigumi Co., Ltd., and Toyota Tsucho Corporation, *Preparatory Survey on Yangon Port in Thilawa Area and Logistics Depot Development in the Republic of the Union of Myanmar, Final Report*, January 2015, p. 197.

[45] In a recent coastal shipping initiative, 185 trucks were sent from Chennai, India, to Mongla, Bangladesh, using roll-on, roll-off (ro-ro) vessels, saving 15–20 days of travel time and 1,500+ km of travel distance. Ministry of Shipping, India, *Sagarmala Programme—Port-Led Prosperity*, 10 November 2017.

As part of its Southern Economic Corridor Project, Thailand has plans (2019–2023) to develop Ranong Port as an alternative gateway for coastal shipping (see Figure 5), including a $550 million railway link to Chumphon, and the development of links to Bangladesh, India, Myanmar, and Bangladesh along the Andaman Sea and Bay of Bengal.

To develop regional trade through international coastal shipping, India and Bangladesh entered into a coastal shipping agreement (the Bangladesh–India Agreement on Coastal Shipping, 2015) to facilitate the movement of commercial goods via river-sea vessels.[46] A similar agreement is contemplated under the BIMSTEC framework, with an ongoing effort (2017–2018) to negotiate a BIMSTEC Coastal Shipping Agreement, including standard operating procedures and coastal shipping regulations.[47]

Box 14: India's Sagarmala Programme

In 2015, the Ministry of Shipping, India, launched the Sagarmala Programme to spearhead national port-led development and harness the prospects of the country's coastline and river network. One of its objectives is to increase the current 6%–7% share of coastal and inland water transport to 12% by 2025, thereby reducing the cost of freight transport through a more optimal transport modal mix. Various initiatives have been pursued for this aim, such as adopting a coastal berth scheme and promoting roll-on, roll-off (ro-ro, including ro-pax) services. The Sagarmala National Perspective Plan, published in 2016, identified key freight commodities (e.g., petroleum, coal, steel) with potential for coastal and inland water transport and proposed measures to promote a modal shift of freight from rail and road. It has been estimated that implementing all Sagarmala-related measures will result in annual savings in logistics of $5.2 billion–$5.9 billion, with most from the use of coastal shipping for coal and other commodities by existing and new industries ($4.0 billion–4.8 billion equivalent).

Sources: http://sagarmala.gov.in/; and Asian Development Bank. 2018. TA-9231 REG: Regional Project Development Support for the South Asia Subregional Economic Cooperation Operational Plan, 2016–2025.

Policy

BIMSTEC recognizes the importance of developing coastal shipping services between and among member states.

Strategy

BIMSTEC supports and promotes the development of coastal shipping between member states.

Projects

Table 13 presents planned flagship projects to develop coastal shipping in the BIMSTEC region. An initial initiative for the development of coastal shipping in the region is an ADB TA study, which is assessing the existing policy and regulatory framework of coastal shipping in the BIMSTEC region to develop an improved or new comprehensive framework for the (sub)sector particularly in facilitating and promoting domestic and international trade through coastal or short-sea routes, building on ongoing efforts spearheaded by the BIMSTEC Secretariat.

---

[46] The agreement is to enable coastal movement of goods and will (i) benefit export-import trade by reducing freight charges, (ii) improve utilization of Indian ports and open new opportunities for Indian coastal vessels, and (iii) help decongest roads especially at the land custom stations and ICPs.

[47] Myanmar has recognized that maritime transport costs can be reduced with implementation of a BIMSTEC Coastal Shipping Agreement, but in assessing such an agreement they are considering issues relating to trade policy, import and export volumes, and transport (including port) infrastructure.

Figure 5: Proposed New Coastal Shipping Routes from Ranong

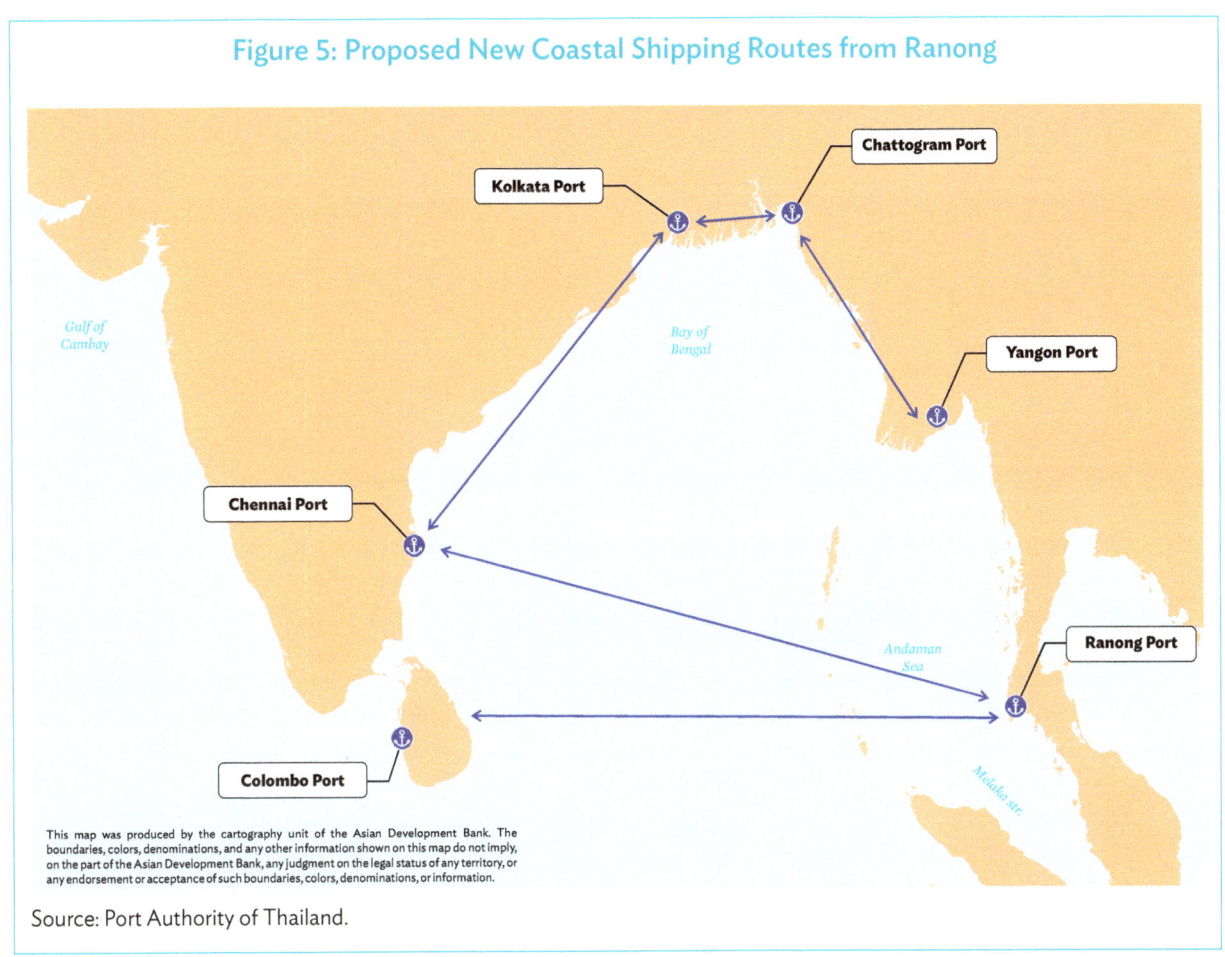

Source: Port Authority of Thailand.

Table 13: Planned Flagship Project for the Development of Coastal Shipping

Code	Project Description	BIMSTEC Development Logic	Estimated Cost, 2018 ($ million)	(Possible) Funding Sources	Timescale
REG-PM-024 (BAN, IND, MYA, SRL, and THA)	Study to develop coastal shipping	Develop regional trade by short-sea shipping	Not yet estimated	Not yet identified, but ADB support for initial study	2018–2028
REG-IW-025 (BAN, IND, MYA, SRL, and THA)	Investment projects to improve coastal shipping in the BIMSTEC region	As above	Not yet estimated	Not yet identified	2020–2023

BAN = Bangladesh, BIMSTEC = Bay of Bengal Initiative for Multi-Sectoral Technical and Economic Cooperation, IND = India, MYA = Myanmar, SRL = Sri Lanka, THA = Thailand.
Source: Asian Development Bank.

VI. Inland Water Transport

Sector Overview

An emerging view is that the inland water transport (sub)sector has a role to play in a comprehensive BIMSTEC regional transport system.[48] An October 2017 subregional conference on the subject concluded that:

(i) the development of a sustainable and economically viable inland waterway transport sector in the subregion can contribute to the achievement of Sustainable Development Goals through poverty reduction and job creation;

(ii) the landlocked BIMSTEC member states—Bhutan and Nepal—might benefit from the inland waterways in India and Bangladesh through multimodal and intermodal connectivity since it provides access to the sea[49];

(iii) multimodal and intermodal connectivity to Myanmar has the potential to increase India's connectivity to Southeast Asia;

(iv) cross-border regulatory barriers should be reduced, and data related to rivers (and seaports) should be shared;

(v) comprehensive research is required on trade prospects, environmental costs, and river management aspects to ensure informed policy decisions on the development of waterways;

(vi) bilateral treaties for trade and transit should include provisions for use of India's waterways for both inbound and outbound cargo, as, for example, does the 2017 Memorandum of Understanding between Bhutan and Bangladesh for Bhutan's use of Bangladesh's inland waterways and river ports for trade purposes[50],

---

[48] For example: (i) UK Aid, Consumer Unity and Trust Society (CUTS) International and The Asia Foundation. *Report of the Sub-Regional Dialogue, Expanding Tradable Benefits of Transboundary Water: Promoting Navigational Usage of Waterways in [the] Ganga and Brahmaputra Basins*. Kolkata, India. 26–27 October 2017. p. 10: stressed "… the need to make inland waterways a part of the transport narrative in the BBIN sub-region with multimodal and intermodal junctures so that this sector becomes economically viable"; and (ii) A. V. Pillai. The Promising Future of Inland Waterway Trade in South Asia. *InAsia*. 19 May 2017: "transboundary inland waterways are an enterprise in dismantling the irrationalities of history and boundaries to focus on the logic of geography".

[49] "Access to the sea" may mean access to seaports where goods can be transshipped since river vessels cannot generally go to the sea. In the cases of Bhutan and Nepal, the distances to the nearest river ports are significant and these nearby ports have virtually no draft since they are located on the headwaters of the Ganges and Brahmaphutra Rivers rather than downstream where there is more draft.

[50] This agreement allows Bhutan to access Chattogram and Mongla Ports through waterways in Bangladesh. On 7 April 2018, the Prime Ministers of India and Nepal reached a "landmark decision" to develop inland water transport for the movement of cargo, within the framework of the Protocol to the Treaty of Transit between India and Nepal, to provide Nepal with additional access to the sea. Ministry of External Affairs, India. India–Nepal Statement on New Connectivity through Inland Waterways. New Delhi, 7 April 2018. However, the costs of dredging the Ganges far upstream would be substantial.

(vii) prospects of local (inland) waterborne trade, e.g., across "immediate, international borders," should be explored; and

(viii) cross-border river tourism offers some potential.[51]

That said, an alternative view is that at this stage the inland waterways sector may not be "sufficiently encompassing of overall transport activities in the member states to support the need for individual modal policies and strategies." The mode is primarily used for domestic rather than international transport. It mainly serves specific markets and is constrained by network geography. It is mainly restricted to lighterage operations and the carriage of low-value products, such as aggregates and some cereals and rice.[52]

Issues

To fully assess the emerging view on the potential importance of the inland waterway transport sector, it will be important to undertake economic and financial analyses comparing the alternative modes, considering life cycle infrastructure costs, operating costs and travel time, and environmental and social impacts.[53]

Specific issues in developing the sector include the need to:

(i) develop inland water transport infrastructure, e.g., maintenance of a least available draft of at least 3.0 m on core sections of the waterway, installation of nighttime navigation aids;

(ii) identify stretches and commodities with trade potential between (and within) member states and design vessels accordingly;

(iii) upgrade a few river vessels to river-sea vessels;[54]

(iv) develop full-fledged border facilities at ferry and entry and exit points along routes designated under the Indo–Bangladesh Protocol on Inland Water Transit and Trade (2015; see Figure 6);[55]

(v) achieve more flexibility in terms of designated routes, jetties, and disembarkation points regarding cross-border tourism between Bangladesh and India;

(vi) improve inter-agency and international cooperation; and

(vii) over the longer term, undertake hydromorphological studies of the subject navigable rivers, on which basis to develop infrastructure and navigable channels.

---

[51] Ministry of External Affairs, India. India–Nepal Statement on New Connectivity through Inland Waterways. New Delhi, 7 April 2018. pp. 3–4, 7.
[52] Asian Development Bank. 2014. *Updating and Enhancement of the BIMSTEC Transport Infrastructure and Logistics Study, Phase II Report.* May. p. 77.
[53] UK Aid, CUTS International, and The Asia Foundation. *Report of the Sub-Regional Dialogue, Expanding Tradable Benefits of Transboundary Water: Promoting Navigational Usage of Waterways in [the] Ganga and Brahmaputra Basins,* Kolkata, India. 26–27 October 2017. p. 8. Citing A. K. Haque, Professor, East-West University, Bangladesh, on the commercial viability of inland water transport.
[54] However, such specialized vessels may not be able to reach inland destinations.
[55] Under this agreement, transshipment of goods to India's Northeast Region through Ashuganj river port in Bangladesh and further through Akhaura–Agartala by road became operational in June 2016. Also worth noting is the 2017 Memorandum of Understanding between India and Bangladesh for fairway development by dredging of the Ashuganj-Zakiganj stretch of the Kushiyara River and Sirajganj-Daikhawa stretch of Jamuna River along an Indo–Bangladesh protocol route.

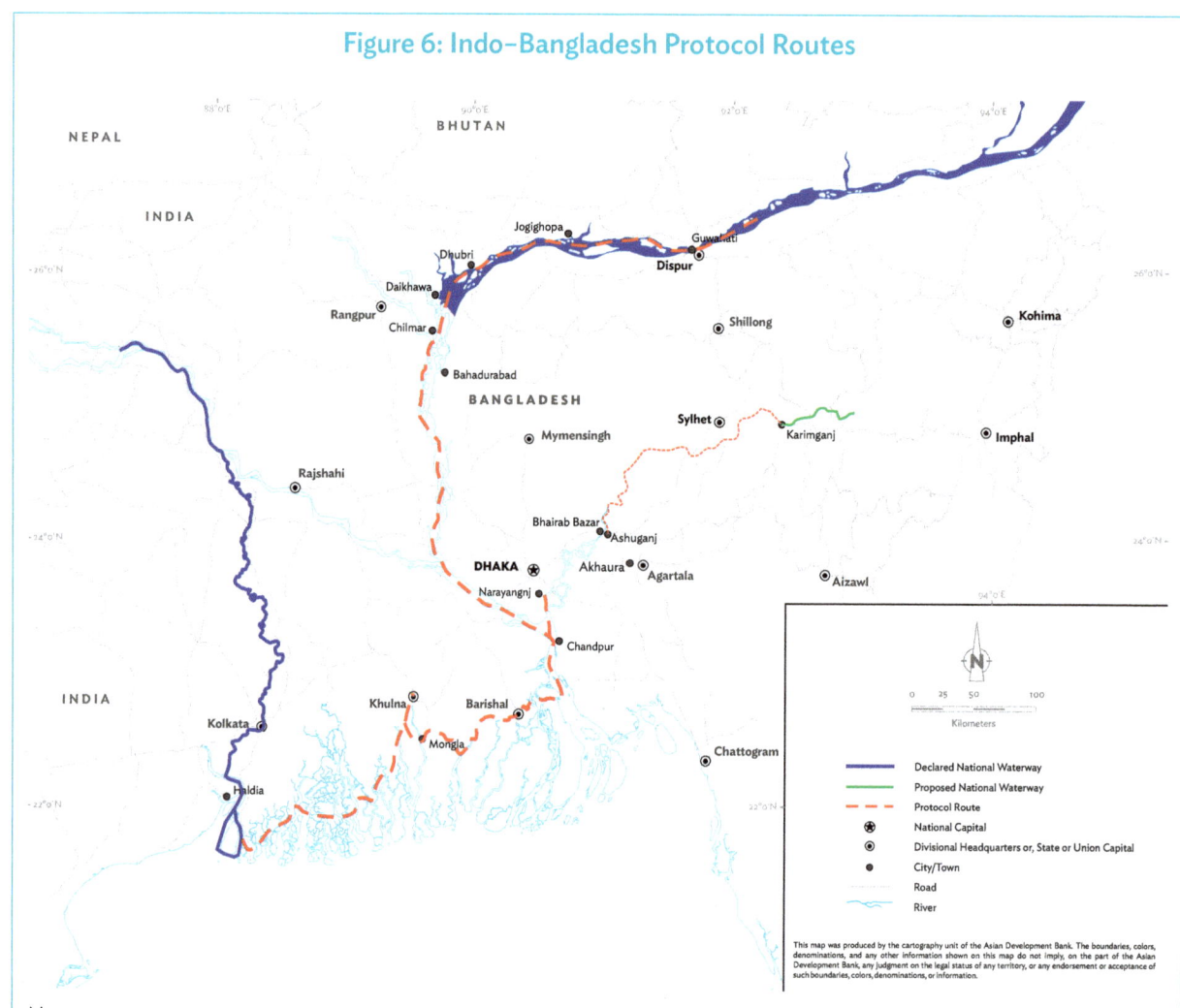

Figure 6: Indo–Bangladesh Protocol Routes

Notes:
1. The existing Indo–Bangladesh Protocol roads, especially the Kolkata–Mongla river route, may be extended or connected to the Roosevelt Jetty, Khulna, for potential benefit.
2. In 2019, a World Bank-supported *Conceptual Plan for Integrating Community-Based Tourism along the Bangladesh–India Protocol Route for Inland Navigation* (with a focus on the Sundarbans), prepared by Consumer Unity and Trust Society International (CUTS), was published.

Source: National Maritime Foundation (Vasudha Chawla). 2017. *India–Bangladesh Maritime Trade Protocol on Inland Water Transit and Trade (PIWTT)*. June. p. 3. http://www.maritimeindia.org/View%20Profile/636331714994487296.pdf.

Policy

BIMSTEC recognizes the potential benefits of developing inland water transport between member states to facilitate and promote intraregional trade for the overall benefit of member states.

Strategy

BIMSTEC will encourage member states to develop sustainable, economically viable inland water transport between them, e.g., by providing multimodal and intermodal connectivity.

Projects

Table 14 presents planned flagship projects to develop international inland water transport in the BIMSTEC region. A number of projects may be considered in the study and follow-on investment(s), e.g., river cruise services linking Kolkata–Dhaka–Guwahati–Jorhat, development of Dhubri on the Bhramaputra River, development of Badarpur on the Barak River, the Maharani–Sonamara–Daukhandi stretch of the Gumti River, the Jirania–Joynagar–Ashuganj stretch of the Howah River, waterways on the Tizu River (Nagaland) flowing into the Chindwin River of Myanmar, and various waterways for the movement of transit cargo to and from Kolkata, Visakhapatnam, Chittagong, and Mongla, and Nepal (e.g., Sagarmala–Barragemala–Haldia–Kolkata–Farakka–Kalughat–Bhimnagar–KoshiBarrage,Sagarmala–Haldia–Kolkata–Farakka–Kalughat–Bhaisalotan–Triveni Dham).

Table 14: Planned Flagship Projects to Develop International Inland Water Transport

Code	Project Description	BIMSTEC Development Logic	Estimated Cost, 2018 ($ million)	(Possible) Funding Sources	Timescale
REG-IW-01 (BAN, BHU, NEP, IND, MYA)	Study of opportunities to improve inland water transport in the BIMSTEC region	Historically important mode, which offers potential for sustainable, economically viable cross-border transport, as well as multimodal and intermodal connectivity	3	Not yet identified	2019–2020
REG-IW-02 (BAN, BHU, NEP, IND, MYA)	Investment projects to improve inland water transport in the BIMSTEC region	As above	Not yet specified	Not yet identified	2020–2023

ADB = Asian Development Bank, BAN = Bangladesh, BHU = Bhutan, BIMSTEC = Bay of Bengal Initiative for Multi-Sectoral Technical and Economic Cooperation, IND = India, MYA = Myanmar, NEP = Nepal, REG = regional.

Source: Asian Development Bank.

Box 18 in the section on multimodal and intermodal transport features the Kaladan Multimodal Transit Transport Project, the most significant project in the region to date involving inland water transport, as well as other modes.

VII. Civil Aviation and Airport Development

Sector Overview

The benefits of civil aviation beyond borders are well established. Aviation generates wealth and employment directly and through value chains and, in particular, is essential for tourism development, which provides substantial economic benefits for participants in tourism value chains. Consider, for example, that Nepal's economy lost $1 million per day due to the disruption after the April 2015 earthquake. Aviation also has numerous social benefits, e.g., facilitation of people-to-people contacts and exchanges,[56] provision of equitable and inclusive educational opportunities, and support for the provision of humanitarian aid after natural disasters.[57]

The BIMSTEC member states have a wide range of air connectivity. According to the Air Connectivity Index (ACI)—which uses network analysis to calculate an index that summarizes a country's ability to connect to global air transport flows—Thailand ranked 26th, India ranked 48th, Bangladesh ranked 108th, Nepal ranked 117th, and Bhutan ranked 133rd, of 154 countries, based on 2012 data (Myanmar and Sri Lanka were not assessed, but Myanmar was ranked 112th and Sri Lanka, 144th in a 2007 assessment of 200+ countries).[58] Of course, even the member states with relatively low rankings maintain international air connectivity.

Civil aviation has been the most dynamic of the transport modes in the region in recent years and has the highest profile internationally. This situation has to a large extent been driven by the rapid growth in low-cost carrier (LCC) operations and the increasing numbers of LCCs. In addition, increased incomes in the region and improved access to flights have substantially increased demand, even for the legacy (full-service) carriers. The focus of this Master Plan has been on infrastructure—particularly on airports and their ability to handle this continued growth—rather than on carriers, which are increasingly private sector operators.

In relation to BIMSTEC's aims and objectives, the aviation industry provides an enabling environment for rapid economic development, accelerates social progress in the region, and provides training and research facilities. However, as with the ports and maritime sector, the situation varies significantly country by country and even airport by airport, thus, potentially limiting the scope for regional coordination and cooperation. Programmed

---

[56] The leaders of the BIMSTEC member states agreed to "explore [the] possibility of establishing appropriate BIMSTEC forums for parliamentarians, universities, academia, research institutes, cultural organizations, and media community to expand the scope of people-to-people contacts." Bay of Bengal Initiative for Multi-Sectoral Technical and Economic Cooperation. *Fourth Summit Declaration, 30–31 August 2018, Kathmandu, Nepal.* p. 9. The development of a BIMSTEC Human Resources Network—analogous to the Asia-Pacific Economic Cooperation (APEC) Education Network—may be considered. Asia-Pacific Economic Cooperation. 2013. *Improving Connectivity in the Asia-Pacific Region: Perspectives of the APEC Policy Support Unit.* September. p. 51.

[57] *Aviation Benefits.* 2017. https://www.icao.int/sustainability/Documents/AVIATION-BENEFITS-2017-web.pdf.

[58] The United States was ranked first and Tonga was ranked last. Developing Trade Consultants (B. Shepherd, A. Shingal, and A. Raj). 2016. *Value of Air Cargo: Air Transport and Global Value Chains, Final Report.* Prepared for the International Air Transport Association. December. pp. 1, 19–22, 83–86; J.-F. Arvis and B. Shepherd. 2016. Measuring Connectivity in a Globally Networked Industry: The Case of Air Transport. *The World Economy.* March. Vol. 39(3). pp. 369–385; World Bank, International Trade Department (J.-F. Arvis and B. Shepherd). 2011. *The Air Connectivity Index: Measuring Integration in the Global Air Transport Network.* June.

airport developments are mainly driven by specific circumstances and demand at each location, rather than being part of published plans.

The most critical issue regarding aviation infrastructure in the region is the continued expansion of airport capacity for both passengers and freight. There are major programs for airport development in all seven member states. An additional issue of common interest is the development of the LCC market, in which high annual growth rates have continued, despite sometimes difficult economic conditions.[59]

The recommended policies, strategies, and projects to address these specific issues are set out below.

Expansion of Airport Capacity

Issues

There are airport capacity expansion programs and projects that were recently completed or are underway in all BIMSTEC member states, including (i) passenger terminal developments, mainly to separate domestic and international flows or separate legacy and LCC traffic; (ii) additional runways and taxiways to handle more flights or reduce delays at peak times; and (iii) apron developments, especially to handle more LCC traffic. Examples of recently completed projects in the (sub)sector include (i) upgrading of a taxiway at Hazrat Shahjalal International Airport, Dhaka, Bangladesh (2009–2015, supported by the Danish International Development Agency, DANIDA); (ii) airport safety and security system improvement, Bangladesh (2014–2018); and (iii) expansion and development of facilities (e.g., development of a new passenger terminal, a new cargo complex, a parallel taxiway) at Paro (55 km from Thimphu), Bhutan, with support of India (2014–2018).

The funding for airport capacity expansion programs and projects has increasingly been provided by the private sector, reflecting a worldwide trend. Over the last decade this trend has been particularly notable in India, and more private sector involvement is programmed in Myanmar, Nepal, and Sri Lanka.

While the BTILS focused on freight traffic, rather than passengers, aviation differs from other modes because passengers and cargo are integrated to a large extent. Most airfreight is carried as underbelly cargo in passenger aircraft and, therefore, passenger operations generate the bulk of freight capacity. Consequently, the development of passenger terminals and runways indirectly benefits freight activities by increasing available freight capacity.

It is important that BIMSTEC as a regional organization have a clear view on the development of this dynamic (sub)sector. It is also important to recognize the linkage between demand and capacity in policy, strategy, and projects, since there are a number of possible airport developments that appear speculative, and it is critical that this sector has a high implementation rate, in view of its high public profile.

---

[59] There is a need to formulate a management plan to construct bays, terminal building(s), and other infrastructure to facilitate LCCs and separate legacy carriers and LCCs. Considering progress in the region in the development of bilateral air services agreements, it was deemed unnecessary to program development of a BIMSTEC air services agreement at this time, although a regional approach may be explored in the future. An incremental approach to freeing up air services—such as has been pursued by India and Sri Lanka—may be effective. S. Kathuria et al. 2018. Reducing Connectivity Costs: Air Travel Liberalization between India, and Sri Lanka. In World Bank Group (ed. S. Kathuria). *A Glass Half Full: The Promise of Regional Trade in South Asia*, South Asia Development Forum. Chapter 4. pp. 159–88.

Policy

BIMSTEC recognizes the need to upgrade and expand airport infrastructure to meet the growing regional demand for air transport, with its ability to promote economic development and social progress in the region.

Strategy

BIMSTEC will promote demand-based development of airport facilities in the member states by encouraging their prioritization in national plans and in discussions with member states and international development partners.

Projects

Appendix 5 includes a long list of planned projects to expand airport capacity in the region, while Table 15 highlights flagship projects in this category selected mainly based on relevance to BIMSTEC intraregional connectivity.

Table 15: Planned Flagship Projects for Expansion of Airport Capacity

Code	Project Description	BIMSTEC Development Logic	Estimated Cost, 2018 ($ million)	(Possible) Funding Sources	Timescale
BAN-CA-003	Hazrat Shahjalal International Airport Expansion Project, Dhaka (Phase 1: construction of Third Passenger Terminal, cargo building, taxiways, apron)	Improved air connectivity with international cities and regional cities of Bangladesh	1,660	JICA	2016–2022
BAN-CA-004	Hazrat Shahjalal International Airport Expansion Project, Dhaka (Phase 2)	As above	Not yet estimated	Not yet identified	2025–2028
BAN-CA-005	Development of Shah Amanat International Airport, Chattogram (strengthening of existing runway and taxiway)	As above	68.5	Government	2018–2020
BAN-CA-012	Development of Bangabandhu Sheikh Mujib International Airport to serve central Bangladesh	As above	Not yet estimated	Not yet specified	2025–2028 and beyond
BHU-CA-013	Further expansion and development of Paro Airport (domestic terminal, runway resurfacing and widening)	Expanded capacity to handle forecast growth including BIMSTEC flights	5	Not yet identified	2018–2023
BHU-CA-014	Expansion of Gelephu Airport (feasibility and design studies, construction of new 3,000-meter runway and associated river diversion, ILS and runway lighting system, apron taxiway, terminal building, hangar, cargo building)	Possible new location for intra-BIMSTEC flights to serve larger aircraft, which would accommodate flight diversions during bad weather at Paro Airport and provide for the transport of supplies during emergencies	200 (including 20 for runway)	As above	2018–2028

continued on next page

Table 15 continued

Code	Project Description	BIMSTEC Development Logic	Estimated Cost, 2018 ($ million)	(Possible) Funding Sources	Timescale
IND-CA-015	Further development of Delhi Airport (into a "Hub Airport of Asia"), with additional runway, terminal expansion, and apron modification (while Terminal 2 has been recommissioned, phased redevelopment of Terminal 1 and expansion of Terminal 3 have been planned)	Additional capacity to handle intra-BIMSTEC flights among others	1,800	PPP	2018–2025
IND-CA-016	Development of Greater Noida Airport, in Uttar Pradesh, about 60 km from Delhi	Greenfield airport that will handle intra-BIMSTEC flights among others	3,100	As above	2019–2022
IND-CA-017	Expansion of Chennai Airport including terminal development	Additional capacity for major BIMSTEC airport hub	Not yet estimated	As above	2019–2020
IND-CA-018	New (Chennai) Sriperumbudur Airport Development Project, as part of Chennai-Bangalore Industrial Corridor Project	As above	Not yet estimated	As above	2020–2023
MYA-CA-021	Construction of new Hanthawaddy International Airport (77 km northeast of Yangon, near Bago), plus road and rail access, and ancillary facilities (e.g., aviation fuel supply; hotel, commercial, and administrative complexes)	Construction of new international airport to serve as a major gateway of Myanmar and regional hub, serving rapidly increasing traffic demand and providing airport users high-quality, world-class airport services	Not yet estimated	PPP, with assistance of the Government of Japan (with the Ministry of Land, Infrastructure and Transport, Japan, as facilitator)	2020–2027
NEP-CA-025	Major development of Kathmandu Airport (Tribhuvan International Airport Capacity Enhancement Investment Program)	Focusing on infrastructure and technology, improvement of air connectivity and enhancement of capacity by attracting larger aircraft, improving terminal facilities, and enhancing safety	59	ADB and Civil Aviation Authority of Nepal	2019–2021
NEP-CA-026	Development of a second international airport on a greenfield site at Nijgadh, Bara, 135 km south of Kathmandu	Provision of a full-fledged international airport to accommodate all types of aircraft; easing of pressure on Tribhuvan International Airport and serving as an alternate airport for all types of aircraft in all weather conditions	650	PPP (spearheaded by the Investment Board of Nepal, as per the Public–Private Partnership and Investment Act, 2019)	2018–2025

continued on next page

Table 15 continued

Code	Project Description	BIMSTEC Development Logic	Estimated Cost, 2018 ($ million)	(Possible) Funding Sources	Timescale
SRL-CA-030	Development of Bandaranaike International Airport, Colombo, including a new passenger terminal with two piers (handling an additional 9 million passengers per year) and construction of new apron and taxiways	Expansion of Sri Lanka's main airport connection with other BIMSTEC countries and which acts as a regional "minihub"	413	JICA	2017–2020
SRL-CA-031	Service delivery improvements at Mattala Rajapaksa International Airport in southeast Sri Lanka	Enhanced regional and local air connectivity with improved operations	To be determined	PPPs with support of the Civil Aviation Authority of India	2020–2028
THA-CA-032	Suvarnabhumi Airport Expansion Project in Bangkok (including third runway)	Expansion of BIMSTEC aviation hub	2,100	Airports of Thailand PLC	2016–2023

ADB = Asian Development Bank, BAN = Bangladesh, BIMSTEC = Bay of Bengal Initiative for Multi-Sectoral Technical and Economic Cooperation, BOT = build–operate–transfer, IND = India, JICA = Japan International Cooperation Agency, km = kilometer, MYA = Myanmar, PLC = public limited company, PPP = public–private partnership, SRL = Sri Lanka, THA = Thailand.
Source: Asian Development Bank.

Box 15 and Box 16 feature the development of notable projects to expand airport capacity in the region (in Dhaka [Box 15] and Colombo [Box 16]), to serve BIMSTEC and wider regional and global traffic. The desirability of developing multiple airports in one metropolitan area is explored in Box 17, looking particularly at recent practice in India.

Box 15: Expansion of Hazrat Shahjalal International Airport, Dhaka, 2019–2022

The Civil Aviation Authority of Bangladesh, in association with the Ministry of Civil Aviation and Tourism, is expanding the Hazrat Shahjalal International Airport in Dhaka to address the continued increase in domestic and international passengers and cargo passing through the facility. Annual passenger traffic is forecast to increase to about 12 million by 2022 and by 22 million to 2025. To meet this demand, including BIMSTEC flights, construction of a third passenger terminal building and other infrastructure will commence in August 2019, with completion scheduled for August 2022. The expansion is to more than double the airport's annual passenger handling capacity from 8 million at present to about 20 million, and the cargo capacity from 200,000 tons to 500,000 tons. The expansion will include the construction of the third passenger terminal building (226,000 m²) known as Terminal 3, as well as a 5,900 m² VIP complex, and a 41,200 m² cargo building and multi-level car parking building with tunnel. In addition, the project includes construction of several exit and connecting taxiways, a parking apron in Terminal 3, new roads to connect the terminal with the airport road, and a drainage system. The project was approved by the Government of Bangladesh in October 2017; the total cost of the expansion is estimated to be JPY192 billion ($1.66 billion), for which JICA will provide a concessionary loan.

BIMSTEC = Bay of Bengal Initiative for Multi-Sectoral Technical and Economic Cooperation, m² = square meter.
Sources: Ministry of Civil Aviation and Tourism, Bangladesh; Hazrat Shahjalal International Airport Expansion, Dhaka. *Airport Technology*. undated. http://www.airport-technology.com/projects/hazrat-shahjalal-international-airport-expansion-dhaka/].

Box 16: Development of Bandaranaike International Airport, Colombo, 2017–2020

Airport and Aviation Services (Sri Lanka) Limited, with support from the Japan International Cooperation Agency (Japanese yen [JPY] 45,428 million or about $413 million), is constructing a new multilevel terminal building (Terminal 2) to be opened in 2020, with an approximate floor area of 180,000 m², where arrivals and departures will be separated vertically. In addition, a new remote apron with 23 parking stands will be developed, as well as a new taxiway.

The project is being developed based on the eco-airport concept with advanced Japanese technology. The concept includes rainwater harvesting for the landscaping works and recycling water from the sewerage treatment plant, photovoltaic power generation, solar energy harvesting, and light-emitting diode (LED) lighting.

After completion of the project, the airport will be able to handle 15 million passengers per annum (mppa). In 2015, Bandaranaike International Airport handled 8.5 mppa, already in excess of its capacity of 6 mppa.

m² = square meter.
Source: Japan International Cooperation Agency. https://www.jica.go.jp/english/news/press/2015/160325_01.html.

Box 17: The Desirability of Developing Multiple Airports in One Metropolitan Area

Since many BIMSTEC airports are experiencing double-digit annual percentage growth in passenger demand, proposals are being put forward for constructing a second airport in these metropolitan areas. Bangkok already has two airports (Suvarnabhumi and Don Mueang) and has adopted a three-airport policy, to meet an expected doubling of passenger traffic in 10 years, with growth to be focused on U-Tapao, 140 km southeast of Bangkok. There are several other examples of cities with multiple airports in Asia (e.g., Tokyo, with Narita and Haneda Airports) and worldwide (e.g., New York City, with three major airports). In the BIMSTEC region, there are now proposals to develop second airports in a number of the member states, e.g., near Delhi and Chennai in India, at Hanthawaddy in Myanmar, and at Nijgadh in Nepal. India has traditionally had a "150 km rule", not permitting the development of a greenfield airport within 150 km of an existing airport, but the Ministry of Civil Aviation, India, is considering relaxing this rule, reducing the distance to 100 km, under its Udan (*udedesh ka aamnagrik*: "let the common citizen of the country fly") regional connectivity scheme.

BIMSTEC = Bay of Bengal Initiative for Multi-Sectoral Technical and Economic Cooperation, km = kilometer.
Sources: This Master Plan; and Handling the Rise in Air Traffic: A Multiple Airport Theory. 2017. *Indian Express*. 28 October.

Development of Airfreight Facilities and Services

Issues

Air cargo is a critical enabler supporting integration of countries into global value chains (GVCs). Speed and reliability are essential in structuring a GVC, and trade in high value-to-weight intermediates is a core GVC activity, which suggests that air cargo can play a transformative role in terms of a country's ability to successfully integrate its firms into GVCs. A 1% increase in the Air Connectivity Index (ACI) is associated with a 6.3% increase in total exports and imports, and air connectivity is strongly associated with participation in GVCs, with a 1% increase in the ACI associated with a 2.9% increase in GVC participation.[60]

---

[60] Developing Trade Consultants (B. Shepherd, A. Shingal, and A. Raj). 2016. *Value of Air Cargo: Air Transport and Global Value Chains, Final Report*. Prepared for the International Air Transport Association. December. pp. iii, 77.

As indicated in the previous section on the expansion of airport capacity, the majority of airfreight in the BIMSTEC region is carried as underbelly cargo in the holds of the legacy (full-service) carriers. LCCs rely on rapid turnaround of their aircraft to maximize aircraft utilization and, therefore, do not generally accept freight traffic, since handling of the cargo can increase turnaround times. Small amounts of parcel traffic are sometimes accepted, as these can be quickly loaded.[61]

All-freighter aircraft activity is generally long-distance intercontinental traffic, with almost no intra-BIMSTEC movements other than cargo imported for specific projects. The exception is the express carriers, such as DHL, UPS, and FedEx, which provide overnight or two-day delivery services. While such operations were initially based on the movement of parcel traffic, they have gradually expanded into the premium air cargo sector with larger consignment sizes. These carriers operate on a hub-and-spoke basis, with specialized facilities to handle the cargo rapidly and priority takeoff slots to meet tight schedules.

At most airports, the handling of freight tends to be low-profile, while the primary public image of the airport is formed by passenger traffic. Although some BIMSTEC airports handle only small volumes of freight, others are expanding their freight operations rapidly. As the region develops economically, the demand for the urgent movement of goods will increase. In addition, as countries expand into the production or processing of higher-value products, aviation will increasingly become a transport option within the supply chain between producers and consumers. Much of the region's airfreight consists of products such as premium or fresh food imports or exports, machinery and electrical goods, fashion garments, and ICT equipment, as well as spare parts and parcel traffic. While it is an indirect relationship, the larger passenger airports within the region also tend to have the largest freight throughputs.

Policy

BIMSTEC recognizes the need for more modern air cargo handling and equipment at the region's main airports to support the growing demand for airfreight movements arising from the region's economic development and the gradual transition toward the production of higher-value exports requiring more rapid travel times.

Strategy

BIMSTEC supports the need for investment in cargo infrastructure and equipment at major airports in the member states and will encourage prioritization for this purpose wherever possible.

Projects

Development plans for cargo facilities at airports in the region are less common than plans for passenger terminal and runway development, but in most cases, some modernization or expansion of existing cargo facilities has been undertaken or is planned as part of the airport capacity expansion projects described in the previous section. For example, a cargo terminal was recently constructed at Paro (Bhutan) and there are plans to construct a cargo terminal in Dhaka (Bangladesh) and Gelephu (Bhutan), to transfer freight operations from Yangon to a new Hanthawaddy Airport in Myanmar, and to add cargo capacity at Bangkok. While these developments may be lower-profile, they reflect the need to develop air cargo facilities in the BIMSTEC region. Other such projects include a new cargo terminal with annual handling capacity of 4,000 tons at Mandalay International Airport (completed

---

[61] That said, there are examples of LCCs having cargo as an important source of revenue. Cargo and LCCs: Cebu Pacific Case Study Shows Cargo Can Pay. 12 March 2018. https://centreforaviation.com/insights/analysis/cargo-and-lccs-cebu-pacific-case-study-shows-cargo-can-pay-404110].

in March 2019) and the development of cargo facilities at Bandaranaike International Airport in Colombo (2018–2019, $21 million).

Development of Support Facilities for Low-Cost Carrier Operations

Issues

Over the last decade, LCC operations have expanded rapidly in the region. As indicated, while the LCCs are generally not players in the freight sector; at many airports, the pressure to develop the infrastructure is mostly coming from the LCCs. The dilemma for airport planners is that while the legacy (full-service) carriers require premium facilities with lounges, comfortable waiting areas, and jetways to be able to market the overall flying experience, LCCs often use only basic facilities to minimize costs, e.g., using external stands with bus transfers rather than paying high jetway charges. Airport operators are attempting to serve two different markets, often within the same building.

However, the rapid growth of LCCs is making it difficult to accommodate the needs of the legacy (full-service) airlines and LCCs within a single structure and there is a gradual trend toward the development of separate LCC terminals or airports. This has already happened at some of the major Indian airports, and the developments at Suvarnabhumi Airport in Bangkok are partly related to supporting some LCC operations rather than having all LCCs operate out of Don Mueang Airport. Other major airports in the region will face a similar dilemma in the coming years and it is important that this trend be addressed in current airport planning.

Policy

BIMSTEC recognizes the importance of the expansion of LCC operations in the region in providing increased access to international air travel between and among BIMSTEC member states, thus, helping to stimulate economic development and social progress in the region.

Strategy

BIMSTEC will promote the development of additional infrastructure where needed at the region's main airports to facilitate the handling of LCC services, without compromising the infrastructure needed for legacy (full-service) carriers.

Projects

A number of the airport capacity expansion projects listed previously and/or listed in Appendix 5 entail development of support facilities for LCC operations: (i) the expansion of Dhaka Airport, including passenger terminal development, runway upgrading, taxiways, and apron development; (ii) further development of Delhi Airport, with an additional runway, terminal expansion, and apron modification; (iii) upgrading of Yangon Airport, including terminal facilities and apron development; (iv) major development of Kathmandu Airport, including terminal facilities improvement; and (v) the Phase 2 (Stage II) development of Bandaranaike International Airport, including a new terminal.

In addition, specific projects to support LCC operations—in Myanmar—are shown in Appendix 5.

VIII. Multimodal and Intermodal Transport

Sector Overview

The seamless movement of freight and passengers across the BIMSTEC region can be achieved by using multiple modes of transport, resulting in lower transport costs. The use of dry ports or ICDs is one way in which this objective can be achieved, as are more ambitious schemes such as the development of a multinational, multimodal transit transport corridor, such as the one linking "mainland" India, Myanmar, and North East India.

Issues

Wherever possible, an integrated approach to the development of transport infrastructure is recommended rather than developing each of the transport modes independently. Appendix 6 lists several multimodal and intermodal corridors (existing and proposed) in the BIMSTEC region. Also worth noting is India's ongoing program to develop 10 multimodal transport hubs, with partnerships between and among the Ministry of Roads and Road Transport, the Ministry of Railways, and the Ministry of Shipping; such hubs provide value-added services (e.g., distribution processing, quality control, customs clearance with bonded storage yards, warehousing management services) as well as multimodal and intermodal transport.

Policy

BIMSTEC recognizes the advantages of multimodal and intermodal transport, to promote efficiency by taking into account the relative advantages and disadvantages of each mode of transport.

Strategy

To establish seamless multimodal and intermodal transport linkages, BIMSTEC will encourage member states to pursue initiatives that efficiently combine the use of different modes of transport, including ICDs and dry ports as well as multimodal transport corridors.

Projects

Table 16 highlights flagship projects in this category selected mainly based on relevance to BIMSTEC intraregional connectivity. In addition, some of the projects are considered in the category including planned projects to develop ICDs. Reference may also be made to the development of automated clearance systems in Section IX, which refers to the provision of connectivity between port(s) and ICD or land border crossings for online clearance.

Table 16: Planned Flagship Projects for Multimodal and Intermodal Transport Development

Code	Project Description	BIMSTEC Development Logic	Estimated Cost, 2018 ($ million)	(Possible) Funding Sources	Timescale
BAN-MM-001	Second rail-connected ICD in Dhaka, at Dhirasram, in Gazipur	For relief of road and (Chattogram) port congestion because the first ICD in Dhaka exceeds capacity	200 (ADB: $100 million)	ADB and PPP	2017–2020
BAN-MM-002	Establishment of road network from economic zones to adjacent land and sea ports through widening of existing roads and national highways	Facilitation of multimodal and intermodal connectivity	To be specified	Not yet identified	To be programmed
BHU-MM-003	Development of Gelephu Transport Hub	Diversification of entry or exit points for BIMSTEC trade and transport	Not yet specified	Not yet identified	2018–2028
MYA-MM-004	Yangon-Dagon ICD	Development of multimodal and intermodal facility to handle container traffic	16	Private	2018–2021
MYA-MM-005	Yangon Region Dry Port (YwaThaGyi)	Linking Yangon Airport, Yangon–Bago rail line, and eventually Hanthawaddy Airport (as well as Yangon inland waterway ports)	40	PPP	2017–2019
MYA-MM-006	Mandalay Region Dry Port (Myitnge)	Linking Mandalay-Yangon Rail Line	40	PPP	2017–2019
MYA-MM-007	Establishment of logistics hub and truck or trailer terminal in the Wartayar Industrial Zone (northwestern Yangon)	Development of multimodal and intermodal facility to handle container traffic	15–20	PPP	To be programmed
REG-MM-009 (IND and MYA)	Kaladan Multimodal Transit Transport Project	Potential use of inland water transport as an alternative to a longer road route	453	India (Ministry of External Affairs)	2008–2020
REG-MM-010	Development of software arrangements for seamless multimodal and intermodal movement (e.g., EDI connectivity between ports and ICDs or land customs stations for online clearance, protocols, use of secure seals)	Facilitation of multimodal and intermodal connectivity	5	Not yet identified	2019–2021

ADB = Asian Development Bank, BAN = Bangladesh, BHU = Bhutan, BIMSTEC = Bay of Bengal Initiative for Multi-Sectoral Technical and Economic Cooperation, ICD = inland clearance/container depot, MYA = Myanmar, PPP = public–private partnership, PPTA = project preparation technical assistance, REG = regional.

Note: The Development of Nganglam Dry Port has been included under the ICD category because of relatively less strong multimodal and intermodal connectivity aspects.

Source: Asian Development Bank.

Box 18 features the Kaladan Multimodal Transit Transport Project, a significant intermodal transport project, involving inland water transport as well as other modes.[62] Also worth noting is the Mekong–India Economic Corridor, which would link Cambodia, Myanmar, Thailand, and Viet Nam, with India, through Dawei Port in Myanmar (see Figure 7), involving road, border crossing, and port improvements listed in other sections.

Box 18: The Kaladan Multimodal Transit Transport Project

Based on a 2 April 2008 Framework Agreement between the Governments of India and Myanmar, the Kaladan Multimodal Transit Transport Project, is notable for featuring inland water transport along with sea shipping and road transport, to provide alternate connectivity for India's northeastern states via Myanmar. It includes (i) a 539 km sea segment from Kolkata Port in India to Sittwe Port in Myanmar; (ii) a 158 km river segment from Sittwe Port to the inland water terminal at Paletwa jetty via the Kaladan River in Myanmar; (iii) a 110 km road segment from the Paletwa inland water terminal to the India and Myanmar border; and (iv) a 90 km road segment from the Indo–Myanmar border at Zorinpui to the Aizawl–Saiha National Highway at Lawngtlai in Mizoram, India, by National Highway (NH) 54, which is part of the East–West Corridor connecting northeastern India with the rest of the country. The following map shows the route.

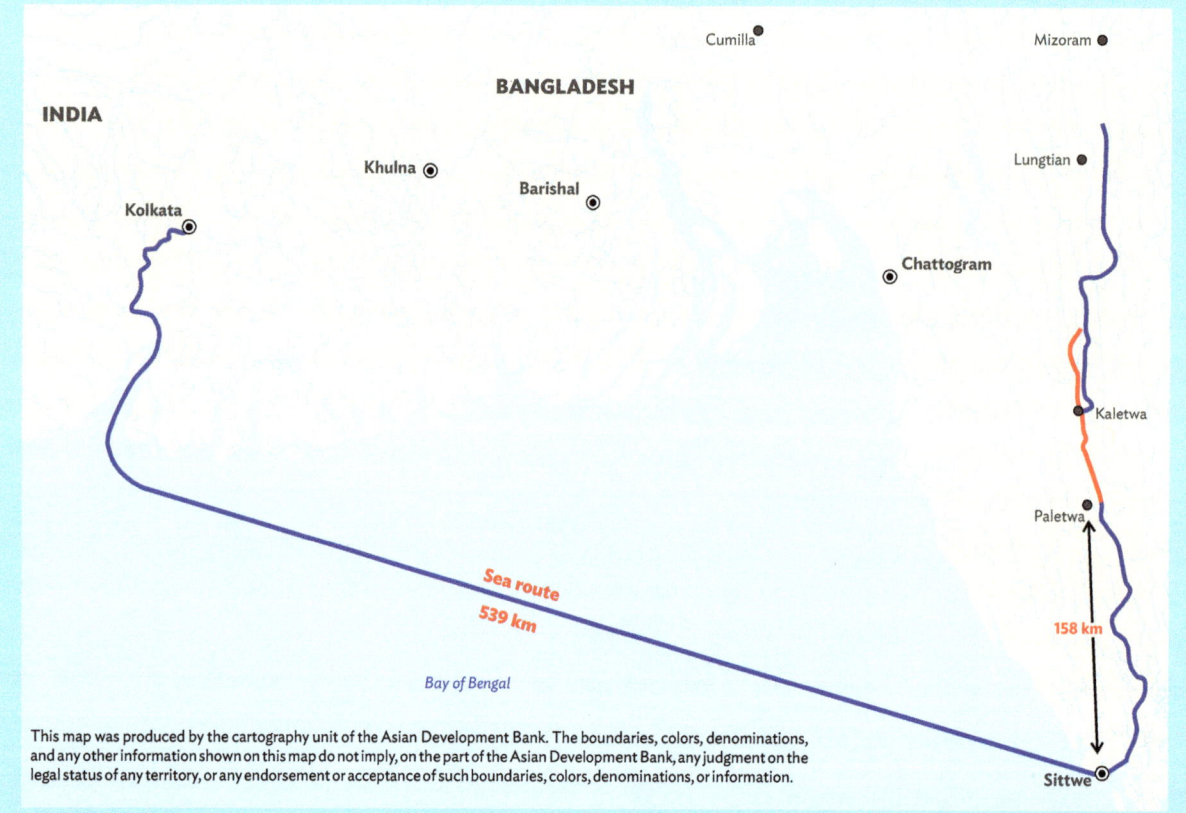

This map was produced by the cartography unit of the Asian Development Bank. The boundaries, colors, denominations, and any other information shown on this map do not imply, on the part of the Asian Development Bank, any judgment on the legal status of any territory, or any endorsement or acceptance of such boundaries, colors, denominations, or information.

km = kilometer.
Sources: www.kaladanmovement.org; Ministry of External Affairs, India. Question No, 6280, Kaladan Multi-Modal Transit Transport. 12 April 2017; http://www.oilseedcrops.org/2013/04/12/indian-look-east-policy-and-the-kaladan-project-of-western-myanmar/.

---

[62] Subject to funding availability, the Government of Myanmar has been exploring the possibility of dredging sections of the Chindwin River, which runs close to the states of Manipur and Nagaland in North East India, but does not currently offer year-round navigability; if appropriate connecting links with other modes (e.g., roads, railways) could be established near the Chindwin River, it may be possible to build a regional multimodal network for both cargo movement and tourism development. V. Vidyadharan and P. Nath. 2017. Connectivity Gains for India's North East via Waterways. 15 December. https://www.thethirdpole.net/en/2017/12/15/connectivity-gains-for-indias-north-east-via-waterways/.

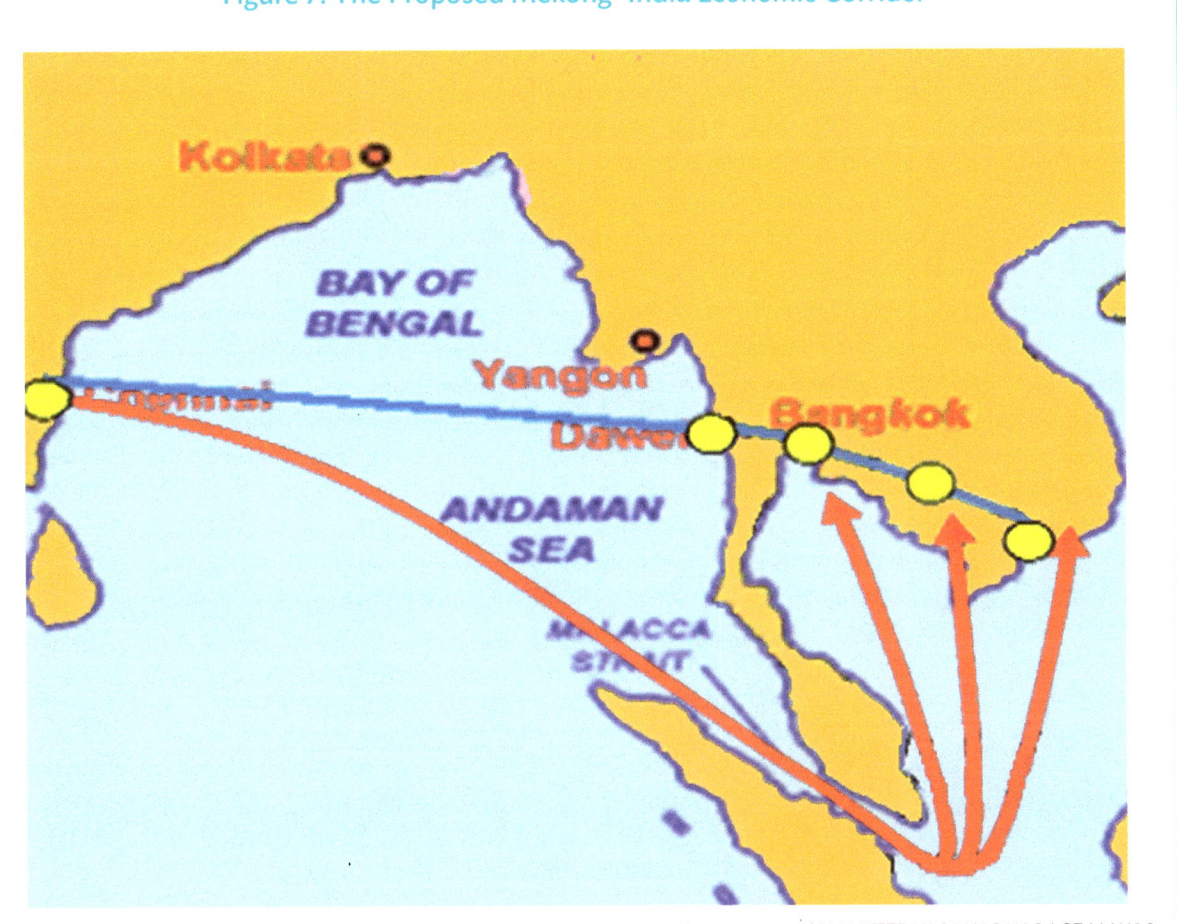

Figure 7: The Proposed Mekong–India Economic Corridor

Source: Economic Research Institute for ASEAN and East Asia. p. 143. http://www.eria.org/CHAPTER%203%20%20ASEAN%20-%20India%20Connectivity%20An%20Indian%20Perspective.pdf.

IX. Trade Facilitation

Sector Overview

A decade ago, the focus on trade facilitation was on the development of physical infrastructure, particularly the facilities at the border crossings and supporting ICDs. This focus was consistent with the overall emphasis on hard infrastructure at that time. However, it has become increasingly clear that border practices and procedures represent a critical non-tariff barrier that is equal to or even more of a constraint on the efficient movement of international traffic through those facilities and is a major cause of border congestion. The two issues of border infrastructure and practices or procedures are linked, because improvements in the physical infrastructure generate only limited benefits unless there are corresponding enhancements in border operations to ensure that cargo moves through those new facilities more quickly.

In the context of BIMSTEC's aims, trade facilitation helps create an enabling environment for rapid economic development by promoting trade, requires active collaboration and mutual assistance on matters of common interest to member states, and involves mutual assistance and cooperation with existing international and regional organizations such as the World Customs Organization (WCO) and other development partners. Trade facilitation is arguably the subject of this Master Plan that relates to most of BIMSTEC's aims because of its specific cross-border orientation and the demand for inter-country cooperation.

Regarding hard infrastructure, the key issues are further development of the main border posts, including associated dry ports, and of ICDs. The soft infrastructure issues mainly relate to customs modernization and the increasing use of ICT, as well as the introduction of new approaches to automation and reductions in trade documentation, and the adoption of advanced logistics. The recommended policies, strategies, and projects to address these specific issues follow.

Development of Border Infrastructure and Facilities

Issues

Border crossings represent a break in the international logistics chain. This occurs not only as a result of the lack of through transport, but also due to complex clearance procedures and, in some cases, the ownership of the products changing at the border. While the application of modern practices and procedures as promoted by the Revised Kyoto Convention of WCO and the Trade Facilitation Agreement of the World Trade Organization (WTO) can minimize these delays, it is critical that there is adequate infrastructure to enable performance of these more advanced procedures in a controlled environment. The modern trend is for the facilities at the border to serve merely as a checkpoint for freight traffic, rather than as a clearance point. This aim is achieved by pre-clearing exports prior to their arrival at the border, with the authorities at the frontier simply checking the paperwork and, if necessary, undertaking a visual inspection of the vehicle. Similarly, for imports the inward paperwork is checked, with inspection of the vehicle and cargo, and the shipment is allowed to proceed inland with transit documents to a point where it is finally cleared. Such checkpoints have simple layouts consisting of separate lanes for passenger and freight traffic with processing booths and adjacent administrative offices.

Unfortunately, this approach has been difficult to implement in the BIMSTEC region (and in developing countries elsewhere) for a variety of reasons. Apart from the lack of through transport, existing practices and procedures combined with the typically large number of small traders mean that most border posts must act as clearance facilities, thus, requiring a more substantial border complex. In some cases, the facility at the border acts as the actual clearance point, while at others, an associated ICD or dry port has been constructed nearby for cargo clearance.

In the last decade, there has been significant investment in new border infrastructure and facilities in the region. In Bangladesh, several new border dry ports have been constructed, with some handed over to the private sector to operate under concession arrangements. The Government of India has commenced a program of constructing integrated check posts (ICPs) or land ports on its borders with Bangladesh, Myanmar, and Nepal, e.g., development of new ICPs at Petrapole (2014–2015), opposite Benapole, Bangladesh; at Agartala (2012–2013), opposite Akhaura in Bangladesh; at Moreh (2017–2018), opposite Tamu in Myanmar. In the case of Nepal, the facility covers both sides of the border, whereas with Bangladesh and Myanmar, it is on the Indian side only. Nepal opened a border ICP at Birgunj in 2018, and new ICPs at several other locations are either under construction or programmed. Myanmar and Thailand are constructing a new Mae Sot–Myawaddy border crossing (2015–2019), plus 21.4 km of road along the Myanmar portion of the Trilateral Highway ($123 million funded by Thailand). Also, Thailand has recently constructed a substantial border facility at Mae Sai, incorporating an ICD within the border security zone.

The concept of simple border checks followed by inland clearance will take time to materialize, which suggests there will be an ongoing need for modernization and development of border complexes, either with clearance facilities within the border control zone or in the immediate vicinity. This control approach minimizes the risk of illegal imports and exports and the non-collection of revenue. There are plans for more border dry ports in Bangladesh, an ICD and dry port at Phuentsholing and Toribari in Bhutan, and additional ICPs in India along its borders with Bangladesh, Bhutan, Myanmar, and Nepal. In Nepal, there will be new ICPs along the Indian border (in addition to the one at Birgunj), with assistance from the Government of India; and in Myanmar, border developments include new border posts and border dry ports at Myawaddy and Tachileik, on its border with Thailand.

A particular issue is the scope for participation of the private sector in the development of border infrastructure, which is examined in Box 19, including the experience of one BIMSTEC member state (Bangladesh).

Box 19: The Scope for Private Sector Participation in the Development of Border Infrastructure

Given the resource constraints facing the public sector in the BIMSTEC region, it may be helpful to consider the scope for the private sector to play a role in the financing of border infrastructure. A private sector entity may earn a return on its capital investment from: (i) rent paid by the public authority combined with a service fee if the entity is also charged with the operational management of the facility; and (ii) an authorization to charge user fees to cover both the repayment of the capital investment and the cost of the operational management of the facility. The concession contract should be transparent and provide a clear and express stipulation regarding the maximum permissible user fee, which is a critical measure to protect users. Also, the facilitation benefit should exceed the cost to users of bringing additional financial and technical resources for this purpose. In the case of six land ports in Bangladesh operated by the private sector, with 25-year concessions commencing in 2009, operations have been less efficient than at government-operated land ports.

Sources: Japan International Cooperation Agency. 2016. *One-Stop Border Post Sourcebook*, 2nd edition, May. p. 7-5; and interview with the Bangladesh Land Port Authority, 28 May 2018.

Policy

BIMSTEC recognizes the need to develop additional infrastructure at the main land borders between the member states to facilitate the movement of intra-BIMSTEC trade and to assist in promoting economic development in those border areas.

Strategy

BIMSTEC will encourage prioritization of the development of border infrastructure at the main BIMSTEC land border crossings, including their inclusion in national development plans and in discussions with the relevant national authorities and international development partners.

Projects

Table 17 highlights flagship projects in this category, which have strong relevance to BIMSTEC intraregional connectivity.

Table 17: Planned Flagship Projects to Develop Border Infrastructure

Code	Project Description	BIMSTEC Development Logic	Estimated Cost, 2018 ($ million)	(Possible) Funding Sources	Timescale
BAN-TF-001	Improvement of Benapole (opposite Petrapole, India) and Burimari (opposite Changrabandha, India) (Road Connectivity Project), plus automation of Benapole land port	Provision of additional processing and storage capacity at busy BIMSTEC border crossings	18 (of 198)	ADB	2013–2019 (June)
BAN-TF-002	Modernization of customs facilities and trade facilitation at seven Land Customs Stations, including laboratories (Banglabandha, Burimari, Hilli, Nakugaon, Sona Masjid, Tamabil, and Teknaf)	Facilitation of intra-BIMSTEC trade	Not yet estimated	ADB	2019–2021
BAN-TF-003	Development of Sheolla, Ramgarh, Bhomra, and Benapole ports (the first two are greenfield sites), under the Bangladesh Regional Connectivity Project 1	As above	87 (75 from World Bank)	World Bank and government	2017–2021
BAN-TF-004	Development of Dhanua Kamalpur land port in Jalmalpur opposite Meghalaya, India	As above	7	Government	2018–2020
IND-TF-005	Development of ICPs, ongoing or planned (Dawki [Bangladesh border], Jaigaon [Bhutan border]; Banbasa, Bhithamore, Panitanki, Rupaidiha, and Sunauli [Nepal border], and Changrabandha, Fulbari, Ghojadanga, Hili, Kawrpuichhuah, Mahadipur, and Sutarkandi, Bangladesh border])	As above	Not fully specified	Government	2018–2028

continued on next page

Table 17 continued

Code	Project Description	BIMSTEC Development Logic	Estimated Cost, 2018 ($ million)	(Possible) Funding Sources	Timescale
IND-TF-006	Development of rail siding logistics hubs within Raxaul, Jogbani, Petrapole, Hili, Nischintapur, and Sabroom land ports	Facilitation of the movement of multimodal container or noncontainer cargo across borders	To be specified	Government	2019–2023
NEP-TF-007	Development of four ICPs at main border crossings with India, including laboratories (Birgunj, Biratnagar, Bhairawaha, and Nepalganj)	Reduction of congestion and transaction costs border crossings	91	India	2012–2023 (Birgunj completed in 2018, Biratnagar completed in 2020)
REG-TF-008 (IND and MYA)	Development of Tamu-Moreh border crossing	Improved border crossing and border access road along the Trilateral India-Myanmar-Thailand Highway	Not yet estimated	India	Not yet programmed
REG-TF-009 (IND and NEP)	Use of electronic cargo tracking system for off-border clearance along selected routes (and associated measures)	Facilitation of movements between India and Nepal	0.5 (TA approved on 3 September 2018 to support this activity and others)	ADB (Trade Facilitation Program)	2018–2019
REG-TF-010 (MYA and THA)	Development of a new Mae Sot–Myawaddy border crossing, including 21.4 km of road (also included in border link project)	Improved border crossing and border access road along the Trilateral India-Myanmar-Thailand Highway	122 (also included in border link project)	Thailand	2015–2019
REG-TF-011 (MYA and THA)	Development of new Htee Kee or Baan Phu Nam Ron border crossing	New border crossing with Thailand to process cargo to and from Dawei	142 (THB 4.5 billion, also included in above in associated road project)	Thailand	2018–2022 (feasibility study under discussion between Ministry of Construction and NEDA, Thailand)

ADB = Asian Development Bank, BAN = Bangladesh, BIMSTEC = Bay of Bengal Initiative for Multi-Sectoral Technical and Economic Cooperation, ICP = integrated check post, IND = India, MYA = Myanmar, NEDA = Neighbouring Countries Economic Development Cooperation Agency (Thailand), REG = regional, TA = technical assistance, THA = Thailand, THB = Thai baht.

Source: Asian Development Bank.

Development of Inland Clearance or Inland Container Depots

Issues

While the concept of land border check posts followed by inland clearance may be difficult to realize in the near term due to transit risks, this difficulty is not necessarily the case with container traffic. Containers with imports can be sealed at the ports and then transported to ICDs located closer to the importer or end user. This practice not only makes clearance easier, but it also enables the inbound container to move rapidly through the port, rather than congesting terminal container yards while awaiting clearance. As trade expands, there will be increasing pressure on the main BIMSTEC ports to increase the percentage of containers that are cleared outside the port area. The primary role of an ICD is as an extension of the container yards, away from the port and closer to the main points of import demand, or in some cases, export demand.

India has developed a national network of ICDs, most of which are served by rail as well as road. Bangladesh has an ICD in Kamlapur, Dhaka (2011–2013) that is linked to Chattogram by rail; Bhutan has recently (2016–2018) developed a mini dry port in Phuentsholing (with ADB support), along with a northern bypass to handle bilateral and third-country imports; Nepal has an ICD in Birgunj that is linked by road and rail to Kolkata; and Thailand has Lat Krabang ICD in eastern Bangkok linked to Laem Chabang. Additional ICD capacity will be required to avoid increased congestion in the ports and to support faster clearance of container traffic. For example, the Dhaka ICD is already at capacity and a second ICD is urgently required. Myanmar does not yet have an ICD, but is planning two, and Sri Lanka has no conventional ICD, but is planning such a facility.

Policy

BIMSTEC recognizes the need for further development of ICDs to reduce the risk of increased congestion at the main seaports (and BCPs) and to facilitate clearance, thus, promoting economic development inland beyond the coastal areas.

Strategy

BIMSTEC will promote the development of ICDs at appropriate locations in the member states by encouraging their inclusion in national development plans and in discussions with relevant authorities and development partners.

Projects

Appendix 5 includes a long list of planned projects to develop ICDs in the region, while Table 18 highlights flagship projects in this category selected mainly based on relevance to BIMSTEC intraregional connectivity.

Table 18: Planned Flagship Projects to Develop Inland Clearance or Inland Container Depots

Code	Project Description	BIMSTEC Development Logic	Estimated Cost, 2018 ($ million)	(Possible) Funding Sources	Timescale
BHU-TF-013	Development of Pasakha Dry Port	Facilitation of clearance at main entry or exit point for BIMSTEC trade and transport	30	Not yet identified (World Bank support for the detailed project report)	2018–2023
BHU-TF-014	Development of Nganglam Dry Port	Diversification of entry or exit points for BIMSTEC trade and transport	Not yet estimated	Not yet identified	2019–2028
NEP-TF-015	Development of ICD in Kanchanpur	Facilitation of southwestern Nepal trade	Not yet estimated	Government	2023–2028
SRI-TF-016	Construction of "cargo village" or customs inspection yard to centralize container freight stations associated with Colombo Port now scattered around the city	Improved performance of Colombo Port, the largest in the BIMSTEC region	100	Not yet identified	2020–2025

ADB = Asian Development Bank, BAN = Bangladesh, BIMSTEC = Bay of Bengal Initiative for Multi-Sectoral Technical and Economic Cooperation, ICD = inland clearance/container depot, IND = India, MYA = Myanmar, PPP = public–private partnership, SRL = Sri Lanka, THA = Thailand.

Note: The project to develop a second rail-connected ICD in Dhaka, at Dhirasram, in Gazipur, Bangladesh, and the Gelephu Transport Hub project in Bhutan, have been included under multimodal and intermodal transport because of their significant multimodal or interconnectivity aspects.

Source: Asian Development Bank.

Simplification and Harmonization of Import–Export and Transit Documentation

Issues

Previous reports have highlighted the adverse trade facilitation environment in the BIMSTEC region, based on the World Bank's Doing Business rankings and logistics performance index (LPI) scores, which are commonly used as international trade facilitation indicators. While these surveys are not perfectly accurate, most of the countries in the region have relatively low rankings, although India and Thailand score well. In the latest LPI rankings (2018), Thailand ranked 32nd, India ranked 44th, Sri Lanka ranked 94th, Bangladesh ranked 100th, Nepal ranked 114th, Myanmar ranked 137th, and Bhutan ranked 149th, of 160 countries.[63] Analysis of the survey data suggests an indirect relationship between the national rankings and the number of documents required to undertake an average import or export transaction in that country.

---

[63] Germany was first and Afghanistan was last. https://lpi.worldbank.org/international/global.

In addition, surveys at BIMSTEC ports have shown that dwell times for container traffic are often dictated by the time taken for the importer or agent to collect the various hard copy documents to enable a declaration to be lodged with customs, rather than the actual physical clearance process. Clearing and forwarding agents at both seaports and land borders often cite the collection and collation of support documents to file a declaration as a major problem. Experience in other regions has shown that reducing the overall number of hard copy documents needed to be presented for clearance directly reduces clearance times and transaction costs. Organizations such as ADB, the World Bank, and WCO have sponsored various national and subregional programs to address this issue in a number of BIMSTEC member states.

The other major area of concern relates to the lack of harmonization of documentation and the clearance requirements. While automation has tended to standardize the layouts of the customs declaration based on variants of the single administrative document used in Europe,[64] there has been little or no standardization of other documents, e.g., for sanitary, phytosanitary, veterinary, and standards requirements. Each country tends to have its own formats and often does not recognize the validity of non-nationally produced documentation and, thus, duplicate documents need to be obtained from various national agencies. There are few mutual recognition agreements between the BIMSTEC member states—the validity of tests and standards undertaken in one BIMSTEC member state is not accepted by another BIMSTEC member state. For example, sanitary or quality certificates generated in member state A will not be acceptable in member state B without member state B redoing those tests. In some member states, testing is required on every individual shipment, as opposed to type-approval certification. The absence of mutual recognition agreements and the need for constant retesting has been identified as a significant non-tariff barrier in the BIMSTEC region, especially for food and electrical products.

Box 20 shows the economic impacts of bottlenecks in trade business processes.

Box 20: Economic Impacts of Bottlenecks in Trade Business Processes

- Each additional day of delay—e.g., because of trade logistics procedures—reduces trade by at least 1%.
- Direct and indirect costs from import or export-related procedures and required documents amount to 1%–15% of product costs

Sources: Organisation for Economic Co-operation and Development. 2013. *Quantitative Assessment of the Benefits of Trade Facilitation*; and P. De (on behalf of the ADB UNESCAP Business Process Analysis [BPA] Study Team). 2012. *Overview of Trade Facilitation and Business Process Analysis*. Asia-Pacific Trade Facilitation Forum. 30–1 October. slide 7.

Policy

BIMSTEC recognizes the need for simplification and harmonization of the regional trade facilitation environment to promote intra-BIMSTEC trade and the resulting economic development.

Strategy

BIMSTEC will encourage member states to review and rationalize their documentation requirements in relation to import and export clearance wherever possible and promote the development of more mutual recognition agreements between member states.

---

[64] That said, a single transit transport document could be productively developed.

Projects

As presented in Table 19, a flagship project to simplify and harmonize import–export and transit documentation in the BIMSTEC region may entail extension of previous work done under the ADB sponsorship to develop business process analysis (BPA) and so-called BPA+.[65] BPA studies were undertaken for specific products in all BIMSTEC member states and provided "proof of concept." In particular, the methodology provides the first technical step in preparing for paperless trade and single window development—e.g., as displayed in Figure 8.

It provides an inventory of processes, documents, data, rules, and regulations; a description of the processes; specifications for harmonizing data and development of electronic documents; and specifications to develop software for the automation of procedures[66] (see the following subsection). Training in trade facilitation—presented in Section 10.3—will support implementation of this project.

And additional flagship project may be implemented to address sanitary-phytosanitary (SPS) and technical barriers to trade (TBT)-related issues, including the development of mutual recognition agreements and developing conformity assessment infrastructure on a hub-and-spoke basis.

Table 19: Planned Flagship Project to Simplify and Harmonize Import–Export Documentation in the Bay of Bengal Initiative for Multi-Sectoral Technical and Economic Cooperation Region

Code	Project Description	BIMSTEC Development Logic	Estimated Cost, 2018 ($ million)	(Possible) Funding Sources	Timescale
REG-TF-017 (Member states along key corridors)	Extension of Prior Business Process Analyses	Rationalization of documentation requirements to reduce the time and costs for import or export-related procedures and required documents	0.5 (TA approved on 3 September 2018 to support this activity and others)	ADB	2019–2021
REG-TF-018 (Member states along key corridors)	SPS or TBT project to develop mutual recognition agreements and conformity assessment infrastructure on a hub-and-spoke basis	Removal of significant non-tariff barrier in the region	0.5	Not yet identified	2020–2022

ADB = Asian Development Bank, BIMSTEC = Bay of Bengal Initiative for Multi-Sectoral Technical and Economic Cooperation, SPS = sanitary-phytosanitary, TA = technical assistance, TBT = technical barriers to trade.
Source: Asian Development Bank.

---

[65] The United Nations Network of Experts for Paperless Trade in Asia and the Pacific (UNNExT) developed the BPA approach based on the "buy-ship-pay model" of the international supply chain introduced in United Nations Center for Trade Facilitation and Electronic Business (UN/CEFACT) Recommendation No. 18. Based on this model, BPA assesses not only the "ship" process along transport routes and at border crossing points, but also trade-related procedures in the "buy" and "pay" stages. BPA+ is built on the BPA methodology complemented by time–cost–distance time and release survey methodologies.

[66] P. De. (on behalf of the ADB UNESCAP Business Process Analysis [BPA] Study Team). 2012. *Overview of Trade Facilitation and Business Process Analysis*. Asia-Pacific Trade Facilitation Forum. 30–31 October. slide 8.

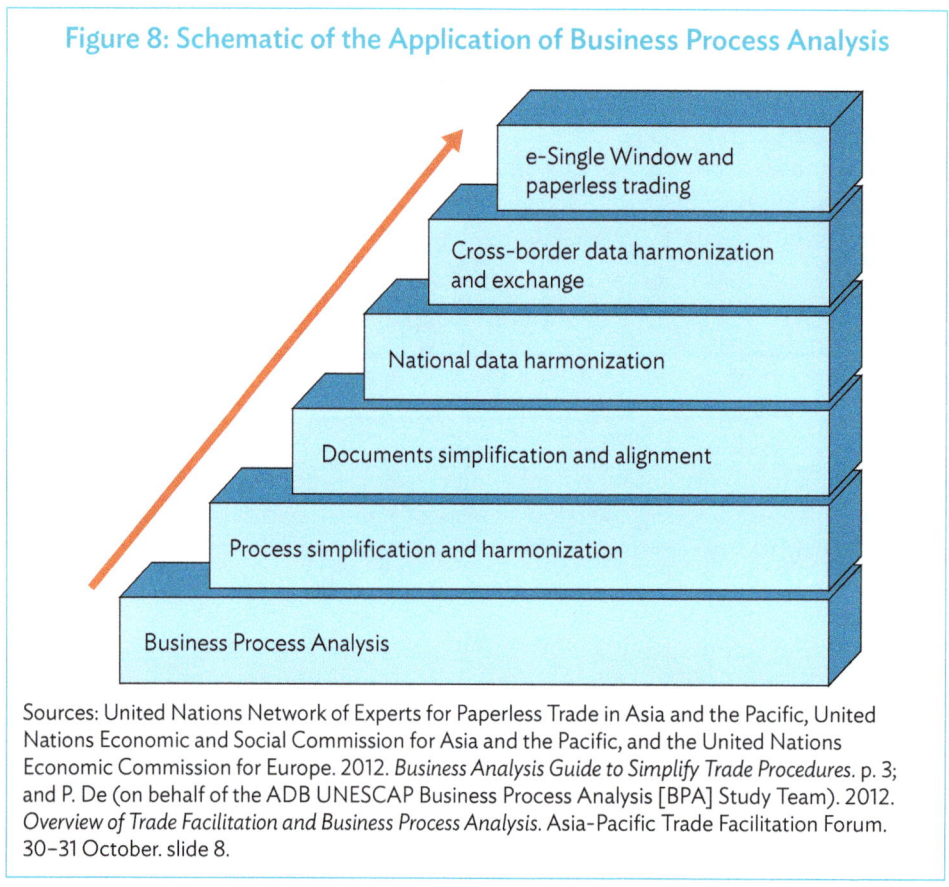

Figure 8: Schematic of the Application of Business Process Analysis

Sources: United Nations Network of Experts for Paperless Trade in Asia and the Pacific, United Nations Economic and Social Commission for Asia and the Pacific, and the United Nations Economic Commission for Europe. 2012. *Business Analysis Guide to Simplify Trade Procedures*. p. 3; and P. De (on behalf of the ADB UNESCAP Business Process Analysis [BPA] Study Team). 2012. *Overview of Trade Facilitation and Business Process Analysis*. Asia-Pacific Trade Facilitation Forum. 30–31 October. slide 8.

Further Development of Automated Clearance Systems

Issues

Trade facilitation in the region has become increasingly reliant on the application of automated clearance systems. All the customs administrations in the BIMSTEC member states either have modern automated ICT systems or are in the process of updating their applications. Bangladesh has migrated from Automated System for Customs Data (ASYCUDA)++ to the web-based ASYCUDA World, and Bhutan has been upgrading its system, both with ADB support. Indian Customs is constantly upgrading its electronic data interchange system and extending its national coverage, Nepal has been introducing ASYCUDA World with ADB assistance, Myanmar has been upgrading the Myanmar Automated Cargo and Port Consolidated System (MACCS)[67] and has extended it from the Yangon Area to the Myanmar–Thailand border (Myawaddy) with the support of JICA, and Sri Lanka has introduced ASYCUDA World.

---

[67] MACCS is based on the Nippon Automated Cargo and Port Consolidated System (NACCS), developed by Japan Customs.

A concern is that in many cases, these systems are used to record transactions rather than to assist in clearance processing. Clearing and forwarding agents or service centers enter the customs declaration online into the system, but these are only validated by the agent or importer or exporter at lodgment by the signing of printouts and the submission of the hard copy supporting documents. The clearance process is then undertaken based on the traditional manual systems with authorization signatures until the goods are finally cleared. Users complain that manual and automated systems are operating in parallel and the workload has actually increased. Most of these systems have processing modules, but often these are not applied and overall clearance times have not decreased appreciably with automation. While this may not be true in some member states, it is the situation in others.

The next phase of automation in trade facilitation is the development of national single windows (NSWs, see Figure 9). An electronic single window is a facility that allows parties involved in trade and transport to lodge standardized information and documents in a single electronic entry point to fulfill all import, export, and transit-related regulatory requirements. If information is electronic, individual data elements should only be submitted once. In essence, all the documentation and information required by the various border agencies is available online in a single database, so that each party can clear shipments electronically and the customs administration that authorizes the final release can verify that all of the other relevant agencies have approved the clearance.[68] The benefits of an NSW are substantial and most countries are committed to developing such systems.

The relatively slow development of the NSWs and the ASEAN Single Window (ASW, a flagship regional initiative in Southeast Asia) demonstrates the challenges in establishing such complex applications. First, it is essential to have a stable customs ICT system to form the core of the NSW system. Second, while customs administrations are relatively highly automated, many of the other border agencies are not, except for immigration and border police. Key agencies (e.g., veterinary, sanitary, phytosanitary, quarantine) have significantly lower use of ICT systems and most do not provide computer-generated certifications online.[69] This situation makes it particularly difficult for these agencies to link into the NSW. However, the greatest problem in the development of the ASW has been institutional, rather than technical—establishing NSW planning committees and agreeing on the scope of participation has not been easy and has delayed implementation.

Despite these difficulties, the establishment of NSWs represents a key trade facilitation goal. Progress is being achieved, e.g., India began implementation of its Single Window Interface for Trade (SWIFT) in 2016 (although it does not include all border agencies), Myanmar recently upgraded the Myanmar Automated Cargo and Port Consolidated System and extended it from the Yangon Area (including the Thilawa SEZ) to the Myanmar–Thailand border area (Myawaddy) in June 2018,[70] Nepal has been implementing a World Bank-supported program to design and build an NSW, Sri Lanka is preparing a National Single Window Blueprint, and Thailand is pursuing its National Single Window Vision 2021.

A BIMSTEC regional single window has not been identified as a target, given its duplication and the major differences in automation status between and among member states. Nevertheless, the NSWs will form the building blocks of any future regional system and, therefore, BIMSTEC should support of efforts to develop such systems in those member states without NSWs and to refine NSWs in member states that have NSWs.

---

[68] Therefore, connectivity is also provided between port(s) and ICD or land border crossings for online clearance.
[69] There are no "off-the-shelf" systems such as ASYCUDA that these other government agencies can introduce (except for the immigration authority), and since the automation process is relatively less complex, it is less likely to be supported by international development partners. Asian Development Bank and Asian Development Bank Institute. 2015. *Connecting South Asia and Southeast Asia.* p. 193.
[70] Myanmar launched MACCS on 12 November 2016 in the Yangon area including the Thilawa SEZ. A survey was undertaken in May 2017 to extend it to the Myawaddy border crossing as an initial extension, which commenced on 5 June 2018. Extensions to additional border areas will be made step by step.

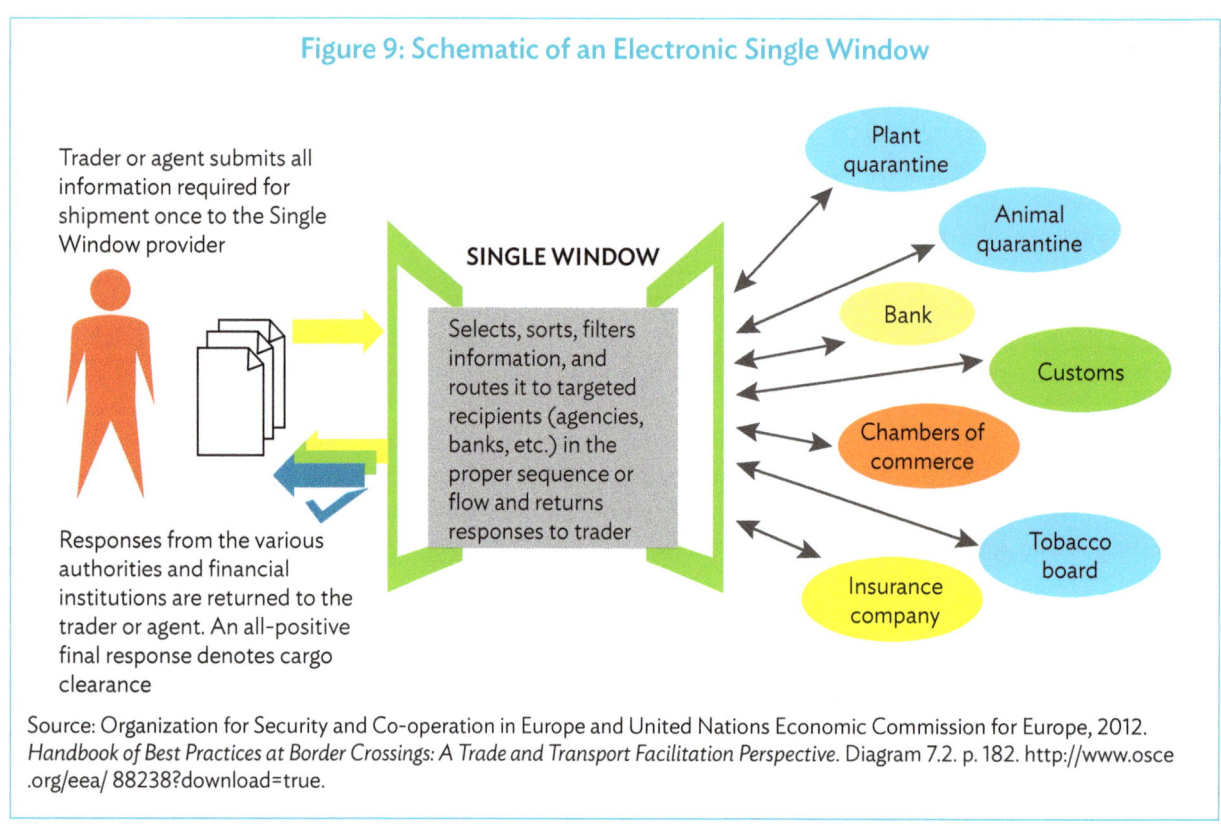

Figure 9: Schematic of an Electronic Single Window

Source: Organization for Security and Co-operation in Europe and United Nations Economic Commission for Europe, 2012. *Handbook of Best Practices at Border Crossings: A Trade and Transport Facilitation Perspective.* Diagram 7.2. p. 182. http://www.osce.org/eea/ 88238?download=true.

Policy

BIMSTEC recognizes the need for further automation in the trade facilitation environment, including implementation of more automated processing applications and the development of national single windows, to promote trade between the BIMSTEC member states and to realize the economic development that such trade can generate.[71]

Strategy

BIMSTEC will encourage the prioritization of upgrading of existing ICT systems within national customs administrations and promote the establishment of national single windows with the relevant national organizations and international development partners.[72]

Projects

Table 20 presents a flagship regional project for the further development of automated systems—to be implemented nationally but within the (sub)regional context. Specific details of national projects in this category (in Bangladesh, Bhutan, Nepal, and Sri Lanka) are included in Appendix 5. Again, training in trade facilitation—presented in Section X—will support implementation of this project.

---

[71] Asian Development Bank. 2018. *Updating and Enhancement of the BIMSTEC Transport Infrastructure and Logistics Study, Final Report.* Manila.
[72] Ibid.

Table 20: Planned Flagship Project for Further Development of Automated Systems

Code	Project Description	BIMSTEC Development Logic	Estimated Cost, 2018 ($ million)	(Possible) Funding Sources	Timescale
REG-TF-021	Development and/or refinement of NSWs	Reduction in time and cost of border crossing through integrated automation of procedures	100	Governments, ADB, World Bank, WCO	2018–2028

ADB = Asian Development Bank, BIMSTEC = Bay of Bengal Initiative for Multi-Sectoral Technical and Economic Cooperation, NSW = national single window, Sri Lanka, WCO = World Customs Organization.
Source: Asian Development Bank.

Advanced Logistics

Issues

Modern or advanced logistics in most BIMSTEC member states lags behind global standards, which is likely a cause of the relatively low performance of most member states in the logistics performance index rankings of the World Bank, as set out in Section IX.

Areas of advanced logistics that could productively be upgraded in the region include:

(i) supply chain management of the flow of goods and services, involving the movement and storage of raw materials, of work-in-process inventory, and of finished goods from point of origin to point of consumption;

(ii) track and trace or shipment visibility;

(iii) enhancement of less than container load (LCL) services, e.g., through a one-stop shop for these services, and the implementation of "milk-run" services (i.e., round trips that facilitate either distribution and/or collection);

(iv) "last-mile (km)" logistics development, relating to the movement of people and goods from a transport hub to the final destination;

(v) development of postal or courier services to support e-commerce;

(vi) cold chain (i.e., temperature-controlled supply chain) development;

(vii) development of fourth-party logistics (4PL) services;

(viii) development of hub-and-spoke systems;

(ix) vendor-managed inventory (VMI) services[73] to meet the demand of new business models and attract investment especially in higher value-added manufacturing;

---

[73] In VMI services, the buyer of a product provides certain information to a supplier (vendor) of that product and the supplier takes full responsibility for maintaining an agreed inventory of the material, usually at the buyer's consumption location.

(x) improvement of publicly provided logistics services, which may be monopolized; and

(xi) green logistics, to minimize the environmental impact of logistics activities, including the forward and reverse flows of freight.[74]

Development of advanced logistics will involve a number of in-country reforms and domestic investment in infrastructure and services, much of it by the private sector, and BIMSTEC as a regional organization may not have much influence on these mainly domestic matters.

Policy

BIMSTEC recognizes the need for developing advanced logistics systems to reduce overall international transport costs and time.

Strategy

BIMSTEC will encourage member states to adopt advanced logistical systems as an approach for reducing the high level of distribution costs and transport time.

Projects

Table 21 presents a proposed regional flagship project for the development of advanced logistics related to connectivity between and among BIMSTEC member states.

Table 21: Project for the Development of Advanced Logistics

Code	Project Description	BIMSTEC Development Logic	Estimated Cost, 2018 ($ million)	(Possible) Funding Sources	Timescale
REG-TF-029	Development of advanced logistics (e.g., supply chain management, LCL services, last mile or kilometer logistics)	Improved logistics performance in BIMSTEC member states	5	Not yet identified (JICA has funded logistics improvement studies in other regions, e.g., Southeast Asia, the Middle East)	2019–2023

BIMSTEC = Bay of Bengal Initiative for Multi-Sectoral Technical and Economic Cooperation, JICA = Japan International Cooperation Agency, LCL = less than container load.
Source: Asian Development Bank.

---

[74] For example, Japan International Cooperation Agency, International Development Center of Japan Inc., and PADECO Co., Ltd. 2018. *The Study on Logistics System Improvement Master Plan in the Kingdom of Cambodia, Final Report.* March. Appendix A1, pp. ii to vii.

X. Human Resource Development

Sector Overview

While progress has been achieved in building capacity in the relevant areas in recent years—with the support of international development partners—further human resource development is required in (i) transport and related sectors, (ii) trade facilitation, and (iii) border management.

Capacity Building in the Transport and Related Sectors

Issues

Capacity building in support of the hard infrastructure development is required, e.g., training in transport planning, road engineering, transport economics, and railway management. Such capacity building should be designed to increase the member states' technical capacities to identify, plan, design, and undertake transport projects without relying heavily on external technical resources. Coordination between and among member states in the planning and implementation of these programs will be beneficial as it will enable a pooling of expertise and resources and a cross-fertilization of approaches. The programs should be tailored to meet the specific requirements of the subsector or field of operation. The needs are greatest in Bhutan and Nepal, particularly if a new mode of transport (i.e., railway) with challenging technical requirements is introduced into these member states, although significant requirements have also been identified for Bangladesh and Myanmar.

Policy

BIMSTEC recognizes the need to enhance the capacity and skill of personnel of member states engaged in transport and related sectors.

Strategy

BIMSTEC encourages the provision of training designed to enhance the capacity and skill of personnel of member states engaged in transport and related sectors. Member states with relatively advanced training facilities may provide training for personnel of member states lacking such facilities.

Projects

Drawn from the long list in Appendix 5, flagship capacity building projects in the transport and related sectors with respect to connectivity between and among BIMSTEC member states are listed in Table 22. The BIMSTEC (Multimodal) Transport Training Institute may include training in different modes (or separate training institute(s) may be established for certain specializations, e.g., railway engineering and railway operation or management) as well as multimodal and intermodal transport. Flexibility will be required in establishing the envisaged BIMSTEC (Multimodal) Transport Training Institute and separate modal training institutes, especially considering the need for complex legal processes, and existing transport training institutes may be involved to the extent possible.

Table 22: Flagship Capacity Building Projects in the Transport and Related Sectors

Code	Project Description	BIMSTEC Development Logic	Estimated Cost, 2018 ($ million)	(Possible) Funding Sources	Timescale
REG-HR-001	Establishment of a BIMSTEC (Multimodal) Transport Training Institute	Enhancement of skills of transport professionals in BIMSTEC member states	5	Not yet identified	2025–2028
BHU-HR-003	Institutional strengthening of engineers of the Department of Roads	Capacity building in the roads sector (e.g., road asset management, climate resilience, slope stabilization)	2.5	Not yet identified	2019–2028
BHU-HR-004	Climate resilience	Enhancing Sustainability and Climate Resilience of Forest and Agriculture Landscape and Community Livelihoods in Bhutan	1.2	Global Environment Facility, Least Developed Countries Fund, and UNDP	2017–2023
BHU-HR-005	Slope disaster prevention	Project for Capacity Development on Countermeasures for Slope Disasters on Roads in Bhutan	0.7 (Government)	JICA and govenment	2019–2022
BHU-HR-006	Climate resilience	Supporting Climate Resilience and Transformational Change in the Agriculture Sector in Bhutan	25.1	Green Climate Fund and government	2020–2025
BHU-HR-007	Training in International Civil Aviation Organization and national standards	Capacity building in the aviation sector, e.g., with respect to aerodrome management, air navigation services, safety, and security	2	As above	2018–2023
BHU-HR-008	Road transport related training	Capacity building for road safety and public transport management or operations	2	As above	2019–2028
MYA-HR-009	Capacity building in airport management and operations, airport security, and aviation information technology network enhancement for Department of Civil Aviation staff	Enable efficient, safe, and secure operation of Myanmar's airports serving BIMSTEC regional traffic	5	Not yet identified	2018–2028

continued on next page

Table 22 continued

Code	Project Description	BIMSTEC Development Logic	Estimated Cost, 2018 ($ million)	(Possible) Funding Sources	Timescale
NEP-HR-010	Adoption of new and innovative technologies for the rapid and efficient development of transport infrastructure including the road and railway subsectors (e.g., design, project management, safety)	Support for development of transport infrastructure for BIMSTEC connectivity	5	ADB and World Bank	2018–2028

ADB = Asian Development Bank, BHU = Bhutan, BIMSTEC = Bay of Bengal Initiative for Multi-Sectoral Technical and Economic Cooperation, JICA = Japan International Cooperation Agency, MYA = Myanmar, UNDP = United Nations Development Programme.
Source: Asian Development Bank.

Capacity Building in Trade Facilitation

Issues

Capacity building for soft infrastructure—in trade facilitation—is required, e.g., training in the Trade Facilitation Agreement of WTO (ratified by all member states, except Bhutan, which is not yet a WTO member), creation of trusted partnerships, reduction of delays at border crossings, rationalization of trade documents and data requirements, and the development of single windows.[75] Recent and ongoing initiatives have achieved successes, but more needs to be done.

Policy

BIMSTEC recognizes the need for enhanced training in trade facilitation to address constraints on trade and transport across BIMSTEC borders.

Strategy

BIMSTEC encourages enhanced training of public and private sector personnel in good and best practices in trade facilitation and the integration of such practices wherever possible.

Projects

Table 23 presents a planned regional flagship project for training in trade facilitation. The project will support the simplification and harmonization of import-export documentation for transit traffic and further development of automated clearance systems (which are both presented in Section IX).

---

[75] For example, United Nations Economic Commission for Europe. 2015. *United Nations Trade Facilitation Implementation Guide.* pp. 12–18.

Table 23: Planned Flagship Project for Training in Trade Facilitation

Code	Project Description	BIMSTEC Development Logic	Estimated Cost, 2018 ($ million)	(Possible) Funding Sources	Timescale
REG-HR-011	Training in trade facilitation (e.g., the TFA, creation of trusted partnerships, customs valuation and procedures, rationalization of trade documents and data requirements, transshipment management, development, and operation of single windows for online clearance and monitoring)	Improved logistics performance	5	WTO and others	2019–2028

BIMSTEC = Bay of Bengal Initiative for Multi-Sectoral Technical and Economic Cooperation, REG = regional, TFA = Trade Facilitation Agreement, WTO = World Trade Organization.
Source: Asian Development Bank.

Training in Border Management

Issues

Efficient border management policies and structures need to be supported by well-trained, professional officers from the various border agencies, to facilitate and foster enhanced movement management at borders. Comprehensive and well-functioning border management structures encompass both security and the facilitation of legitimate cross-border flows of people and goods—the two aspects complement and do not contradict each other.[76]

A recent development is integrated and coordinated border management (IBM and CBM), which is an inclusive approach for connecting stakeholders that actively encourages customs administrations to further improve their collaboration with partner agencies responsible for border operations. IBM and CBM have been actively promoted globally to effectively cope with the complex nature and substantial increase in the volume of international and regional trade, which must be handled by not only customs authorities, but also by other trade facilitation agencies, requiring good teamwork within a government.[77]

Policy

BIMSTEC recognizes the need for enhanced training of border personnel to facilitate trade and transport across BIMSTEC borders.

---

[76] For example, International Organization for Migration, Immigration and Border Management. https://www.iom.int/immigration-and-border-management.

[77] Indeed, over time, the emphasis should be shifted from customs reforms to addressing non-customs issues (e.g., quarantine, sanitary-phytosanitary, veterinary, trading standards). Asian Development Bank and Asian Development Bank Institute. 2015. *Connecting South Asia and Southeast Asia*. pp. 24 and 223. http://www.wcoomd.org/en/topics/facilitation/activitiesand-programmes/coordinated-border-management.aspx.

Strategy

BIMSTEC encourages enhanced training of border personnel in good and best practices in modern border management and the implementation of such practices wherever possible.

Projects

Table 24 presents a planned flagship regional project for training in border management and related aspects, focusing on BIMSTEC priority routes.

Table 24: Planned Flagship Project for Training in Border Management

Code	Project Description	BIMSTEC Development Logic	Estimated Cost, 2018 ($ million)	(Possible) Funding Sources	Timescale
REG-HR-015	Training in border (and ICD) management, including IBM and CBM, focusing on BIMSTEC priority routes, and including the exchange of good practices, using existing infrastructure in member states	Improved performance at BIMSTEC borders	4	WCO, IOM, ADB, World Bank, INTERPOL	2019–2023

ADB = Asian Development Bank, BIMSTEC = Bay of Bengal Initiative for Multi-Sectoral Technical and Economic Cooperation, CBM = coordinated border management, IBM = integrated border management, ICD = inland clearance/container depot, INTERPOL = International Criminal Police Organization, IOM = International Organization for Migration, REG = regional, WCO = World Customs Organization.

Source: Asian Development Bank.

XI. Implementation

Critical Success Factors

Several critical success factors for the Master Plan have been identified:

(i) political will and commitment by the member states, which may be demonstrated by cooperation between and among participating states, budgeting for identified projects, and including projects in national development plans;

(ii) creation of an appropriate policy and regulatory framework for implementation, e.g., with through-transport agreements, access agreements for developing coastal shipping services between and among member states;

(iii) development of a pipeline of bankable projects, with economic and financial viability, accelerate the implementation of infrastructure projects;

(iv) addressing of social and environmental concerns;

(v) development of human resources and associated capacity;

(vi) partnership with the private sector in infrastructure development, as addressed in Section 11.3, in view of budget constraints and the needs in other socioeconomic sectors; and

(vii) robust monitoring, as addressed in Section XI.

Project Financing

Issues

As shown in Appendix 7 (Parts C and D), the resources to implement the "flagship" (or "signature") projects in the Master Plan have been estimated at (as of 2018) $47.0 billion (141 projects) including ongoing projects, and $22.0 billion (73 projects) excluding ongoing projects in 2018 values. Half or more (50%–61%) of these amounts would be in the roads and road transport (sub)sector.[78]

---

[78] As shown in Appendix 7 (Parts A and B), the resources to implement the longlist projects in the Master Plan have been estimated as $124.4 billion and $53.3 billion in 2018 values, including and excluding ongoing projects (as of 2018), respectively. About two-fifths (40–44%) of these amounts would be in the roads and road transport (sub)sector. As noted in the appendix, some projects have not been costed and therefore could not be included in the estimate.

The Master Plan does not provide detailed financing proposals since these depend on considerations that will become clearer during the implementation period. However, given the breadth and magnitude of funding requirements, it will be critical to ensure that full funding potentials are mobilized. A separate study on financing for BIMSTEC transport connectivity is ongoing with the support of ADB.

While it is recognized that international development partners play a critical role in committing financial resources to projects, active participation by the private sector as a "top-up" is required, although it is not necessarily a panacea. One constraint is that cross-border financing vehicles are not available since private investors are risk-averse and hesitant to cross borders.[79] Box 21 further examines the potential of public–private partnerships for financing transport connectivity infrastructure in the BIMSTEC region.

While regional projects (as regional public goods) are generally justified when the net benefits for the participating countries exceed the net costs, it will be necessary for projects to be perceived as "win-win" (or "win-win-win" with three countries, and others), which may require a financial sharing mechanism (e.g., the financing of roads in Myanmar by India and Thailand, to provide "a bridge linking South and Southeast Asia").[80]

Where applicable, it will be helpful to adopt the user pays principle, to at least provide funds for infrastructure maintenance and operation.

Policy

BIMSTEC recognizes the need to promote overall and closer coordination with its development partners on financing and technical assistance, such as international financial institutions and development banks as well as the private sector through existing frameworks.

Strategy

BIMSTEC will facilitate and promote overall and closer coordination with its development partners on financing and technical assistance.

Monitoring

Issues

The BIMSTEC Secretariat and the BTCWG have formulated a monitoring framework for the development of transport connectivity that focuses on processes rather than on project results (i.e., outputs, outcomes, impacts). Therefore, for the purposes of monitoring, the goals are the projects and initiatives the completion of which will demonstrate progress in achieving the implementation of particular policies and strategies, and which can, therefore, be used as output indicators. BIMSTEC is a regional cooperation initiative rather than an implementation

---

[79] Asian Development Bank and Asian Development Bank Institute. 2015. *Connecting South Asia and Southeast Asia*. pp. 139–180.
[80] Bay of Bengal Initiative for Multi-Sectoral Technical and Economic Cooperation. 2018. *Fourth Summit Declaration. 30–31 August 2018*. Kathmandu, Nepal. p. 2; J.-F. Gautrin. Land-Based Cross-Border Infrastructure. In M. G. Plummer, P. J. Morgan, and G. Wignaraja. 2016. *Connecting Asia: Infrastructure for Integrating South and Southeast Asia*. Asian Development Bank Institute. p. 66.

> **Box 21: The Potential of Public–Private Partnerships for Financing Transport Connectivity Infrastructure in the Bay of Bengal Initiative for Multi-Sectoral Technical and Economic Cooperation Region**
>
> Public–private partnerships have become a useful tool to complement government initiatives to develop transport connectivity and other infrastructure in the BIMSTEC region. India is now the world's largest PPP market and the Government of India has applied the PPP model with success in the transport sector, as shown in the *Infrastructure Journal Database* (http://www.ijonline.com/data). That said, there have been some disappointing experiences due to inadequate project preparation, a lack of proper feasibility studies (e.g., due to overestimation of project demand), flawed project appraisals (e.g., due to overestimation of project demand), a lack of competitive tendering, poor contract design, and difficulties in land acquisition. However, in recent years, the PPP development model has been undergoing changes, with the private sector becoming more particular about minimizing development and execution risks, and asking governments to present better-structured, easily financeable, and ready-to-construct project propositions for competitive bidding. For example, there has been an emphasis on unbundling operational risks and allocating external risks to project entities, internal risks to project sponsors, and residual risks to government shareholders.
>
> The following improvements are required to increase the success rate of PPPs:
>
> (i) adoption of global good and best practices to ensure transparency and accountability (e.g., by fully disclosing bid criteria);
> (ii) development of units based on international good and best practices, to facilitate the PPP procurement and delivery process;
> (iii) creation of an independent regulatory environment;
> (iv) investment in human resources for PPPs to improve skills and knowledge across a variety of specialties (e.g., institutional, technical, finance) by partnering with experienced countries.
>
> BIMSTEC = Bay of Bengal Initiative for Multi-Sectoral Technical and Economic Cooperation, PPP = public–private partnership.
> Sources: Asian Development Bank and Asian Development Bank Institute. 2015. *Connecting South Asia and Southeast Asia*. pp. 154–155; and S. Ray. Infrastructure Finance and Financial Sector Development for Cross-Border Connectivity. In M. G. Plummer, P. J. Morgan, and G. Wignaraja. 2016. *Connecting Asia: Infrastructure for Integrating South and Southeast Asia*. Asian Development Bank Institute. pp. 106–109.

agency, and along with other similar cooperation initiatives, the physical realization of its strategies largely depends on actions by the member states, in some cases, supported by international development partners.[81]

Based on this understanding, Appendix 8 presents monitoring formats or "scorecards" for the Master Plan projects and initiatives to be used by the member states and the BTCWG, including a tabular format for monitoring of overall status, a project profile format for project-specific monitoring, and a simplified time-based implementation monitoring spreadsheet for each project.[82]

Recognizing the importance of robust institutional arrangements to effectively steer regional integration,[83] the member states recognize that a results monitoring framework should be developed at a later stage. For example,

---

[81] *Concept Paper for Master Plan on BIMSTEC Transport Connectivity*, discussed and agreed by the 2nd Meeting of the BTCWG. Bangkok, Thailand. 13–14 November 2017 (updated in March 2018), para. 60; and *The Proposed BTCWG Work Plan and Monitoring Framework*, presented at the Inception Meeting of the BIMSTEC Transport Connectivity Working Group. Bangkok, Thailand. 30–31 August 2016. p. 2.
[82] Building on the second source in the previous footnote.
[83] Bay of Bengal Initiative for Multi-Sectoral Technical and Economic Cooperation. *Fourth Summit Declaration*. 30–31 August 2018. Kathmandu, Nepal. p. 2.

such a results framework may evaluate changes in travel times along major routes and corridors, turnaround times at major land and sea ports, increases in cross-border trade and the share of intra-BIMSTEC trade to total BIMSTEC member state trade, and the number of new air routes developed. To support implementation of such a framework, surveys (e.g., travel time surveys, time release studies at borders) will be required, both before and after implementation of the flagship projects.

Policy

BIMSTEC recognizes the need to monitor the implementation of the projects in the Master Plan based on agreed monitoring formats.

Strategy

With inputs from the member states, the BIMSTEC Secretariat and the BTCWG will take the lead in monitoring implementation of the Master Plan projects.

References

Arvis, Jean-François, and Ben Shepherd. 2016. Measuring Connectivity in a Globally Networked Industry: The Case of Air Transport. *The World Economy.* Vol. 39 (3). pp. 369–385.

Asian Development Bank. 2010. *Technical Assistance for Regional Transport Development in South Asia.* October.

———. 2014. *Updating and Enhancement of the BIMSTEC Transport Infrastructure and Logistics Study, Phase II Report.* May.

———. 2018. *Major Change in Technical Assistance: Regional Project Development Support for the South Asia Subregional Economic Cooperation Operational Plan, 2016–2025.* Manila.

Asia-Pacific Economic Cooperation. 2013. *Improving Connectivity in the Asia Pacific Region: Perspectives of the APEC Policy Support Unit.* September.

Asian Development Bank and Asian Development Bank Institute (ADBI). 2015. *Connecting South Asia and Southeast Asia.* ADBI: Tokyo.

Bangladesh–India Memorandum of Understanding Relating to the use of Chittagong and Mongla Ports, 2015.

Bay of Bengal Initiative for Multi-Sectoral Technical and Economic Cooperation (BIMSTEC). *Fourth Summit Declaration. 2018.* 30–31 August. Kathmandu, Nepal.

———. 2014. *Updating and Enhancement of the BIMSTEC Transport Infrastructure and Logistics Study, Phase I Final Report.* March.

Centre for Aviation. 2018. Cargo and LCCs: Cebu Pacific Case Study Shows Cargo Can Pay. 12 March. https://centreforaviation.com/insights/analysis/cargo-and-lccs-cebu-pacific-case-study-shows-cargo-can-pay-404110.

Chawla, Vasudha. 2017. *India–Bangladesh Maritime Trade: Protocol on Inland Water Transit and Trade (PIWTT).* National Maritime Foundation. 16 June. p. 3. http://www.maritimeindia.org/View%20Profile/636331714994487296.pdf.

Concept Paper for Master Plan on BIMSTEC Transport Connectivity, discussed and agreed on during the 2nd Meeting of the BTCWG.2017. Bangkok, Thailand. 13–14 November (updated in March 2018).

De, P. (on behalf of the ADB UNESCAP Business Process Analysis [BPA] Study Team. 2012. *Overview of Trade Facilitation and Business Process Analysis.* Asia-Pacific Trade Facilitation Forum. 30–1 October.

Egis International and Egis India. *2013. ADB TA-7650 (REG): Regional Transport Development in Asia, Final Report.*

Export–Import Bank of India. 2017. *India's Engagements with CLMV [Cambodia–Lao PDR–Myanmar–Viet Nam]: Gateway to ASEAN Markets.* February 2017.

Goldman Sachs. 2005. How Solid are the BRICS? *Global Economics Paper.* No. 134. 1 December.

Gautrin, Jean-François. Land-Based Cross-Border Infrastructure. In Michael G. Plummer, Peter. J. Morgan, and Ganeshan Wignaraja, eds. 2016. *Connecting Asia: Infrastructure for Integrating South and Southeast Asia.* Asian Development Bank Institute.

Indian Express. Handling the Rise in Air Traffic: A Multiple Airport Theory. 2017. 28 October.

International Air Transport Association. 2016. Developing Trade Consultants (B. Shepherd, A. Shingal, and A. Raj). *Value of Air Cargo: Air Transport and Global Value Chains, Final Report.* December.

International Organization for Migration, Immigration and Border Management. https://www.iom.int/immigration-and-border-management.

Japan International Cooperation Agency. 2016. *One-Stop Border Post Sourcebook*, 2nd edition, May.

———, International Development Center of Japan Inc., and PADECO Co., Ltd. 2018. *The Study on Logistics System Improvement Master Plan in the Kingdom of Cambodia, Final Report.* March.

———, Kamigumi Co., Ltd., and Toyota Tsucho Corporation, *Preparatory Survey on Yangon Port in Thilawa Area and Logistics Depot Development in the Republic of the Union of Myanmar, Final Report.* January 2015.

——— and PADECO Co., Ltd. 2014. *Data Collection Survey on Transport Infrastructure Development for Regional Connectivity in and around South Asia.* March.

Kasturi, Charu Sudan. 2018. Bangladesh Bets on Connectivity for Its Next Economic Leap. *OZY.* 4 May.

Logistics Blog. 2015. Difference between Intermodal Shipping and Multimodal Shipping. Retrieved from http://logisticsportal.org/community/blogs/-/blogs/difference-between-intermodal-shipping-and-multimodal-shipping.

Ministry of Construction, Myanmar. 2014. *The Preparatory Survey for The Project for Construction of Bago River Bridge.* Japan International Cooperation Agency. March.

Ministry of External Affairs. 2018. India–Nepal Statement on Expanding Rail Linkages: Connecting Raxaul in India to Kathmandu in Nepal. New Delhi. 7 April.

———. 2018. India–Nepal Statement on New Connectivity through Inland Waterways. New Delhi. 7 April.

Ministry of Shipping, Bangladesh; W. Shepard. Bangladesh's Deep Sea Port Problem. *The Diplomat.* 7 June 2016.

Ministry of Shipping, India. 2017. *Sagarmala Programme – Port-Led Prosperity.* 10 November.

Observer Researcher Foundation. 2017. *ORF Issue Brief*. Issue No. 171. February.

Organisation for Economic Co-operation and Development. 2013. *Quantitative Assessment of the Benefits of Trade Facilitation*.

Oxera Consulting Ltd. 2010. *Understanding The Theory of International Connectivity*. Oxford: Oxera.

Pillai, Aditya Valiathan. 2017. The Promising Future of Inland Waterway Trade in South Asia. *In Asia*. 19 May.

Rahman, Mohammad Masudur, and Chanwhan. Kim. 2016. Prospects for Economic Integration of BIMSTEC: Trade and Investment Scenario. *International Journal of u- and e- Service, Science and Technology*. Vol. 9, No. 4. pp. 235–248. http://dx.doi.org/10.14257/ijunesst.2016.9.4.24

Ray, Shubhomoy. Infrastructure Finance and Financial Sector Development for Cross-Border Connectivity. In M. G. Plummer, P. J. Morgan, and G. Wignaraja, eds. 2016. *Connecting Asia: Infrastructure for Integrating South and Southeast Asia*. Asian Development Bank Institute.

Report of the Second Meeting of the BIMSTEC Transport Connectivity Working Group. 2017. Bangkok, Thailand. November 2017.

Shrestha, Chandra B. 2014. Kathmandu–Terai Fast Track: From Non-Starter to National Project. *Spotlight Nepal*. Vol. 8, No. 12. December.

South Asia Subregional Economic Cooperation and Asian Development Bank. 2017. SASEC Powering Asia in the 21st Century. p. 32. https://www.adb.org/sites/default/files/publication/233646/sasec-powering-asia.pdf.

UK Aid, Consumer Unity and Trust Society (CUTS) International, and The Asia Foundation. 2017. *Report of the Sub-Regional Dialogue, Expanding Tradable Benefits of Transboundary Water: Promoting Navigational Usage of Waterways in [the] Ganga and Brahmaputra Basins*. Kolkata, India. 26–27 October.

UN-Habitat, United Nations Environment Programme (UNEP), and SLoCaT. 2015. Partnership on Sustainable, Low Cost, Carbon Transport. *Analysis of the Relevance of Each of the 17 SDGs*. Draft. 24 September. https://sustainabledevelopment.un.org/content/documents/8656Analysis%20of%20transport%20relevance%20of%20SDGs.pdf.

United Nations Economic Commission for Europe. 2015. *United Nations Trade Facilitation Implementation Guide*. http://tfig.unece.org.

United Nations Network of Experts for Paperless Trade in Asia and the Pacific, United Nations Economic and Social Commission for Asia and the Pacific, and the United Nations Economic Commission for Europe. 2012. *Business Analysis Guide to Simplify Trade Procedures*.

Vidyadharan, Veena, and Prithviraj Nath. 2017. Connectivity Gains for India's North East via Waterways. *thethirdpole.net*. 15 December. https://www.thethirdpole.net/en/2017/12/15/connectivity-gains-for-indias-north-east-via-waterways/.

Wignall, David, and Mark Wignall. 2014. Seaborne Trade between South Asia and Southeast Asia. *ADBI Working Paper Series*. No. 508. December.

World Bank, International Trade Department (Arvis, Jean-Francois, and Ben Shepherd). 2011. *The Air Connectivity Index: Measuring Integration in the Global Air Transport Network*. June.

World Bank. 2014. *A Vision for Nepal, Policy Notes for the Government, Synthesis Report*.

Xavier, Constantino. 2018. *Bridging the Bay of Bengal: Toward a Stronger BIMSTEC*. Carnegie India. February.

Appendix 1
Relevance of Transport in the Agenda for Sustainable Development

Transport has become more important in the global development agenda in recent years. In the *2030 Agenda for Sustainable Development*, sustainable transport is mainstreamed across several Sustainable Development Goals (SDGs) and targets, especially those related to food security, health, energy, economic growth, infrastructure, and cities and human settlements. Transport-related targets are included in 8 of the 17 SDGs (Goals 2, 3, 6, 7, 9, 11, 12, and 13), illustrating the cross-cutting role that transport plays in sustainable development. In the context of the SDGs, transport is not only a matter of developing transport infrastructure and services, but also encompasses the ease of reaching destinations in terms of proximity, convenience, and safety. The following table sets out the relevance of transport to selected SDGs.

Table A1: Relevance of Transport to Selected Sustainable Development Goals

SDG Goal	Relevance of Transport
Goal 1: End poverty in all its forms everywhere	Transport reduces absolute poverty through economic efficiency—by lowering costs and enhancing opportunities, improving access to services and markets, and enhancing social well-being of communities, building productive capacity, as well as promoting trade and regional and global integration.
Goal 2: End hunger, achieve food security and improved nutrition and promote sustainable agriculture	The correlation between transport and food security is particularly visible in the context of rural accessibility. Strong attention to "food-transit connections" is, furthermore, vital to keep consumer prices affordable. Logistics improvements can also be effective in the management of food price risks, shocks, and instabilities. Improved access in remote areas will additionally increase the outreach of extension workers.
Goal 3: Ensure healthy lives and promote well-being for all at all ages	The transport sector is a major source of air pollution in cities and often the largest source of small particulate matter (PM) and nitrogen oxide (NOx) emissions that drastically affect public health. Some of the main policies that can reduce air pollution by up to 95% include (re)designing cities such that active and public transport is the main mode of transport; and providing cleaner fuels and implementing vehicle emission standards for light-duty and heavy-duty vehicles.
Goal 6: Ensure availability and sustainable management of water and sanitation for all	Reliable, low-cost, and efficient transport infrastructure and services can improve physical access to water and sanitation facilities—particularly in rural areas.
Goal 7: Ensure access to affordable, reliable, sustainable, and modern energy for all	Transportation accounts for approximately 25% of the world's energy demand and for about 61.5% of all the oil used each year. Various types of actions that can be taken to improve the efficiency of transport fuel use, like improving road conditions, providing high-quality fuels, promoting eco-driving, better vehicle technologies including promoting electric vehicles, and the overall improvement of urban transport systems.

continued on next page

Table A1 continued

SDG Goal	Relevance of Transport
Goal 9: Resilient Infrastructure, sustainable industrialization and innovation	To achieve sustainable industrialization, transborder connections and transport development corridors for spatial inclusion of and connectivity between economic hubs play a crucial role. A robust and resilient transportation infrastructure is an essential element for a resilient supply chain as disruption to the global, interregional, national and local trade lanes could impact development, as transport costs could be increased and delivery of products delayed.
Goal 11: Make cities and human settlements inclusive, safe, resilient, and sustainable	Transport ensures access to services, goods, and opportunities. Compact city planning can reduce the need to travel. Affordability of transport for the urban poor and accessibility of all, including for people with disabilities, women, the elderly, and other vulnerable groups are essential for the city to be inclusive.
Goal 12: Ensure sustainable consumption and production patterns	The shortage of reliable rural transport services is responsible for food crops not reaching the market at all and holding back farmers to expand food production for the market.
Goal 13: Take urgent action to combat climate change and its impacts	Sustainable transport solutions offer significant mitigation potential and are essential in meeting the 2°C goal to minimize the impacts of climate change. To achieve this target, comprehensive sustainable transport solutions have to be pursued. Actions also have to be prioritized toward adaptation or enhancing the resilience of transport infrastructure and services.

SDG = Sustainable Development Goal.

Source: UN-Habitat, United Nations Environment Programme (UNEP), and SLoCaT 2015. Partnership on Sustainable, Low Cost, Carbon Transport. *Analysis of the Relevance of Each of the 17 SDGs*. 24 September. https://sustainabledevelopment.un.org/content/documents/8656Analysis%20of%20transport%20relevance%20of%20SDGs.pdf.

Appendix 2
Synergies between the BIMSTEC Master Plan for Transport Connectivity and Other Selected Connectivity Frameworks

I. The ASEAN Secretariat, Master Plan on ASEAN Connectivity 2025 (MPAC 2025, August 2016)

The Association of Southeast Asian Nations (ASEAN) has 10 members, including BIMSTEC member states Myanmar and Thailand, along with Brunei Darussalam, Cambodia, Indonesia, the Lao People's Democratic Republic, Malaysia, the Philippines, Singapore, and Viet Nam.

The *Master Plan on ASEAN Connectivity 2025*, published in 2016, encompasses physical (e.g., transport, information and communication technology [ICT], and energy), institutional (e.g., trade, investment, and services liberalization), and people-to-people linkages (e.g., education, culture, and tourism), which are considered to be the "foundational supportive means to achieving the economic, political-security, and socio-cultural pillars of an integrated ASEAN Community.

The vision for ASEAN Connectivity 2025 is "to achieve a seamlessly and comprehensively connected and integrated ASEAN that will promote competitiveness, inclusiveness, and a greater sense of Community."

MPAC 2025 focuses on five strategic areas: (i) sustainable infrastructure, (ii) digital innovation, (iii) seamless logistics, (iv) regulatory excellence, and (v) people mobility.

"To make it happen," the approach of *MPAC 2025* includes (i) a strong focus and targets; (ii) clear governance and ownership; (iii) clear and aligned plans; (iv) the presence of core skills, incentives, and finance; (v) proactive stakeholder engagement; and (vi) robust performance management.

Specific synergies between the *MPAC 2025* and this BIMSTEC Master Plan for Transport Connectivity include the following:

(i) similar vision statements, for the seven-country BIMSTEC and the 10-country ASEAN regional organizations, which have two overlapping members (i.e., Myanmar and Thailand);

(ii) overlapping strategies for achieving physical connectivity (i.e., completion of the ASEAN Highway Network, which is based on Asian Highway [AH] system, and which includes part of AH 1, i.e., Tamu–Mandalay–Meiktila–Yangon–Bago–Payagyi–Thaton–Myawaddy, and AH 2, i.e., Meiktila–Loilem–Kyaing Tong–Tachilek);

(iii) overlapping strategies for establishing an integrated and seamless multimodal and intermodal transport system, including the development of effective networks of dry ports;

(iv) overlapping strategies for achieving an integrated, efficient, and competitive maritime transport system, including improved institutional arrangements (e.g., customs, immigration, and quarantine) and enhanced port capacity; and

(v) overlapping strategies for seamless logistics and transport facilitation, including the development of regional agreements (e.g., the ASEAN Framework Agreement Facilitation of Goods in Transit), and the development of single windows.

II. ACMECS Five-Year Master Plan 2019–2023

The Ayeyawaddy–Chao Phrya–Mekong Economic Cooperation Strategy regional grouping includes two BIMSTEC member states (Myanmar and Thailand), as well as Cambodia, the Lao People's Democratic Republic, and Viet Nam.

The *ACMECS Master Plan (2019–2023)*, published in 2018, includes three goals, the first of which is seamless connectivity, including multimodal transport, covering roads, bridges, railways, ports, air transport, maritime transport, and inland water transport.

Specific synergies between the *ACMECS Master Plan (2019–2023)* and this BIMSTEC Master Plan for Transport Connectivity include the following:

(i) prioritized road projects for 2019–2020, e.g., the Eindu–Kawkareik Road Improvement Project, the Mae Sot–Myawaddy Border Crossing Project and associated infrastructure improvements, the Thaton–Eindu Road Section Project, the Bang Yai–Kanchanaburi Intercity Motorway Project, the Kanchanaburi–Ban Phu Nam Ron (Thailand and Myanmar border) Intercity Motorway Project;

(ii) prioritized rail project feasibility studies for 2019–2020, e.g., for the missing link of Dawei–Htiki–Ban Phu Ron, for upgrading the Dawei–Mawlamyine line;

(iii) prioritized air transport projects for 2019–2020, e.g., the Yangon International Airport Development Project, Mae Sot Airport Development Project;

(iv) prioritized port projects for 2019–2020, e.g., Ranong port development; and

(v) identified missing links, e.g., Dawei–Myittar and Myittar–Myanmar and Thailand border road links along AH 123, Tamu–Mandalay–Meiktila–Yangon–Bago–Payagyi–Thaton–Myawaddy (along AH 1).

Appendix 3
Major Routes/Corridors in the BIMSTEC Region

Major corridors that have been identified in the BIMSTEC region from prior initiatives are set out below:

(i) The **major BIMSTEC corridors (trade routes) identified during the BTILS Updating and Enhancement Study** are as follows: (a) Land Route 1: Kolkata–Siliguri–(Jaigaon-Phuentsholing)–Guwahati–Imphal–Moreh/Tamu–Mandalay–Bago–Myawaddy/Mae Sot–Tak–Bangkok–Laem Chabang; (b) Land Route 2: Kolkata–Petrapole/Benapole–Jashore–Dhaka–Chattogram; and (c) Land Route 3: Kolkata–Raxaul/Birgunj–Kathmandu. In addition, there are direct or indirect sea routes between all of the main BIMSTEC ports, and in the case of civil aviation, some of the main BIMSTEC airports are linked with each other by direct airline services.

(ii) **Asian Highway (AH) routes**, developed under the auspices of the United Nations Economic and Social Commission for Asia and the Pacific (UNESCAP), include (a) AH 1, linking Thailand, Myanmar, Bangladesh, and India, including Tak/Myawaddy, Mandalay, Tamu/Moreh, and Kolkata; (b) AH 2, linking Myanmar, Bangladesh, India, and Nepal, including Mae Sai/Tachilek, Mandalay, Tamu/Moreh, Dawki/Tamabil, Dhaka, Banglabandha, Fulbari, Siliguri, Panitanki, and Kakarbitta; (c) AH 3, linking Thailand and Myanmar, including Chiang Rai and Mong La; (d) AH 41, traversing Bangladesh, and providing connectivity for Chattogram and Mongla Ports; (e) AH 42, linking Nepal and India, including Kathmandu and Birganj/Raxaul; (f) AH 43, linking India and Sri Lanka; (g) AH 44, within Sri Lanka; (h) AH 45–47, within India; and (i) AH 48, linking Bhutan and India, including Thimphu, Phuenthsholing/Jaigaon, and Changrabandha.

(iii) **Trans-Asian Railway (TAR) routes** have also been developed under the auspices of UNESCAP; the TAR Southern Corridor links India, Myanmar, and Thailand, although there are missing links between India and Myanmar, and between Myanmar and Thailand.

(iv) **Road corridors identified by the South Asian Association for Regional Cooperation (SAARC)** include (a) SAARC Highway Corridor (SHC) 1, which links India and Bangladesh, including Kolkata, Petrapole/Benapole, Dhaka, and Akhaura/Agartala; (b) SHC 2, which links Nepal and India, including Kathmandu, Birgunj/Raxaul, and Kolkata/Haldia; (c) SHC 3, which links Bhutan and India, including Thimphu–Phuentsholing/Jaigaon, and Kolkata/Haldia; (d) SHC 4, which links Nepal, India, and Bangladesh, including Kathmandu, Kakarbitta, Phulbari, Banglabandha, and Mongla/Chattogram; (e) SHC 5, linking Bhutan, India, and Bangladesh, including Sandrupjongkhar, Guwahati, Shillong, Sylhet, Dhaka, and Kolkata; (f) SHC 6, linking India and Bangladesh, linking Agartala, Akhaura, and Chittgaong; (g) SHC 7, linking Nepal and India, including Kathmandu, Nepalganj, and New Delhi; (h) SHC 8, linking Bhutan, India, and Bangladesh, including Thimphu, Phuentsholing/Jaigaon, Burimari, and Mongla/Chattogram; (i) SHC 9, linking India and Bangladesh, including Maldha, Shibanj, and the Jamuna Bridge; and (j) SHC 10, linking Nepal and India, including Kathmandu, Bhairahara, Sunauli, and Lucknow.

(v) **Railway corridors identified within SAARC** include (a) SAARC Railway Corridor (SRC) 1, linking India and Bangladesh, including Delhi, Dhaka, Mahishasan, and Imphal; (b) SRC 3, linking Nepal and India, including Birgunj/Raxaul and Haldia/Kolkata; (c) SRC 4, linking Nepal, India, and Bangladesh, including Birgunj/Raxaul, Katihar, Rohanpur, and Chattogram, with links to Jogbani and Agartala; and (d) SR 5, linking Sri Lanka and India, including Colombo and Chennai (to be linked by ferry).

(vi) **Inland water transport corridors identified within SAARC** include (a) SAARC Inland Waterways Corridor (SIWC) 1, linking India and Bangladesh, including Kolkata, Haldia, Raimongal, Mongla, Kaukhali, Barishal, Hizla, Chandpur, Narayanganj, Aricha, Sirajganj, Bahadurabad, Chilmari, and Pandu; and (b) SIWC 2, also linking India and Bangladesh, including Kolkata/Haldia, Raimongal, Mongla, Kaukhali, Barishal, Hizla, Chandpur, Narayanganj, Bhairabbazar, Ajmiriganj, Markuli, Sherpur, Fenchuganj, Zakiganj, and Karimganj.

Note: Priority projects may be expected to be found along these corridors, but projects along newer routes are conceivable as long as they have relevance to the development of the BIMSTEC region.

Source: Asian Development Bank. 2014. *Updating and Enhancement of the BIMSTEC Transport Infrastructure nd Logistics Study (BTILS), Final Report.* June 2014 (and issued formally in July 2018). pp. 30–32.

Appendix 4
Schematic Map of Development of Bay of Bengal Initiative for Multi-Sectoral Technical and Economic Cooperation Road Corridors

Corridors and Subcorridors

Road Corridor 1: Kathmandu–Birgunj (NEP)/Raxaul–Kolkata–Petrapole (IND)/Benapole–Jashore–Bhanga–Dhaka–Agartala–Sabroom–Feni Bridge–Baraierhat–Chattogram–Keranirhat–Bandarban–Thanchi (BAN)/Paletwa (MYA)

Subcorridor 1.1: Bhanga–Barishal–Patuakhali–Kuakata with link to Payra Deep Sea Port (BAN)

Subcorridor 1.2: Jashore–Khulna–Mongla (BAN)

Road Corridor 2: Kathmandu–Kakarbitta (NEP)/Panitanki–Siliguri–Fulbari (IND)/Banglabandha–Rangpur–Hatikumrul–Dhaka–Chattogram–Cox's Bazar–Teknaf (BAN) –Maungdaw (MYA)

Subcorridor 2.1: Hatikumrul–Banpara–Khustia–Jenaidah–Jashore–Khulna–Mongla (BAN)

Subcorridor 2.2: Balukhali–Gundum (BAN)/Taunbro–Baulibazar–Kyauktaw–Mandalay (MYA)

Road Corridor 3: Dhaka–Sylhet–Tamabil (BAN)/Dawki–Shillong–Guwahati–Kohima–Imphal (IND)/ Moreh/Tamu–Kale–Mandalay–Myawaddy (MYA) –Mae Sot–Bangkok–Laem Chabang (THA)

Subcorridor 3.1: Sylhet–Sheola (BAN)/Sutarkandi–Shilchar–Imphal (IND)

Road Corridor 4: Kolkata–Siliguri–Guwahati–Imphal (IND)/Moreh–Mandalay (MYA)[c]

Subcorridor 4.1: Siliguri–Chengrabandha (IND)/Burimari–Lalmonirhat–Rangpur (BAN)

Road Corridor 5: Chattogram–Feni–Cumilla–Akhaura (BAN)/Agartala–Silchar–Guwahati (IND)

Subcorridor 5.1: Silchar–Harangajao–Guwahati[d](IND)

Road Corridor 6: Thimphu–Phuentsholing (BHU)/Jaigaon–Hasimara–Siliguri–Kolkata (IND)[e]

Subcorridor 6.1: Phuentsholing (BHU)/Jaigaon–Hasimara–Chengrabandha (IND) – Burimari–Lalmonirhat–Rangpur–Dhaka–Chattogram/Mongla (BAN)

Subcorridor 6.2: Phuentsholing (BHU) –(Siliguri–Guwahati Highway [IND})–Samdrupjongkhar (BHU)

Subcorridor 6.3: Phuentsholing (BHU)/Hasimara–Siliguri–Panitanki (IND)/Kakarbitta (NEP)

Road Corridor 7: Samdrupjongkhar (BHU)/Rangia–Guwahati–Shillong–Dawki (IND)/Tamabil–Sylhet–Dhaka–Bhanga–Jashore–Benapole(BAN)/Petrapole–Kolkata (IND)[f]

Subcorridor 7.1a: Samdrupjongkhar–Thimphu–Phuentsholing(BHU)/Jaigon–Chengrabandha (IND)/Burimari–Rangpur–Hatikamrul–Dhaka–Chattogram (BAN)

Subcorridor 7.1b: Samdrupjongkhar–Thimphu–Phuentsholing(BHU)/Jaigon–Chengrabandha (IND)/Burimari–Rangpur–Hatikamrul–Banparaa–Kushtia–Jenaida–Jashore–Khulna–Mongla (BAN)

Subcorridor 7.2: Gelephu (BHU)/Hathisar–Samthaibari–Rangia (IND)/Samdrupjongkhar (BHU)

Subcorridor 7.3: Gelephu (BHU) –Samthaibari/Hasimara (India)/Phuentsholing (BHU)

Subcorridor 7.4: Samdrupjongkhar (BHU)/Rangia-Siliguri-Panitanki (IND)/Kakarbitta (NEP)

BAN = Bangladesh, BHU = Bhutan, IND = India, MYA = Myanmar, NEP = Nepal, and THA = Thailand.
a   Subcorridors may be considered as feeder or complementary to main corridors.
b   Reflecting inputs of the Bangkok Workshop on the Second Draft of the Master Plan, 17–18 September 2018; inputs of BAN dated 27 September 2018 and 15 September 2019; and inputs of BHU dated 3 October 2018.
c   Corridors and subcorridors serving BHU are part of Road Corridors 6 and 7.
d   Alternate route to the East–West Corridor.
e   Designated Corridor 4 in input of BHU.
f   Designated Corridor 6 in input of BHU.
Source: Asian Development Bank.

Appendix 5
Long List of Master Plan Projects

No.	Code	Project Description	BIMSTEC Development Logic	Estimated Cost, 2018 ($ million)	(Possible) Funding Sources	Timescale
1. Roads and Road Transport						
1.1 Enhancement of Arterial Links to Borders and Ports						
1	BAN-RD-001	Improvement of the Jatrabari intersection (Mawa) on the Dhaka–Khulna Highway and the Pantchchar–Bhanga road section to four lanes	Enhancing and accommodating future traffic flow between Dhaka and Kolkata along AH 1 and BIMSTEC Road Corridor 1 as well as connecting southwestern parts of Bangladesh (especially Greater Faridpur, Barishal, and Khulna) with the capital, resulting in significant reductions in transport times and costs between and among BIMSTEC member states	1,295	Government	2016–2020
2	BAN-RD-002	Four-laning Daulatdia–Magura–Jhneidha–Jashore–Khulna (212 km)	Upgrading of main border corridor linking Bangladesh and India, a key trade link	1,800	World Bank and other sources to be identified	2021–2025
3	BAN-RD-003	Four-laning Paturia to Nabinagar, including Manikganj bypass	Improved connection of Dhaka with Benapole through the existing route	400	Not yet identified	2020–2024
4	BAN-RD-004	Construction of the Padma Multipurpose Bridge at Mawa	Linking of Dhaka and the Indian border near Kolkata, as well as connecting southern parts of the country, resulting in significant reductions in transport times and costs for trade between and among BIMSTEC states	3,706	Government	2009–2019
5	BAN-RD-005	Construction of the Dhaka Elevated Expressway	Uninterrupted road communication between the Dhaka–Chattogram Highway and the Dhaka–Tangail–Hatikamrul Highway through the proposed Dhaka–Ashulia elevated expressway along AH 2	1,132	PPP	2011–2021

continued on next page

Table continued

No.	Code	Project Description	BIMSTEC Development Logic	Estimated Cost, 2018 ($ million)	(Possible) Funding Sources	Timescale
6	BAN-RD-006	Construction of the Dhaka-Ashulia Elevated Expressway	Uninterrupted road communication between the Dhaka–Chattogram Highway and the Dhaka–Tangail–Hatikamral Highway through the ongoing Dhaka Elevated Expressway along A12	2,098	PRC (China Exim Bank) and government	2017–2023
7	BAN-RD-007	Construction of the Dhaka East–West Elevated Expressway	Linking of the Dhaka-Aricha Highway (NH 5) and the Dhaka–Chattogram Highway (NH 1) with a connection to the Dhaka-Mawa Highway, which links directly with the Padma Bridge	2,049	Malaysia and government	2018–2024
8	BAN-RD-008	Road Connectivity Project Joydevpur–Chandra–Tangail–Elenga to four-lane highway	Connection of northwestern Bangladesh with northeastern India, Bhutan, and Nepal	682	ADB, OFID, ADFD	2013–2018
9	BAN-RD-009	Road Connectivity Project II (Four-laning Elenga–Hatikamrul–Rangpur, 190.4 km)	Connection of northwestern Bangladesh with northeastern India, Bhutan, and Nepal	1,494	ADB	2016–2021
10	BAN-RD-010	Construction of the second Katchpur, Meghna, and Gomti Bridges and rehabilitation of existing bridges (total bridge length of 2,736 m)	Development of the country's main arterial trade link between Chattogram Port and Dhaka	1,035	Government and JICA	2013–2021
11	BAN-RD-011	Construction of the Dhaka–Chattogram Expressway (217 km)	Provision of faster access between the capital and the main port of Bangladesh	3,701	PPP, with proposal for ADB viability gap financing under process of approval	2019–2023
12	BAN-RD-012	Improvement of the Ashuganj River Port–Sarail–Dharkhar–Akhaura Land Port Road as a four-lane national highway (50.6 km)	Linking to the northeastern states of India and beyond	430	ILOC	2017–2020
13	BAN-RD-013	Upgrading of the Cumilla (Moynamati)–Brahmanbaria (Dharkar) four-lane national highway (51 km)	Connection of Dhaka with India's northeastern states and Myanmar	718	ILOC	2020–2023

continued on next page

Table continued

No.	Code	Project Description	BIMSTEC Development Logic	Estimated Cost, 2018 ($ million)	(Possible) Funding Sources	Timescale
14	BAN-RD-014	Four-laning of the Dhaka (Katchpur)–Sylhet Highway (226 km, NH 2)	Provision of connectivity down the eastern side of Bangladesh for traffic from India's northeastern states to Dhaka and Chattogram	1,800	Government and other funding sources to be identified	2019–2023
15	BAN-RD-015	Construction of Bridge along the Bhulta-Araihazar-Banchrampur-Nabinagar Road over the Meghna River	As above	231	Malaysia and government	2022–2026
16	BAN-RD-016	Four-laning Rangpur to Banglabandha (196 km)	Connection with Siliguri and Nepal and Bhutan	1,500	ADB	2021–2025
17	BAN-RD-017	Four-laning of the Khulna-Mongla Highway (37 km)	As above	300	As above	2021–2025
18	BAN-RD-018	Four-laning Bhanga [Faridpur]-Barishal (130 km) and four-laning Barishal-Patuakhali-Kuakata (106 km) with a link to Payra deep sea port	Linking of Payra deep seaport through Padma Bridge with a connection to Benapole	2,000	ADB (four-laning Bhanga [Faridpur] – Barishal) Not yet identified (four-laning Barishal-Patuakhali-Kuakata)	2019–2024
19	BAN-RD-019	Construction of a Bridge along the Patuakhali-Amtoli-Barguna Road over the Payra River	Linking of Payra deep seaport through Patuakhali-Barguna-Perojpur-Jashore-Benapole to India	200 (to be refined in ongoing feasibility study)	Not yet identified	To be determined after completion of feasibility study in June 2019
20	BAN-RD-020	Construction of Bridge on Barguna-Pathorghata Road over the Bishkhali River	As above	250 (to be refined in ongoing feasibility study)	Not yet identified	As above
21	BHU-RD-021	Upgrading of the Gelephu-Trongsa National Highway (before 244 km, but shortened to 201 km), including four bridges	Improved north–south connection to NH 31 in India and also to Gelephu Airport	82	Funding sources to be identified	2018–2023
22	BHU-RD-022	Kharbandi–Pasakha–Gedu (55 km, including Singye Bridge)	Provision of an alternate route for the Thimphu–Phuentsholing Highway	18	Not yet identified	2018–2028

continued on next page

Table continued

No.	Code	Project Description	BIMSTEC Development Logic	Estimated Cost, 2018 ($ million)	(Possible) Funding Sources	Timescale
23	IND-RD-023	Upgrading of Imphal–Moreh NH 39	Improved connectivity between India and Myanmar along AH 1 and AH 2	180	Government (National Highways and Infrastructure Development Corporation) and ADB	2017–2020
24	IND-RD-024	Hapachara–Tulungia–Jogighopa–Gendera–Paikan Road	Improved connectivity for India's new gateway to Southeast Asia and the rest of the North East	228	Government	2019–2023
25	IND-RD-025	Paikan–Dudhnoi–Guwahati	Improved connectivity in Assam	450	As above	As above
26	IND-RD-026	Jogighopa-Bilasipara	Improved connectivity for India's new gateway to Southeast Asia and the rest of the North East above	200	As above	As above
27	IND-RD-027	Two-lane road bridge in Jogighopa across the Brahmaputra River	As above	Cost not yet estimated	As above	As above
28	IND-RD-028	Guwahati and Jorabat Bypass	Improved connectivity in Assam	As above	As above	As above
29	MYA-RD-029	Improvement of the Yagyi-Kalewa road (139 km)	Reconstruction of a key section of the India–Myanmar–Thailand Trilateral Highway	174 (INR 11.77 billion)	India (grant)	2015–2021
30	MYA-RD-030	Construction of Kawkareik–Eindu Road	Enhancing access to a primary BIMSTEC east-west trade corridor along the India–Myanmar–Thailand Trilateral Highway	131.8 (including 110 from ADB, 20 from AIF, and 1.8 from government)	ADB, AIF, and government	2015–2021
31	MYA-RD-031	Provision of 69 new bridges along the Kalewa-Tamu Road	Development of the northern section of the India–Myanmar–Thailand Trilateral Highway	54	India (grant)	2014–2024
32	MYA-RD-032	Construction of Bago NH 1 bypass road	Elimination of a highly congested bottleneck along the primary north-south artery	25	Regional government (Bago)	2019–2020
33	MYA-RD-033	Construction of new Bago–Kyaikto road	Economic corridor connecting with Trilateral Highway	526.43 (including 483.3 from ADB and 42.54 from Government)	JICA grant for construction following ADB prefeasibility study	2018–2020
34	MYA-RD-034	Gyaing (580 m), Kawkarait (796 m), and Zathapyin (480 m) bridges	As above	308 (JPY 33.86 billion)	JICA Loan	2016-2024

continued on next page

Table continued

No.	Code	Project Description	BIMSTEC Development Logic	Estimated Cost, 2018 ($ million)	(Possible) Funding Sources	Timescale
35	MYA-RD-035	Yangon–Mandalay Expressway improvement project from Yangon to Payagyi (65 km)	Serving Tamu–Mandalay–Yangon–Thailand traffic	57	ADB loan	2018–2022
36	MYA-RD-036	Yangon–Mandalay Expressway improvement Project Mandalay portion (502 km, km 65 to 567)	As above	Not yet estimated	PPP	2025–2028
37	MYA-RD-037	Development of new Htee Kee (Myanmar)/Baan Phu Nam Ron (Thailand) border crossing road	Provision of a new east-west connection, linking with a new Dawei Port	142 (THB 4.5 billion)	Thailand (NEDA)	2018–2024 (feasibility study under discussion between Ministry of Construction and NEDA, Thailand)
38	NEP-RD-038	Kathmandu–Terai Fast Track Road, including construction of a new four-lane expressway between Kathmandu and Nijgadh (76.2 km) and upgrading of Nijgadh–Pathalaiya segment from two to four lanes (18 km)	Provision of an arterial trade link between Kathmandu and the main border crossing with India; also enabling the development of a new airport	2,000	Government (and Nijgadh–Pathalaiya section by the World Bank)	2016–2024
39	NEP-RD-039	Nijgadh–Pathalaiya–Birgunj road upgrade	Improvement of arterial road to the Nepal–India border	200	Government	2018–2024 (Pathlaiya–Birgunj ICP, 2018–2022, and Nijgadh–Pathlaiya, 2020–2024)
40	NEP-RD-040	Widening of Dharan–Biratnagar (Nepal)–Jogbani (India) road link to six lanes	Additional capacity for trade route in eastern Nepal	136	Government	2016–2023
41	NEP-RD-041	Upgrading of Narayanghat–Mungling–Kathmandu road (146 km) and studies on axle load control and road safety measures	Improvement of a critical section of an existing trade corridor	700	World Bank and government	2013–2024 (Narayanghat–Mungling completed in 2018; Mungling–Kathmandu to be undertaken in 2020–2024)
42	NEP-RD-042	Upgrading of East–West Highway (1,028 km)	Improvement of an important section of AH 2, serving international trade and traffic	2,010	ADB, World Bank, and the government	2016–2025

continued on next page

Table continued

No.	Code	Project Description	BIMSTEC Development Logic	Estimated Cost, 2018 ($ million)	(Possible) Funding Sources	Timescale
43	NEP-RD-043	Two-laning and intermediate laning of Postal Highway (950–1,031 km), parallel and south of the East–West Highway (near the Indian border)	Development of an important domestic connection carrying some international traffic	350–500	Governments of India and Nepal	2016–2022
44	SRL-RD-044	Central Expressway, Phases I–IV, including Kadawata, Mirigama, Kurunagala, and Dambulla	Improved connectivity between Colombo port and the northern part of the country	800–1,000	PRC (China Exim Bank) and others	2017–2025
45	SRL-RD-045	Intelligent Transport System for Colombo Suburban Area	Improved transport system efficiency in major BIMSTEC port metropolis	400 (60 for bridge and 340 for the extension)	JICA (bridge); funding source not yet identified for the extension	2018–2025 (bridge, 2018–2020)
46	THA-RD-046	Four-laning of the Mae Sot–Tak Highway (51 km, Route 12 mountain section)	Expediting trade between Thailand and Myanmar	90	Government	2015–2019
47	THA-RD-047	Improvement of the Bangkok–Kanchanaburi–Dawei road corridor by developing the Bang Yai-Kanchanaburi motorway	Provision of a new east-west connection, linking with a new Dawei Port	1,700	PPP	Project including timing subject to further confirmation by MYA and THA
48	THA-RD-048	Improvement of the Bangkok–Kanchanaburi–Dawei road corridor by developing the section from Kanchanaburi to the Thailand and Myanmar border at Ban Phu Nam Ron	As above	1,300	PPP	As above
49	REG-RD-049 (IND and NEP)	Nepal–India Transit Roads (e.g., Biratnagar, Birgunj, Bhairahawa, and Nepalgunj Roads connecting with Visakhapatnam, and Kolkata–Kanchanpuri (Bhimdatta) linkage	Provision of transit and road connectivity for transit cargo of Nepal	Not yet estimated	Not yet identified	2018–2028
50	REG-RD-050 (IND and NEP)	Kolkata–Kalughat–Raxual, and Biratnagar–Sahibganj(–Bangladesh) linkages	As above	2,000	Government(s)	2016–2024

continued on next page

Table continued

No.	Code	Project Description	BIMSTEC Development Logic	Estimated Cost, 2018 ($ million)	(Possible) Funding Sources	Timescale
1.2 Border Roads						
51	BAN-RD-051	Four-laning of the Bhanga–Bhatiapara–Kalna–Lohagora–Narail–Jashore–Highway (135 km)	Upgrading of the main border corridor linking Bangladesh and India, a key trade link	1,100	ILOC	2019–2024
52	BAN-RD-052	Four-laning of the Chattogram–Cox's Bazar–Teknaf Highway	Connecting Chattogram Port and Myanmar	1,270	Government-to-government PPP with Japan, ADB, and government	2018–2023
53	BAN-RD-053	Four-laning of the Sylhet to Tamabil Highway (65 km)	Border link with Bhutan and the northeastern states of India	400	AIIB	2020–2023
54	BAN-RD-054	Four-laning of the Rangpur to Burimari Highway (128 km)	Connection with Changrabandha (India) and Bhutan	960	ADB	2019–2023
55	BAN-RD-055	Construction of direct road link between Bangladesh and Myanmar (Gundum [Bangladesh]/Taungbro–Bawlibazaar–Kyauktaw [Myanmar] (135 km)	Improved connectivity between Bangladesh and Myanmar	Not yet estimated	Not yet identified (Bangladesh to construct 25 km inside Myanmar territory according to 2007 agreement)	Not yet determined
56	BAN-RD-056	Construction of a tunnel under the Karnaphuli River	Linking of Dhaka–Chattogram–Cox's Bazar with the Myanmar border through AH 41	1,056	PRC (China Exim Bank) and government	2015–2022
57	BHU-RD-057	Construction of Samrang–Jomotsangkha section (58 km)	Improved accessibility along the southern Bhutan border with India	21 (roads and 19 bridges)	Government of India	2023
58	BHU-RD-058	Construction of the Lhamoizhingkha–Sarpang section of the SEWH (75 km, including about 14 bridges)	As above	52	Not yet identified	2018–2028
59	BHU-RD-059	Construction of the Gelephu–Panbang section of the SEWH (74 km)	As above	57	As above	2018–2028
60	BHU-RD-060	Construction of the Nganglam–Dewathang section of the SEWH (75 km)	Improved accessibility to a major export area	48	As above	2018–2028

continued on next page

Table continued

No.	Code	Project Description	BIMSTEC Development Logic	Estimated Cost, 2018 ($ million)	(Possible) Funding Sources	Timescale
61	IND-RD-061	Four-laning Kolkata–Siliguri corridor NH 34	Upgrading of arterial trade links between Kolkata and Bhutan, Nepal, and Myanmar	1,220	Government (under Bharatmala Pariyojana)	2014–2020
62	IND-RD-062	Upgrading of Wangjing–Khudenthabi section in Manipur	Improved connectivity in Manipur State	95	ADB	2019–2023
63	IND-RD-063	Upgrading of the NH 44 Silchar–Agartala–Sabroom in Assam and Tripura (NH 53 and NH 44) with Karimganj–Sutrakhandi spur of NH 151 to the India–Bangladesh border	Improved connectivity between India and Bangladesh	610	Government (National Highways and Infrastructure Development Corporation) and JICA	2019–2023
64	IND-RD-064	Two-laning from the Assam/Meghalaya border, Dudhanai to Dalu, via Bagmara, NH 62	As above	227	JICA	2021–2022
65	IND-RD-065	Improvement of NH 208 between Teliamura and Harina (158 km) in Tripura	As above	285	JICA	2021–2022
66	IND-RD-066	Upgrading road between Kolkata and Bongaon near Petrapole on the India–Bangladesh border	As above	130	Government and ADB	2021–2022
67	IND-RD-067	Two-laning of alternate route between Barak Valley (Silchar) to Guwahati via Harangajao-Turuk in Assam	As above	452	As above	2021–2022
68	IND-RD-068	Development of link roads between Srirampu–Dhubri and Phulbari to Tura with a new bridge across the Brahamputra River on NH 127B	As above	825	JICA	2024–2025
69	IND-RD-069	Improvement of Manu-Simlung, NH 44 in Tripura	As above	170	As above	2021–2022

continued on next page

Table continued

No.	Code	Project Description	BIMSTEC Development Logic	Estimated Cost, 2018 ($ million)	(Possible) Funding Sources	Timescale
70	IND-RD-070	Improvement of NH 51 between Tura and Dalu connecting with the India-Bangladesh border	As above	79	As above	2018–2020
71	IND-RD-071	Shillong–Dawki (NH 40) including rehabilitation of the Dawki bridge on the India-Bangladesh border	As above	31	Government (National Highways and Infrastructure Development Corporation) and JICA	2018–2022
72	IND-RD-072	Construction of a new extradosed bridge over the Feni River at Sabroom in southern Tripura, connecting India and Bangladesh	As above`	13	Government	2017–2020
73	IND-RD-073	Khowai–Agartala link road	As above	85	Government	2019–2023
74	IND-RD-074	Improvement of NH 512 between km 82.4 and km 99.5, and between km 104.2 and km 106.6	As above	21	Government	2017–2022
75	IND-RD-075	Maram–Peren–Dimapur road in Manipur and Nagaland	Improved connectivity between India and Myanmar	360	As above	2019–2023
76	IND-RD-076	Four-laning of Imphal–Moirang, NH-150 in Manipur	As above	100	ADB	2021–2022
77	IND-RD-077	Hafflong–Tamelong via Lia Sang and Tavesam in Assam and Manipur	Improved connectivity within Assam and Manipur	300	As above	2019–2023
78	IND-RD-078	Divided four-lane road linking the Kohima and Kedima, Kromg, and Imphal section of NH 39 in Manipur	Improved connectivity between India and Myanmar	280	ADB	2021–2022
79	IND-RD-079	Ukhrul–Tolloi–Tadubi in Manipur	As above	230	As above	2021–2022
80	IND-RD-080	Ukhrul–Jessami, NH 202 in Manipur	As above	230	As above	2019–2023
81	IND-RD-081	Jiribam–Tipaimukh in Manipur	As above	210	As above	As above

continued on next page

Table continued

No.	Code	Project Description	BIMSTEC Development Logic	Estimated Cost, 2018 ($ million)	(Possible) Funding Sources	Timescale
82	IND-RD-082	Aizawl–Tuipang connecting with the Kaladan multimodal transport corridor	As above	946	JICA	2021–2022
83	IND-RD-083	Improvement of Imphal–Kangchup–Tamenglong–Tousem–Haflong	As above	184	Government and ADB	2021–2022
84	IND-RD-084	Development of the Gangtok Highway (Bagrakot–Menia) in Sikkim	Improved connectivity in Sikkim State	150	Government and ADB	2021–2022
85	IND-RD-085	Construction and upgrading of alternate highway to Gangtok from Bagrakot to Kafer	Improved connectivity between India, Bhutan, and Nepal	48	Government	2018–2020
86	IND-RD-086	Development of the Siliguri–Mirik–Darjeeling link road	Improved connectivity between India and Nepal	150	ADB	2020–2021
87	IND-RD-087	Gelephu (Bhutan) to Samthaibari (near Hapachara in Assam)	Improved connectivity between Bhutan and India	117	India	2019–2021
88	IND-RD-088	Additional approach roads to ICPs or land ports (ICP Raxual, Bihar approach road [7 km], ICP Bihar; Jogbani, Bihar approach road [1 km]; ICP Rupaidiha, Uttar Pradesh approach road [1.5 km]; ICP Sunaulli approach road [0.5 km], ICP Moreh approach road [3 km])	Links to border crossings through ICPs	To be specified	India	2018–2020
89	IND-RD-089	Upgrading of Paikan–Tura	Improved connectivity in Assam and Meghalaya States	205	Government of India	2020–2021
90	IND-RD-090	Four-laning of Forbesganj–Jogbani section (9.3 km) along NH 57A in Bihar	Improved connectivity between India, Bhutan, and Nepal	38	Government	2018–2019
91	NEP-RD-091	Connection between the ICP and the ICD bypass road at Birgunj	Linking of main border development with national road network	12	Government, and Birgunj Municipality	2018–2020

continued on next page

Table continued

No.	Code	Project Description	BIMSTEC Development Logic	Estimated Cost, 2018 ($ million)	(Possible) Funding Sources	Timescale
92	NEP-RD-092	Widening of Belhiya (Nepal) and Sunauli (India) to Bhairahawa–Butawal Road (23 km) to six lanes to improve trade route in west	Provision of extra capacity on an important trade route in western Nepal	58	Government	2012–2019
93	NEP-RD-093	Construction of Mahakali Bridge border link to India	Reduction in transport costs for bilateral traffic	36	Government	2016–2020
94	NEP-RD-094	Bardibas–Janakpur–Jaynagarand–Dhalkebar–Janakpur–Bhittamond Roads	Improvement of border link road in eastern Nepal	65+	Government	2012–2025
95	NEP-RD-095	Widening of the Birgunj bypass to four lanes	Provision of extra capacity for traffic generated by ICD volumes	47	ADB and government	2016–2021
96	NEP-RD-096	Madan Bhandari Highway (1,200 km)	Improvement of important domestic connection to enhance trade	1,940	Not yet specified	2016–2023
97	REG-RD-097 (IND and NEP)	Construction of Mechi Bridge	Improved connectivity between India and Nepal	25	ADB and India	2016–2021
98	REG-RD-098 (MYA and THA)	Border link project between Mae Sot (Thailand) and Myawaddy (Myanmar), including a bypass road and new border checkpoints	Expediting trade between Thailand and Myanmar	122	Government of Thailand	2015–2019
1.3 Port Access Roads						
99	BAN-RD-099	Chattogram Port Access Road (13 km)	Link to Chattogram Port, a major BIMSTEC gateway	150	ADB	2021–2023
100	IND-RD-100	Elevated expressway to Chennai Port, along a new alignment	Improved access to major BIMSTEC port gateway	200	Government	2020–2023
101	MYA-RD-101	Improvement of Thilawa-East Dagon Road (8.7 km, two lanes)	Linking the port and SEZ with Yangon and the national road network	42 (JPY 4.613 billion)	JICA loan	2015–2019
102	SRL-RD-102	Southerly extension of Colombo-Katunayake Expressway with a new six-lane Kelani Bridge at Peliyagoda, plus associated roadway	Improved connectivity to port access road from the north	400 (60 for the bridge and 340 for the extension)	JICA (bridge); funding source not yet identified for the extension	2018–2020 (bridge) and 2018–2025 (extension)

continued on next page

Table continued

No.	Code	Project Description	BIMSTEC Development Logic	Estimated Cost, 2018 ($ million)	(Possible) Funding Sources	Timescale
103	SRL-RD-103	Port Access Elevated Highway Project (5.8 km)	Reduction of urban congestion and transport costs at access point to major BIMSTEC port	592	ADB	2018–2021
104	SRL-RD-104	Phase III of the Outer Circular Highway (9.0 km, including 5.5 km elevated)	Improvement of connectivity with both the port and the international airport	500	PRC (China Exim Bank)	2017–2019 (50% completed as of May 2018)
105	SRL-RD-105	Colombo Elevated Expressway Program to connect the Outer Circular Highway with the center of the city (100% elevated)	Reduction of traffic in congested area near port	950	PPP	2018–2022
106	SRL-RD-106	Stage 4 of Southern Expressway connecting Matara with the Hambantota seaport and the new Mattala International Airport	Linking of new seaport and new airport	1,600	PRC (China Exim Bank)	2016–2020 (50% completed as of May 2018)
107	SRL-RD-107	Ratmalana (Colombo) Airport to Southern Expressway (10 km)	Connecting airport to port(s)	600	Not yet identified	2020–2025
108	SRL-RD-108	Eastern Expressway (Dambulla–Trincomalee, 90 km)	Connection to new eastern port	540	Not yet identified	2025–2030
1.4 Road-Based Buddhist and Temple Tourism Circuits						
109	REG-RD-109	Technical assistance to identify road-based Buddhist and temple tourism circuits	Promotion of intra-BIMSTEC tourism and cultural exchange(s) based on historical cultural ties	0.5	Not yet identified	2019
1.5 Coordination of Road Programs						
110	REG-RD-110	Sharing of relevant road planning data through a BIMSTEC database	Increasing efficiency of road investments by ensuring availability of data on road projects and conditions in neighboring member states	0.5	Not yet identified	2019–2020 (initial development)
1.6 Through-Transport Agreements						
111	REG-RD-111	Formulation of a regional through-transport agreement among BIMSTEC member states	Increasing efficiency of international road transport by avoiding the need for transshipment at border crossings	1 (for costs associated with meetings)	Member states	2019–2020 (negotiations and finalization)

continued on next page

Table continued

No.	Code	Project Description	BIMSTEC Development Logic	Estimated Cost, 2018 ($ million)	(Possible) Funding Sources	Timescale
112	REG-RD-112	Phased implementation of through-transport agreements	As above	3 (for costs associated with meetings)	As above	2021–2028 (phased implementation)
2. Railways and Rail Transport						
2.1 Rail Connectivity between Ports, Dry Ports, and Borders, and Their Hinterlands						
113	BAN-RW-001	Construction of third and fourth dual gauge lines between Dhaka and Tongi and dual gauge double line between Dhaka and Joydevpur	Improved rail connectivity with India	133	India dollar line of credit	2012–2019
114	BAN-RW-002	Construction of dual-gauge, double rail line and conversion of existing rail line into dual gauge between Akhaura and Laksham	Mainline upgrading to increase freight and passenger capacity between the largest port and capital of Bangladesh; potential link to North East India	784	ADB and EIB	2014–2020
115	BAN-RW-003	Construction of Sheikh Mujib Railway Bridge (parallel to the Jamuna Bridge) with twin dual-gauge lines	Improved rail connectivity with India by removing current restrictions	1,173	JICA	2016–2023 (including project preparation)
116	BAN-RW-004	Padma Bridge Rail Link	Improved rail connectivity with India	4,216	PRC	2016–2022
117	BAN-RW-005	Construction of single line dual gauge railway track from Dohazari to Cox's Bazar via Ramu to Gundum near Myanmar	Improved connectivity between India and Myanmar	2,173	ADB	2010–2022
118	BAN-RW-006	Construction of Khulna-Mongla Port rail line	Increased freight and passenger capacity and improved rail connectivity with India through construction of mainline link between port and the capital	458	ILOC	2010–2020
119	BAN-RW-007	Construction of broad gauge double track line in section between Khulna and Darshana junction	Improved rail connectivity with India	446	ILOC	2018–2020
120	BAN-RW-008	Construction of double track high-speed railway from Dhaka to Chattogram via Cumilla–Laksham	Provision of a high-speed rail link between the largest port and capital of Bangladesh	3,734	ADB	2021–2025

continued on next page

Table continued

No.	Code	Project Description	BIMSTEC Development Logic	Estimated Cost, 2018 ($ million)	(Possible) Funding Sources	Timescale
121	BAN-RW-009	Introduction of electric traction (including overhead catenary and substation) along the Narayanganj–Dhaka–Joydevpur rail section	Modernization of rail link between the largest port and capital of Bangladesh	67	Not yet identified	2018–2020
122	BAN-RW-010	Construction of dual gauge railway between Bogura and Shahid M. Monsur Ali	Improved rail connectivity with India	796	ILOC	2017–2022
123	BAN-RW-011	Construction of second rail cum road bridge on Karnaphuli River at Kalurghat	Connection to the south and Myanmar	241	Economic Development Cooperation Fund (Republic of Korea)	2018–2020
124	BAN-RW-012	Construction of broad gauge rail line from Bhanga junction (Faridpur) to Payra Port via Barishal	Mainline facilities to link major new port and the capital, increasing freight capacity	3,414	Not yet identified	2018–2020
125	BAN-RW-013	Construction of broad gauge rail line between Chilahati and Chilahati border	Improved rail connectivity with India	10	Government	2018–2020
126	BAN-RW-014	Conversion of existing meter gauge double line to dual gauge between Tongi and Bhairab	Increased freight and passenger capacity with mainline facilities between port and capital city, and improved rail connectivity with India	751	Not yet identified	2021–2025
127	BAN-RW-015	Conversion of meter gauge double line to dual gauge between Bhairab Bazar and Akhaura including rebuilding of the existing Bhairab and Titas bridges	As above	387	As above	2021–2025
128	BAN-RW-016	Conversion of existing meter gauge double line to dual gauge between Laksam and Chattogram	As above	1,521	As above	2021–2025
129	IND-RW-017	Eastern Dedicated Freight Corridor, I and II	Providing dedicated freight capacity on busy route from Kolkata	3,109	World Bank, government, and PPP	2014–2019
130	IND-RW-018	Double tracking Bongaigaon–Kamakhya in Assam	Providing additional connectivity between India and Bangladesh	320	Government	2017–2019

continued on next page

Table continued

No.	Code	Project Description	BIMSTEC Development Logic	Estimated Cost, 2018 ($ million)	(Possible) Funding Sources	Timescale
131	IND-RW-019	Dhubri in Assam to Medhnipathar in Meghalaya with a double line rail cum road bridge over the Brahmaputra River at Dhubri (79 km)	Providing additional connectivity between India and Bangladesh	1,100	India	Timing not yet specified
132	IND-RW-020	New Belonia–Feni line connecting with the India-Bangladesh border	As above	Not yet estimated	India	Timing not yet specified, but survey completed
133	IND-RW-021	Radhikapur–Birol rail link	As above	Not yet estimated	India	Timing not yet specified, but survey ongoing
134	MYA-RW-022	Yangon–Mandalay Railway Improvement Project (620 km)	Increasing capacity on primary north-south rail link	2,500	JICA	2017–2025
135	MYA-RW-023	Upgrading of Yangon–Pyay rail line (226 km)	Increasing capacity on primary western North-South rail link	Under negotiation	ADB	Feasibility study ongoing (by ADB TA team); construction not yet programmed
136	NEP-RW-024	Construction of East–West Railway (945 km)	Provision of new international linkage with time and cost savings	7,000	Not yet specified	2018–2028
137	NEP-RW-025	Construction of Birgunj–Kathmandu Railway (115 km)	Provision of linkage with India and other member states	2,500	Not yet identified	2018–2028
138	SRL-RW-026	Matara to Kataragama Railway Extension Project (120 km)	Enhanced rail connectivity with sea and airports in southern Sri Lanka, including Hambantota seaport and Mattala Rajapaksa Airport	278	PRC (China Exim Bank) for Phase 1 (Matara–Beliatta, 26 km)	2014–2028
139	SRL-RW-027	Kurunegala to Habarana new rail project (80 km)	Connection of hinterlands and air and sea ports; improved rail connectivity between western, northwestern, and north central and eastern provinces of Sri Lanka, and serving as a catalyst for proposed East–West economic corridor linking Colombo and Trincomalee	980	Not yet identified	2014–2028
140	SRL-RW-028	Colombo Suburban Railway Development Project	Development of multimodal transport hubs and new rail and road links connecting major air and sea ports in the Colombo Metropolitan Area, thus, improving connectivity with BIMSTEC countries	1,134	ADB	2018–2028

continued on next page

Table continued

No.	Code	Project Description	BIMSTEC Development Logic	Estimated Cost, 2018 ($ million)	(Possible) Funding Sources	Timescale
141	THA-RW-029	Double tracking of East Coast line linking Chachoengsao–Klong Sip Kao–Kaeng Khoi	Improving rail access from the north of Laem Chabang	303	Government (State Railway of Thailand)	2016–2019
142	THA-RW-030	Increased efficiency of railway transport through double tracking of BIMSTEC-relevant lines	Serving increased passenger and freight transport demand	To be confirmed.	Government (State Railway of Thailand)	2018–2025
143	REG-RW-031 (BAN and IND)	Akhaura-Agartala rail link (new 12-km line)	Improved rail connectivity between Bangladesh and India	144	India	2016–2021
144	REG-RW-032 (BAN and IND)	New line linking Haldibari-Chilahati (10 km)	Improved rail connectivity between Bangladesh and India, and with Bhutan	12 (for segment in IND)	India	2019–2021
145	REG-RW-033 (IND and MYA)	New lines linking Jiribam-Imphal (125 km) in Manipur, Imphal-Moreh (111 km) connecting with the India–Myanmar border, and a new line linking Moreh–Tamu–Kalay (128 km) onward to Mandalay	Linking of India and Myanmar by rail	Not yet estimated (1,000 for Jiribam-Imphal)	As above	2017–2028 (to be confirmed)
146	REG-RW-034 (MYA and THA)	Laem Chabang–Dawei Rail Link via Kanchanaburi	Linking of two major port sites	5,100 (upgrading estimated to 2015 cost to 2018 values; about 55% of the cost would be in THA, and 45% of the cost would be in MYA)	Thailand and other development partner(s) (Myanmar seeks assistance for Dawei-Hteekkhee segment)	Initially postponed due to low rate of return in 2015 feasibility study; another feasibility study may be conducted in 2019 after the plans for the Eastern Economic Corridor becomes firm
2.2 Rail Connectivity for Landlocked member states							
147	REG-RW-035 (IND and BHU)	Development of Kokhrajhar (Assam)-Gelephu (Bhutan) (57 km), Pathsala (Assam) –Nanglam (Bhutan)(51 km), Rangiya (Assam) –Samdrupjongkhar (Bhutan)(48 km),	Project to provide Bhutan with intermodal transport options	To be estimated	India	2019–2028 and beyond

continued on next page

Table continued

No.	Code	Project Description	BIMSTEC Development Logic	Estimated Cost, 2018 ($ million)	(Possible) Funding Sources	Timescale
		Banarhat (West Bengal) –Samtse (Bhutan)(23 km), and Hasimara (West Bengal)–Phuentsholing (Bhutan)(18 km)				
148	REG-RW-036 (IND and NEP)	Development of (i) Jaynagar–Bardibas (69 km, including 3 km in India and 66 km in Nepal), (ii) Jogbani–Biratnagar (19 km), (iii) Nepalganj–Nepalganj Road (12 km), (iv) Nautanwa–Bhairahawa (15 km), and (v) New Jalpaiguri–Kakarbitta (46 km)	Project to provide Nepal with multimodal/intermodal transport options on more routes to Kolkata (and onward to other BIMSTEC countries)	900+	India	2018–2025; the first two (sub) projects are ongoing
2.3 Rail-Based Buddhist and Temple Tourism Circuits						
149	REG-RW-037	Technical assistance to identify rail-based Buddhist and temple tourism circuits	Promotion of intra-BIMSTEC tourism and cultural exchange(s) based on historical cultural ties	0.5	Not yet identified	2019
2.4 Coordination of Railway Programs						
150	REG-RW-038	Sharing of relevant railway planning data through a BIMSTEC database	Increasing efficiency of railway investments by ensuring availability of data on railway projects and conditions in neighboring member states	0.3	Not yet identified	2019–2020 (initial development)
3. Ports and Maritime Development						
3.1 Development of Deeper Water Ports						
3.2 Improvement of Container Handling Performance						
151	BAN-PM-001	Patenga container terminal at Chattogram	New container facilities in congested port handling BIMSTEC traffic	220	Government (Port Authority)	2017–2019
152	BAN-PM-002	Karnaphuli Container Terminal at Chattogram	As above	200	As above	2022–2026
153	BAN-PM-003	Construction of Laldia multipurpose terminal at Chattogram, about 4 km upstream of Karnaphuli River	Greenfield container and bulk cargo terminal potentially serving BIMSTEC traffic	Estimation at final stage	PPP	2019–2021
154	BAN-PM-004	Development of Matarbari Port in Cox's Bazar	As above	320 (JPY 3.5 billion)	JICA	2020–2023

continued on next page

Table continued

No.	Code	Project Description	BIMSTEC Development Logic	Estimated Cost, 2018 ($ million)	(Possible) Funding Sources	Timescale
155	BAN-PM-005	Bay multipurpose terminal on west coast of Chattogram, 6 km from Chattogram Port (one multipurpose and two container terminals)	Facilitation of growing external trade, including trade to BIMSTEC member states	2,100	Not yet finalized	2019–2021
156	BAN-PM-006	Payra Port Development Project (first terminal, connecting road, bridge over the Andermanik River and related facilities)	New sea port to serve southern Bangladesh and possibly Bhutan and Nepal	474	Government	2018–2021
157	BAN-PM-007	Upgrading of Mongla Port (e.g., construction of container terminals including cargo handling equipment, tower, container delivery yard)	Improvement of Bangladesh's second port, which serves Bhutan, India, and Nepal	656	Government and ILOC	2018–2021
158	IND-PM-008	Development of Haldia Port	Assistance of shipments for bulk traffic from BIMSTEC countries	280	Kolkata Port Trust	2019–2025
159	IND-PM-009	Development of major port in Kanyakumari District, Tamil Nadu	Provision of additional port capacity, in South East Asia	3,059 (Phase 1: 1,064)	SPV (30% equity, 70% external loan)	2021–2025
160	IND-PM-010	V.O. Chidambaranar Port Trust, Tuticorin (deepening harbor basin and approach channel, construction of breakwater and bubble protection bund, strengthening of berths 1–6, widening of port entrance channel)	As above	462	Government and ADB	2021–2025
161	IND-PM-011	Development of deep sea port at Tajpur (near Digha) along the coast of West Bengal	Provision of additional container traffic capacity to take larger vessels than at Diamond Harbour	747	EPC or PPP mode, and government for funding gap	2021–2025
162	IND-PM-012	Expansion of Inner Harbour at Paradip Port, 210 nautical miles south of Kolkata and 260 nautical miles north of Visakhapatnam	Provision of additional port capacity, in South East Asia	226	Government and ADB	2021–2025

continued on next page

Table continued

No.	Code	Project Description	BIMSTEC Development Logic	Estimated Cost, 2018 ($ million)	(Possible) Funding Sources	Timescale
163	IND-PM-013	Expansion of Outer Harbour near the south breakwater at Paradip Port	As above	2,450	Government and ADB	2021–2025
164	IND-PM-014	Augmentation of capacity of Haldia Dock Complex, Kolkata Port Trust (new lock gate in existing dock and basin and modification of existing lock gate)	Increased capacity at major BIMSTEC gateway	200	Government and ADB	2021–2025
165	IND-PM-015	Development of a new port at Sirkazh, Tamil Nadu	Provision of additional port capacity, in South East Asia	450	Not yet specified	2021–2025
166	MYA-PM-016	New port facilities at Thilawa Special Economic Zone	New port complex to handle intra-BIMSTEC trade	175 (JPY 19.087 billion)	Government, JICA, and PPP	2016–2019
167	MYA-PM-017	New port facilities at Dawei	Potential new maritime link between South and Southeast Asia	3,050	Investor	Not yet programmed
168	MYA-PM-018	Development of deep sea port at Kyaukphyu	Construction of a new container port in western Myanmar	1,050	Investor	Not yet programmed
169	MYA-PM-019	Improvement of container handling performance of ports	Improved port efficiency	Not yet estimated	PPP	2014–2025
170	SRL-PM-020	Extension of East Terminal at Colombo	Facilitation of the handling of international cargo, including transshipment and bilateral traffic with other BIMSTEC members states	430–1,150	Government (Sri Lanka Ports Authority; 400 m of container yard) and BOT	2014–2022
171	SRL-PM-021	Construction of West Terminal at Colombo	Provision of additional capacity to handle mega container ships	840	BOT	2023–2026
172	SRL-PM-022	Business development plan covering Colombo, Hambantota, and Trincomalee ports, identifying their specific niches and how to attract new business	Clarification of the roles of the ports in handling BIMSTEC traffic	0.35 (0.25 for Colombo and Trincomalee and 0.10 for Hambantota)	(PRC for Hambantota); no funding yet for other two	2019–2020
173	THA-PM-023	Development of Phase III at Laem Chabang	Provision of additional capacity, including for handling of BIMSTEC traffic	1,500	Port Authority of Thailand and others	2019–2022 (feasibility study now under review)

continued on next page

Table continued

No.	Code	Project Description	BIMSTEC Development Logic	Estimated Cost, 2018 ($ million)	(Possible) Funding Sources	Timescale
3.3 Development of Coastal Shipping						
174	REG-PM-024 (BAN, IND, MYA, SRL, and THA)	Study to develop coastal shipping	Develop regional trade by short-sea shipping	Not yet estimated	Not yet identified, but ADB support for initial study	2018–2028
175	REG-PM-025 (BAN, IND, MYA, SRL, and THA)	Investment projects to improve coastal shipping in the BIMSTEC region	As above	Not yet estimated	Not yet identified	2020–2023
4. Inland Water Transport						
176	REG-IW-001 (BAN, BHU, NEP, IND, MYA)	Study of opportunities to improve inland water transport in the BIMSTEC region	Historically important mode, which offers potential for sustainable, economically viable cross-border transport, and multimodal/ intermodal connectivity	3	Not yet identified	2019–2020
177	REG-IW-002(BAN, BHU, NEP, IND, MYA)	Investment projects to improve inland water transport in the BIMSTEC region	As above	Not yet specified	Not yet identified	2020–2023
178	IND-IW-003	Development of National Waterway 1 (Allahabad–Haldia, 1,620 km)	Improved connectivity between India and Bangladesh	800	World Bank and the Government of India	
179	IND-IW-004	Development of National Waterway 2 on the Brahmaputra River from India–Bangladesh border at Dhubri to Sadiya (891 km)	As above	Not yet estimated	As above	2019–2023
5. Civil Aviation and Airports Development 5.1 Expansion of Airport Capacity 5.2 Air Freight Facilities and Services 5.3 Support Facilities for LCC Operations						
180	BAN-CA-001	Improvement of parking aprons for cargo at Hazrat Shahjalal International Airport, Dhaka	Improved air connectivity with international cities and regional cities of Bangladesh	21.16	Government	2016–2019

continued on next page

Appendix 5 123

Table continued

No.	Code	Project Description	BIMSTEC Development Logic	Estimated Cost, 2018 ($ million)	(Possible) Funding Sources	Timescale
181	BAN-CA-002	Airport safety and security system improvement, Bangladesh	As above	25.23	JICA and government	2014–2018
182	BAN-CA-003	Hazrat Shahjalal International Airport Expansion Project, Dhaka (Phase 1: construction of Third Passenger Terminal, cargo building, taxiways, apron)	As above	1,660	JICA	2016–2022
183	BAN-CA-004	Hazrat Shahjalal International Airport Expansion Project, Dhaka (Phase 2)	As above	Not yet estimated	Not yet identified	2025–2028
184	BAN-CA-005	Development of Shah Amanat International Airport, Chattogram (strengthening of existing runway and taxiway)	As above	68.5	Government	2018–2020
185	BAN-CA-006	Further development of Shah Amanat International Airport, Chattogram (construction of parallel taxiway)	As above	Not yet estimated	Not yet identified	2020–2024
186	BAN-CA-007	Development of Osmani International Airport, Sylhet (strengthening of existing runway and taxiway)	As above	54.4	Government	2017–2019
187	BAN-CA-008	Development of international airport at Cox's Bazar (extension of runway and provision of communication equipment, and construction of terminal building)	As above	143.8	Government and Civil Aviation Authority of Bangladesh	2009–2019
188	BAN-CA-009	Expansion of Cox's Bazar Airport (Phase 2: runway extension)	As above	452.9	Government	2019–2021

continued on next page

Table continued

No.	Code	Project Description	BIMSTEC Development Logic	Estimated Cost, 2018 ($ million)	(Possible) Funding Sources	Timescale
189	BAN-CA-010	Expansion of Osmani International Airport, Sylhet (Phase 1: passenger terminal building, cargo complex, fire station, control tower, maintenance building, apron, and taxiway)	As above	289.2	Government	2019–2021
190	BAN-CA-011	Upgrading of Saidpur Airport	As above	756.3	ILOC	2020–2024
191	BAN-CA-012	Development of Bangabandhu Sheikh Mujib International Airport to serve central Bangladesh	As above	Not yet estimated	As above	2025–2028 and beyond
192	BHU-CA-013	Further expansion and development of Paro Airport (domestic terminal, runway resurfacing and widening)	Expanded capacity to handle forecast growth including BIMSTEC flights	5	As above	2018–2023
193	BHU-CA-014	Expansion of Gelephu Airport (feasibility and design studies, construction of new 3,000 m runway and associated river diversion, ILS and runway lighting system, apron taxiway, terminal building, hangar, cargo building)	Possible new location for intra-BIMSTEC flights to serve larger aircraft, to serve larger aircraft, which would accommodate flight diversions during bad weather at Paro Airport and provide for the transport of supplies during emergencies as directed	200 (including 20 for runway)	As above	2018–2028
194	IND-CA-015	Further development of Delhi Airport (into a "Hub Airport of Asia"), with additional runway, terminal expansion, and apron modification (while Terminal 2 has been recommissioned, phased redevelopment of Terminal 1 and expansion of Terminal 3 have been planned)	Additional capacity to handle intra-BIMSTEC flights among others	1,800	PPP	2018–2025
195	IND-CA-016	Development of Greater Noida Airport, in Uttar Pradesh, about 60 km from Delhi	Greenfield airport that will handle intra-BIMSTEC flights among others	3,100	As above	2019–2022

continued on next page

Table continued

No.	Code	Project Description	BIMSTEC Development Logic	Estimated Cost, 2018 ($ million)	(Possible) Funding Sources	Timescale
196	IND-CA-017	Expansion of Chennai Airport including terminal development	Additional capacity for major BIMSTEC airport hub	Not yet estimated	As above	2019–2020
197	IND-CA-018	New (Chennai) Sriperumbudur Airport Development Project, as part of Chennai–Bangalore Industrial Corridor Project	As above	As above	As above	2020–2023
198	IND-CA-019	Guwahati Airport Expansion Project	Development of major airport in North East India as a regional hub under the Udan project (with planned air connectivity to/from Bangkok, Dhaka, Kathmandu, Kuala Lumpur, Singapore, and Yangon)	As above	As above	To be specified
199	MYA-CA-020	Expansion of Yangon International Airport (construction and expansion of new international and domestic terminal, aprons, and related facilities)	Increased capacity at airport in Myanmar's largest city, including for intra-BIMSTEC flights and possible hub role	666	PPP	2014–2019
200	MYA-CA-021	Construction of new Hanthawaddy International Airport (77 km northeast of Yangon, near Bago), plus road and rail access, and ancillary facilities (e.g., aviation fuel supply; hotel, commercial, and administrative complexes)	Construction of new international airport to serve as a major gateway of Myanmar and regional hub, serving rapidly increasing traffic demand and providing airport users high-quality, world-class airport services	Not yet estimated	PPP, with assistance of the Government of Japan (with the Ministry of Land, Infrastructure and Transport, Japan, as facilitator)	2020–2027
201	MYA-CA-022	Development of new cargo terminal at Mandalay International Airport	Accommodation of high-density, scheduled international flights at an airport in central Myanmar, establishing a direct air route and new aviation cargo hub, linking Europe and points in Asia	4.8	Private	2018–2019
202	MYA-CA-023	Development of LCC terminal at the new Hanthawaddy Airport	Dedicated terminal to support LCC operations	Not yet estimated	Not yet identified	2019–2024
203	MYA-CA-024	Introduction of regulatory framework for LCC operations	Formulation and implementation of necessary regulatory framework and practices for LCC operations	1.0	As above	2019–2020

continued on next page

Table continued

No.	Code	Project Description	BIMSTEC Development Logic	Estimated Cost, 2018 ($ million)	(Possible) Funding Sources	Timescale
204	NEP-CA-025	Major development of Kathmandu Airport (Tribhuvan International Airport Capacity Enhancement Investment Program)	Focusing on infrastructure and technology, improvement of air connectivity and enhancement of capacity by attracting larger aircraft, improving terminal facilities, and enhancing safety	59	ADB and Civil Aviation Authority of Nepal	2019–2021
205	NEP-CA-026	Development of a second international airport on a greenfield site at Nijgadh, Bara, 135 km south of Kathmandu	Provision of a full-fledged international airport to accommodate all types of aircraft; easing of pressure on Tribhuvan International Airport and serving as an alternate airport for all types of aircraft in all weather conditions	650	Not yet identified	2018–2025
206	NEP-CA-027	Expansion and upgrading of Gautam Buddha Airport, about 280 km west of Kathmandu (including an action plan, in collaboration with the private sector, for airport operation)	Upgrading of the facility to an international airport (Category E as per ICAO guidelines)	65 (as part of the South Asia Tourism Infrastructure Project with ADB support)	ADB (80%), OPEC (10%), government (10%); bill of quantities model contract	2013–2019
207	NEP-CA-028	Construction of a new regional/international airport at Pokhara (including an action plan, in collaboration with the private sector, for airport operation)	Promotion of connectivity with BIMSTEC countries and to promote tourism	230	PRC (China Exim Bank)	2017–2022
208	NEP-CA-029	Air Freight Facilitation Project	Promotion of air freight traffic at Tribhuvan International Airport and other airports in Nepal	Not yet specified	Not yet identified	2023–2025
209	SRL-CA-030	Development of Bandaranaike International Airport, Colombo, including a new passenger terminal with two piers (handling an additional 9 million passengers per year) and construction of new apron and taxiways	Expansion of Sri Lanka's main airport connection with other BIMSTEC countries, which acts as a regional "minihub"	413	JICA	2017–2020
210	SRL-CA-031	Service delivery improvements at Mattala Rajapaksa International Airport in southeast Sri Lanka	Enhanced regional and local air connectivity with improved operations	To be determined	PPPs with support of the Civil Aviation Authority of India	2020–2028

continued on next page

Table continued

No.	Code	Project Description	BIMSTEC Development Logic	Estimated Cost, 2018 ($ million)	(Possible) Funding Sources	Timescale
211	THA-CA-032	Suvarnabhumi Airport Expansion Project in Bangkok (including third runway)	Expansion of major BIMSTEC aviation hub	2,100	Airports of Thailand PLC	2016–2023
212	THA-CA-033	Development of Mae Sot (International) Airport (new passenger terminal, runway strengthening and extension, construction of apron and taxiways)	Improved air connectivity with Thai regional city on the border with Myanmar, along the India–Myanmar–Thailand Trilateral Highway	36.4	Government	2016–2021
6. Multimodal and Intermodal Transport						
213	BAN-MM-001	Second rail-connected ICD in Dhaka, at Dhirasram, in Gazipur	For relief of road and (Chattogram) port congestion because the first ICD in Dhaka exceeds capacity	200 (100 from ADB, and 100 from PPP)	ADB and PPP	2017–2020
214	BAN-MM-002	Establishment of road network from economic zones to adjacent land and sea ports through widening of existing roads and national highways	Facilitation of multimodal and intermodal connectivity	Not yet specified	Not yet identified	To be programmed
215	BHU-MM-003	Development of Gelephu Transport Hub	Diversification of entry or exit points for BIMSTEC trade and transport	Not yet specified	Not yet identified	2018–2028
216	MYA-MM-004	Yangon–Dagon ICD	Development of multimodal and intermodal facility to handle container traffic	16	Private	2018–2021
217	MYA-MM-005	Yangon Region Dry Port (YwaThaGyi)	Linking Yangon Airport, Yangon–Bago rail line, and eventually Hanthawaddy Airport (as well as Yangon inland waterway ports)	40	PPP	2017–2019
218	MYA-MM-006	Mandalay Region Dry Port (Myitnge)	Linking Mandalay–Yangon Rail Line	40	PPP	2017–2019
219	MYA-MM-007	Establishment of logistics hub and truck or trailer terminal in the Wartayar Industrial Zone (northwestern Yangon)	Development of multimodal and intermodal facility to handle container traffic	15–20	PPP	To be programmed
220	SRL-MM-008	Pettah (Colombo) Multimodal Transport Hub	Facilitation of multimodal and intermodal connectivity	5,000	PPP with gap financing (if required) by government plus 1.1 from for feasibility study financed by AFD	2018–2028

continued on next page

Table continued

No.	Code	Project Description	BIMSTEC Development Logic	Estimated Cost, 2018 ($ million)	(Possible) Funding Sources	Timescale
221	REG-MM-009 (IND and MYA)	Kaladan Multimodal Transit Transport Project	Potential use of inland water transport as an alternative to a longer road route	453	India (Ministry of External Affairs)	2008–2020
222	REG-MM-010	Development of software arrangements for seamless multimodal and intermodal movement (e.g., EDI connectivity between ports and ICDs or land customs stations for online clearance, protocols, use of secure seals)	Facilitation of multimodal/intermodal connectivity	5	Not yet identified	2019–2021
7. Trade Facilitation						
7.1 Development of Border Infrastructure and Facilities						
223	BAN-TF-001	Improvement of Benapole (opposite Petrapole, India) and Burimari (opposite Changrabandha, India) (Road Connectivity Project), plus automation of Benapole land port	Provision of additional processing and storage capacity at busy BIMSTEC border crossings	18 (of 198)	ADB	2013–2019
224	BAN-TF-002	Modernization of customs facilities and trade facilitation at seven Land Customs Stations, including laboratories (Banglabandha, Burimari, Hilli, Nakugaon, Sona Masjid, Tamabil, and Teknaf)	Facilitation of intra-BIMSTEC trade	Not yet estimated	ADB	2019–2021
225	BAN-TF-003	Development of Sheolla, Ramgarh, Bhomra, and Benapole ports (the first two are greenfield sites), under the Bangladesh Regional Connectivity Project 1	As above	87 (75 from World Bank)	World Bank and government	2017–2021
226	BAN-TF-004	Development of Dhanua Kamalpur land port in Jalmalpur opposite Meghalaya, India	As above	7	Government	2018–2020

continued on next page

Table continued

No.	Code	Project Description	BIMSTEC Development Logic	Estimated Cost, 2018 ($ million)	(Possible) Funding Sources	Timescale
227	IND-TF-005	Development of ICPs, ongoing or planned (Dawki [Bangladesh border], Jaigaon [Bhutan border]; Banbasa, Bhithamore, Panitanki, Rupaidiha, and Sunauli [Nepal border], and Changrabandha, Fulbari, Ghojadanga, Hili, Kawrpuichhuah, Mahadipur, and Sutarkandi, Bangladesh border])	As above	Not fully specified	Government	2018–2028
228	IND-TF-006	Development of rail siding logistics hubs within Raxaul, Jogbani, Petrapole, Hili, Nischintapur, and Sabroom land ports	Facilitation of the movement of multimodal container or noncontainer cargo across borders	To be specified	Government	2019–2023
229	NEP-TF-007	Development of four ICPs at main border crossings with India, including laboratories (Birgunj, Biratnagar, Bhairawaha, and Nepalganj)	Reduction of congestion and transaction costs border crossings	91	India	2012–2023 (Birgunj completed in 2018, Biratnagar completed in 2020)
230	REG-TF-008 (IND and MYA)	Development of Tamu–Moreh border crossing	Improved border crossing and border access road along the Trilateral India–Myanmar–Thailand Highway	Not yet estimated	India	Not yet programmed
231	REG-TF-009 (IND and NEP)	Use of electronic cargo tracking system for off-border clearance along selected routes (and associated measures)	Facilitation of movements between India and Nepal	0.5 (TA approved on 3 September 2018 to support this activity and others)	ADB (Trade Facilitation Program)	2018–2019
232	REG-TF-010 (MYA and THA)	Development of a new Mae Sot–Myawaddy border crossing, including 21.4 km of road (also included in under border link roads)	Improved border crossing and border access road along the Trilateral India–Myanmar–Thailand Highway	122 (also indicated in above border link project)	Thailand	2015–2019

continued on next page

Table continued

No.	Code	Project Description	BIMSTEC Development Logic	Estimated Cost, 2018 ($ million)	(Possible) Funding Sources	Timescale
233	REG-TF-011 (MYA and THA)	Development of new Htee Kee and Baan Phu Nam Ron border crossing	New border crossing with Thailand to process cargo to and from Dawei	142 (THB 4.5 billion, also included in associated road project)	Thailand	2018–2022 (feasibility study under discussion between Ministry of Construction and NEDA, Thailand)
7.2 Development of ICDs						
234	BHU-TF-012	Construction of Allay Land Customs Station and access road (1.2 km) to Pasakha Industrial Estate	Reduction of congestion in Phuentsholing, at main entry or exit point for BIMSTEC trade and transport	17.45	ADB (operations and management under PPP)	2016–2019
235	BHU-TF-013	Development of Pasakha Dry Port	Facilitation of clearance at main entry or exit point for BIMSTEC trade and transport	30	Not yet identified (World Bank support for the detailed project report)	2018–2023
236	BHU-TF-014	Development of Nganglam Dry Port	Diversification of entry or exit points for BIMSTEC trade and transport	Not yet specified	Not yet identified	2019–2028
237	NEP-TF-015	Development of ICD in Kanchanpur District	Facilitation of southwestern Nepal trade	Not yet estimated	Government	2023–2028
238	SRI-TF-016	Construction of "cargo village" or customs inspection yard to centralize container freight stations associated with Colombo Port now scattered around the city	Improved performance of Colombo Port, the largest in the BIMSTEC region	100	Not yet identified	2020–2025
7.3 Simplification and Harmonization of Import-Export and Transit Documentation						
239	REG-TF-017 (Member states along key corridors)	Extension of Prior Business Process Analyses	Rationalization of documentation requirements to reduce the time and costs for import/export-related procedures and required documents	0.5 (TA approved on 3 September 2018 to support this activity and others)	ADB	2019–2021
240	REG-TF-018 (Member states along key corridors)	SPS and TBT project to develop mutual recognition agreements and conformity assessment infrastructure on a hub-and-spoke basis	Removal of significant non-tariff barrier in the region	0.5	Not yet identified	2020–2022

continued on next page

Table continued

No.	Code	Project Description	BIMSTEC Development Logic	Estimated Cost, 2018 ($ million)	(Possible) Funding Sources	Timescale
241	NEP-TF-019	Customs reform and modernization—upgrading of ICT, simplification and harmonization of procedures and documentation, and development of a national single window	Reduction of cross-border transaction costs to facilitate trade	Not yet estimated for the entire period	ADB and World Bank	2012–2028
242	NEP-TF-020	Nepal-India Regional Trade and Transport Project (e.g., modernization of transport and transit arrangements, institutional capacity strengthening, and development of a trade portal)	Improvement of transit and processing arrangements to facilitate trade	99 (including the Kathmandu Container Freight Station above)	World Bank	2013–2019
7.4 Further Development of Automated Clearance Systems						
243	REG-TF-021	Development and/or refinement of NSWs	Reduction in time and cost of border crossing through integrated automation of procedures	100	Governments, ADB, World Bank, WCO	2018–2028
244	BAN-TF-022	Development of National Single Window, under Bangladesh Regional Connectivity Project 1	Reduction in time and cost of border through integrated automation of procedures	67	World Bank	2018–2020
245	BHU-TF-023	Development of a national trade portal	Facilitation of BIMSTEC trade through dissemination of comprehensive trade information	1	Not yet identified (ADB financed the feasibility study)	2018–2023 (a 2-year project within this period)
246	BHU-TF-024	Development of a national single window	Reduction in time and cost of border crossing through integrated automation of procedures	7	Not yet identified	2019–2028
247	BHU-TF-025	Development of Customs Management System	As above	6	Not yet identified	2018–2023
248	NEP-TF-026	Extending automation to additional border crossings with India (currently, 15 of 25 are automated)	Increased efficiency of BIMSTEC trade	To be estimated	Government	2017–2021

continued on next page

Table continued

No.	Code	Project Description	BIMSTEC Development Logic	Estimated Cost, 2018 ($ million)	(Possible) Funding Sources	Timescale
249	SRL-TF-027	Development of national single window linking the relevant government agencies and the trading community, following a national single window blueprint	Reduced transaction costs by expediting clearance procedures	To be estimated	World Bank (study portion ongoing, to be followed by implementation)	2017–2018 (study only); 2019–2028 (implementation)
250	SRL-TF-028	Risk management system study and capacity building for customs	Reduced physical inspection rate from the current 80+%, which will facilitate intra-BIMSTEC trade	1.25	ADB	2019–2021
7.5 Advanced Logistics						
251	REG-TF-029	Development of advanced logistics (e.g., supply chain management, LCL services, last mile or km logistics)	Improved logistics performance in BIMSTEC member states	5	Not yet identified (JICA has funded logistics improvement studies in other regions, e.g., Cambodia, Myanmar, the Middle East)	2019–2023
8. Human Resource Development						
8.1 Capacity Building in Transport and Related Sectors						
252	REG-HR-001	Establishment of a BIMSTEC (Multimodal) Transport Training Institute	Enhancement of skills of transport professionals in BIMSTEC member states	5	Not yet identified	2025–2028
253	BAN-HR-002	Establishment of public aviation university in Bangladesh	Enhancement of skills of aviation professionals	Not yet estimated	As above	2025–2028
254	BHU-HR-003	Institutional strengthening of engineers of the Department of Roads	Capacity building in the roads sector (e.g., road asset management, climate resilience, slope stabilization)	2.5	As above	2019–2028
255	BHU-HR-004	Climate resilience	Enhancing Sustainability and Climate Resilience of Forest and Agriculture Landscape and Community Livelihoods in Bhutan	1.22	Global Environment Facility, Least Developed Countries Fund, and UNDP	2017–2023
256	BHU-HR-005	Slope disaster prevention	Project for Capacity Development on Countermeasures for Slope Disasters on Roads in Bhutan	0.7 (Government)	JICA and government	2019–2022

continued on next page

Table continued

No.	Code	Project Description	BIMSTEC Development Logic	Estimated Cost, 2018 ($ million)	(Possible) Funding Sources	Timescale
257	BHU-HR-006	Climate resilience	Supporting Climate Resilience and Transformational Change in the Agriculture Sector in Bhutan	25.14	Green Climate Fund and government	2020–2025
258	BHU-HR-007	Training in International Civil Aviation Organization and national standards	Capacity building in the aviation sector, e.g., with respect to aerodrome management, air navigation services, safety, and security	2	As above	2018–2023
259	BHU-HR-008	Road transport related training	Capacity building for road safety and public transport management and operations	2	As above	2019–2028
260	MYA-HR-009	Capacity building in airport management and operations, airport security, and aviation IT network enhancement for Department of Civil Aviation staff	Enable efficient, safe, and secure operation of Myanmar's airports serving BIMSTEC regional traffic	5	Not yet identified	2018–2028
261	NEP-HR-010	Adoption of new and innovative technologies for the rapid and efficient development of transport infrastructure including the road and railway subsectors (e.g., design, project management, safety)	Support for development of transport infrastructure for BIMSTEC connectivity	5	ADB and World Bank	2018–2028
8.2 Capacity Building in Trade Facilitation						
262	REG-HR-011	Training in trade facilitation (e.g., the TFA, creation of trusted partnerships, customs valuation and procedures, rationalization of trade documents and data requirements, transshipment management, development and operation of single windows for online clearance and monitoring)	Improved logistics performance	5	WTO and others	2019–2028

continued on next page

Table continued

No.	Code	Project Description	BIMSTEC Development Logic	Estimated Cost, 2018 ($ million)	(Possible) Funding Sources	Timescale
263	BAN-HR-012	Career planning and training in customs facilitation (e.g., AEO, PCA, advance rulings), including training of trainers	Enhancement of skills of customs professionals	Not yet estimated	Not yet identified	2019–2024 (first phase) and 2025–2028 (second phase)
264	BHU-HR-013	Institutional strengthening of the Department of Trade	Capacity building in evidence-based trade policy making and market research for export promotion	1.5	Not yet identified	2018–2023
265	BHU-HR-014	Training in the operation and management of ICDs and dry ports	Facilitation of clearance at entry or exit points for BIMSTEC trade and transport	Not yet specified	Not yet identified	2018–2023
266	REG-HR-015	Training in border (and ICD) management, including IBM and CBM, focusing on BIMSTEC priority routes, and including the exchange of good practices, using existing infrastructure in member states	Improved performance at BIMSTEC borders	4	WCO, IOM, ADB, World Bank, INTERPOL	2019–2023
267	BHU-HR-016	Capacity building in handling border processing equipment	As above	1	As above	2019–2023

Flagship projects have been shaded green.

ADB = Asian Development Bank, ADFD = Abu Dhabi Fund for Development, AFD = Agence Française de Développement (French Development Agency), AH = Asian Highway, AIF = ASEAN Infrastructure Fund, AIIB = Asian Infrastructure Investment Bank, BAN = Bangladesh, BHU = Bhutan, BIMSTEC = Bay of Bengal Initiative for Multi-Sectoral Technical and Economic Cooperation, BOT = build–operate–transfer, CBM = coordinated border management, China Exim Bank = Export-Import Bank of China, EIB = European Investment Bank, EPC = engineering, procurement, and construction, IBM = integrated border management, ICD = inland clearance/container depot, ICP = integrated check post, ILOC = Indian Line of Credit, IND = India, INTERPOL = International Criminal Police Organization, IOM = International Organization for Migration, JICA = Japan International Cooperation Agency, JPY = Japanese yen, km = kilometer, LCC= low-cost carrier, LCL = less than container load, m = meter, MYA = Myanmar, NEDA = Neighbouring Countries Economic Development Cooperation Agency (Thailand), NEP = Nepal, NH = National Highway, NSW = national single window, OFID = OPEC Fund for International Development, OPEC = Organization of Petroleum Exporting Countries, PLC = public limited company, PPP = public–private partnership, PRC = People's Republic of China, REG = regional, SEZ = special economic zone, SPS = sanitary-phytosanitary, SPV = special purpose vehicle, SRL = Sri Lanka, TA = technical assistance, TBT = technical barriers to trade, THA = Thailand, THB = Thai baht, WCO = World Customs Organization, WTO = World Trade Organization.

Notes:
1. Data in this table may not reflect the latest developments. The main work for the preparation of the Master Plan was undertaken in 2018, and accordingly 2018 was the base year. Periodic updates were made between September 2018 and the fourth quarter of 2020 based on inputs from BIMSTEC member states. However, since not all projects were updated, some data may not reflect the current status of project development and implementation.
2. Bridge costs have not (yet) been estimated for (border) road projects in Bhutan, except for the Singye Bridge in the Kharbandi–Pasakha–Gedu project.
3. The project to develop a second rail-connected ICD in Dhaka, at Dhirasram, in Gazipur, Bangladesh, and the Gelephu Transport Hub project in Bhutan, have been included under multimodal and intermodal transport because of their significant multimodal or interconnectivity aspects. The Development of Nganglam Dry Port has been included under the ICD category because of relatively less strong multimodal and intermodal connectivity aspects.
4. Considering the establishment of the Mongla Export Processing Zone, a project to establish multimodal transport linkages may be developed around Mongla Port.

Source: Asian Development Bank.

Appendix 6
Existing and Proposed Multimodal and Intermodal Transport Corridors in the BIMSTEC Region

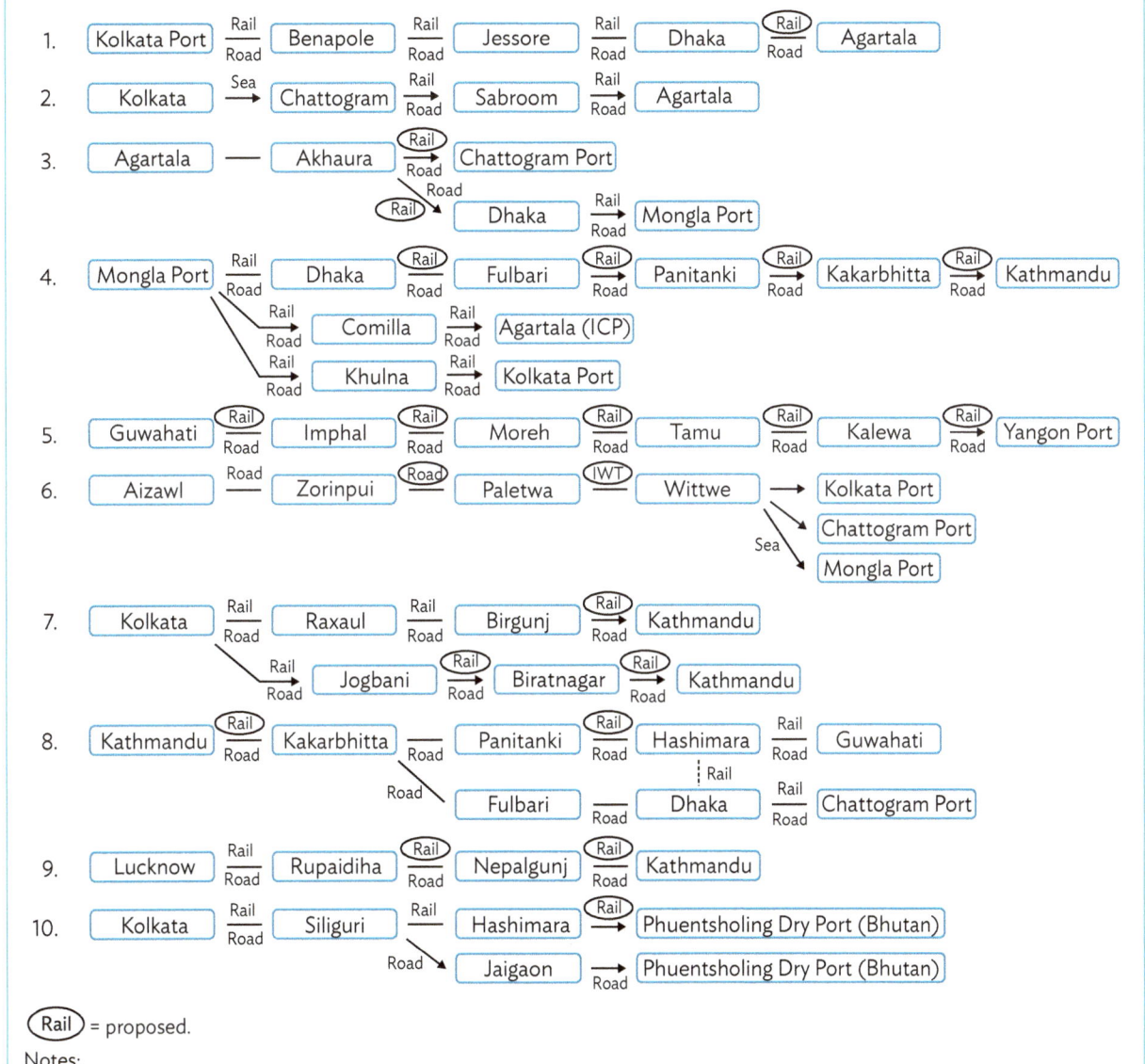

Appendix 7
Resources to Implement the Projects in the Master Plan, 2018, ($ billions)

Table A7.1: Long List Projects (Including Ongoing Projects, as of 2018), 2018–2028

Sector	Short Term (2018–2020)	Medium Term (2020–2024)	Long Term (2025–2028)	Total
Roads and Road Transport	20.092	25.710	3.368	49.170 (112 projects)
Railways and Rail Transport	13.933	14.838	9.532	38.303 (38 projects)
Ports and Maritime Transport	4.773	10.415	3.550	18.737 (25 projects)
Inland Water Transport	0.221	0.291	0.291	0.803 (4 projects)
Aviation and Airports	4.751	3.782	2.953	11.486 (33 projects)
Multimodal and Intermodal Transport	1.687	1.824	1.818	5.329 (10 projects)
Trade Facilitation	0.331	0.102	0.083	0.518 (29 projects)
Human Resource Development	0.013	0.026	0.021	0.060 (16 projects)
Total	45.804	56.985	21.616	124.405 (267 projects)

Notes:
1. Some of the projects have not been costed and, therefore, could be included in the table.
2. Costs of ongoing projects (as of 2018) incurred before 2018 are also not included.
3. Totals may not add up exactly due to rounding.

Source: Asian Development Bank.

Table A7.2: Long List Projects (Excluding Ongoing Projects, as of 2018), 2018–2028

Sector	Short Term (2018–2020)	Medium Term (2020–2024)	Long Term (2025–2028)	Total
Roads and Road Transport	5.141	15.389	2.904	23.434 (59 projects)
Railways and Rail Transport	0.309	5.674	1.679	7.662 (14 projects)
Ports and Maritime Transport	3.428	9.957	3.550	16.934 (18 projects)
Inland Water Transport	0.222	0.291	0.291	0.803 (4 projects)
Aviation and Airports	1.201	1.644	1.286	4.130 (17 projects)
Multimodal and Intermodal Transport	0.003	0.002	0.000	0.005 (3 projects)
Trade Facilitation	0.196	0.054	0.047	0.297 (12 projects)
Human Resource Development	0.008	0.020	0.009	0.037 (10 projects)
Total	10.507	33.030	9.765	53.302 (137 projects)

Notes:
1. Some of the projects have not been costed and, therefore, could not be included in the table.
2. Totals may not add up exactly due to rounding.

Source: This Master Plan.

Table A7.3: Flagship Projects (Including Ongoing Projects, as of 2018), 2018–2028

Sector	Short Term (2018–2020)	Medium Term (2020–2024)	Long Term (2025–2028)	Total
Roads and Road Transport	9.803	13.091	0.805	23.699 (60 projects)
Railways and Rail Transport	3.465	2.434	0.187	6.086 (13 projects)
Ports and Maritime Transport	1.948	1.908	0.540	4.396 (11 projects)
Inland Water Transport	0.003	0.000	0.000	0.003 (2 projects)
Aviation and Airports	4.198	3.618	4.238	12.054 (16 projects)
Multimodal and Intermodal Transport	0.323	0.006	0.000	0.329 (9 projects)
Trade Facilitation	0.149	0.142	0.111	0.401 (19 projects)
Human Resource Development	0.010	0.022	0.012	0.045 (11 projects)
Total	19.899	21.220	5.894	47.012 (141 projects)

Notes:
1. Some of the projects have not been costed and, therefore, could not be included in the table.
2. Costs of ongoing projects (as of 2018) incurred before 2018 are also not included.
3. Totals may not add up exactly due to rounding.

Source: Asian Development Bank.

Table A7.4: Flagship Projects (Excluding Ongoing Projects, as of 2018), 2018–2028

Sector	Short Term (2018–2020)	Medium Term (2020–2024)	Long Term (2025–2028)	Total
Roads and Road Transport	3.757	9.189	0.422	13.368 (30 projects)
Railways and Rail Transport	0.009	0.164	0	0.174 (6 projects)
Ports and Maritime Transport	0.750	1.450	0.460	2.660 (6 projects)
Inland Water Transport	0.003	0.000	0.000	0.003 (2 projects)
Aviation and Airports	1.589	1.260	2.790	5.639 (9 projects)
Multimodal and Intermodal Transport	0.003	0.002	0.000	0.005 (3 projects)
Trade Facilitation	0.014	0.048	0.044	0.106 (10 projects)
Human Resource Development	0.002	0.005	0.009	0.016 (7 projects)
Total	6.127	12.117	3.726	21.971 (73 projects)

Notes:
1. Some of the projects have not been costed and, therefore, could not be included in the table.
2. Totals may not add up exactly due to rounding.

Source: Asian Development Bank.

Appendix 8
Monitoring Formats for the Master Plan Flagship Projects and Initiatives

Table A8.1: Overall Status Report

Project Description	BIMSTEC Development Logic	Estimated Cost (2018 $ million)	(Possible) Funding Sources	Year(s)	Physical Progress	Financial Progress	Remarks/ Comments
1. Roads and Road Transport							
1.1 Roads to Enhance Arterial Links to Ports and Borders							
1.2 Upgrading of Border Roads							
1.3 Upgrading of Port Access Roads							

continued on next page

Table A8.1 continued

Project Description	BIMSTEC Development Logic	Estimated Cost (2018 $ million)	(Possible) Funding Sources	Year(s)	Physical Progress	Financial Progress	Remarks/ Comments
1.4 Development of Road-Based Buddhist Tourism and Temple Circuits							
1.5 Coordination of Road Programs							
1.6 Formulation and Implementation of Through-Transport Agreements							
2. Railways and Rail Transport							
2.1 Enhanced Rail Connectivity between Ports, Dry Ports, and Borders, and Their Hinterlands							
2.2 Rail Connectivity for Landlocked Countries							
2.3 Development of Rail-Based Buddhist Tourism and Temple Circuits							
2.4 Coordination of Railway Programs							
3. Ports and Maritime Transport							
3.1 Development of Deeper Water Ports							
3.2 Improvement of Container Handling Performance at Ports							

continued on next page

Table A8.1 continued

Project Description	BIMSTEC Development Logic	Estimated Cost (2018 $ million)	(Possible) Funding Sources	Year(s)	Physical Progress	Financial Progress	Remarks/ Comments
3.3 Development of Coastal Shipping							
4. Inland Water Transport							
5. Civil Aviation and Airport Development							
5.1 Expansion of Airport Capacity 5.2 Air Freight Facilities and Services 5.3 Support Facilities for LCC Operations							
6. Multimodal and Intermodal Transport							
7. Trade Facilitation							
7.1 Development of Border Infrastructure							
7.2 Development of ICDs							
7.3 Simplification and Harmonization of Export-Import Documentation							

continued on next page

Table A8.1 continued

Project Description	BIMSTEC Development Logic	Estimated Cost (2018 $ million)	(Possible) Funding Sources	Year(s)	Physical Progress	Financial Progress	Remarks/ Comments
7.4 Further Development of Automated Systems							
7.5 Development of Advanced Logistics							
8. Human Resource Development							
8.1 Capacity Building Projects in Transport and Related Sectors							
8.2 Training in Trade Facilitation							
8.3 Training in Border Management							

BIMSTEC = Bay of Bengal Initiative for Multi-Sectoral Technical and Economic Cooperation, ICD = inland clearance/container depot, LCC= low-cost carrier.

Note: There may be some overlapping between arterial roads and border or port access roads when arterial roads approach border or port areas. It may (somewhat arbitrarily) be considered that border and port access link roads are (mainly) within, say, 50 kilometers of the ports.

Source: After *The Proposed BTCWG Work Plan and Monitoring Framework*, presented at the Inception Meeting of the BIMSTEC Transport Connectivity Working Group, Bangkok, Thailand. 30–31 August 2016. Appendix A. pp. 4–7.

Table A8.2: (Flagship) Project Profile Format

Project Title / Description:	Year(s):
Member State(s):	(Sub)-Sector:

Implementing Agency/Agencies:

Background and Rationale:

[Describe the project context, i.e., the underlying conditions that make the project necessary, the issues that the project is intended to address, and the benefits or outcomes expected to result from the project. The rationale or development logic of the project should be explained in the BIMSTEC context. At the same time, it should be stated if the project is part of national and local development plans.]

Objectives:

[Indicate both short-term and long-term objectives as applicable.]

Scope:

[Indicate project components and geographic/location focus.]

Estimated Cost (2018 $ equivalent):

[Indicate estimated cost in 2018 $, for easy comparison across member states.]

Project Financing:

[Indicate financing source(s), indicate if the financing is firm, i.e., budgeted or earmarked, in the case of domestic financing, or committed by an international development partner in the case of external financing, or whether financing is only at the proposal stage or not yet identified.]

Other Information:

[Please provide other relevant information on the project (e.g., economic and/or financial rates of returns, environmental and social considerations, resettlement requirements).]

BIMSTEC = Bay of Bengal Initiative for Multi-Sectoral Technical and Economic Cooperation.
Source: After *The Proposed BTCWG Work Plan and Monitoring Framework,* presented at the Inception Meeting of the BIMSTEC Transport Connectivity Working Group, Bangkok, Thailand. 30–31 August 2016. Appendix B. p. 8.

Table A8.3: Simplified Time-Based Implementation Monitoring Spreadsheet for Each Flagship Project

			TCD[a]	Year				Year				Year				Year			
				Q1	Q2	Q3	Q4	Q1	Q2	Q3	Q4	Q1	Q2	Q3	Q4	Q1	Q2	Q3	Q4
A	Project Development Phase																		
1	Project identification																		
2	Studies, pre-FS / FS/ DE																		
3	Securing of pre-implementation approvals																		
4	Securing of funding																		
5	Awarding of contracts																		
B	Implementation Phase																		
1	Construction																		
2	Completion/ commissioning																		

Project:
Country: **(Sub)Sector:** **Implementing Agency:**
Remarks on the status reported on this sheet:
(Describe briefly in this row the most recent status being reported. Indicate physical and financial progress.)

Prepared by: Email: Office Tel: Mobile Tel:
(Name, Position, and Department)
Date:

Instructions: (i) Indicate the target completion date ("TCD"; quarter/year) for each stage of the project. (ii) For each stage of the project, mark with a "C" if the stage has been completed, a "U" if the stage is underway (ongoing), or a "NYS" if the stage or preparatory activity has not yet started. (iii) Mark with a bar the period covered up to the TCD. (iv) If TCDs are revised, please explain in a footnote. (v) Approvals may include approvals for land acquisition, environmental and social clearance(s), and the like. (vi) The sheet should be updated quarterly or as requested by the BIMSTEC Secretariat.

C = completed, NYS = not yet started, Q = quarter, TCD = target completion date, U = underway.

Source: After *The Proposed BTCWG Work Plan and Monitoring Framework*, presented at the Inception Meeting of the BIMSTEC Transport Connectivity Working Group, Bangkok, Thailand. 30–31 August 2016. Appendix C. p. 9.

www.ingramcontent.com/pod-product-compliance
Lightning Source LLC
Chambersburg PA
CBHW061207230426

43664CB00030B/2942